Benjamin Ridsdale

Scenes and Adventures in Great Namaqualand

Benjamin Ridsdale

Scenes and Adventures in Great Namaqualand

ISBN/EAN: 9783337177621

Printed in Europe, USA, Canada, Australia, Japan

Cover: Foto ©ninafisch / pixelio.de

More available books at **www.hansebooks.com**

SCENES AND ADVENTURES

IN

GREAT NAMAQUALAND.

BY THE

REV. BENJAMIN RIDSDALE.

LONDON:

T. WOOLMER, 2, CASTLE STREET, CITY ROAD, E.C.
AND 66, PATERNOSTER ROW, E.C.

1883.

LONDON:
PRINTED BY BEVERIDGE AND MILLER,
HOLBORN PRINTING WORKS, FULLWOOD'S RENTS, W.C.

CONTENTS.

CHAPTER I.

HAVING offered my services to the Wesleyan Missionary Society for missionary work abroad, I received an appointment to South Africa, and with my wife left England in the *Persia* for the Cape of Good Hope on the 4th of September, 1843. In due time we arrived safely at Cape Town, after a fair passage, and a day or two afterwards it was arranged that I should proceed to Nisbett Bath, in Great Namaqualand, to carry on the work so hopefully begun by the late Rev. E. Cook. Preparations for the journey were instantly commenced. Everything demanded haste. The travelling season was already past, and every day the sun was gathering fresh power, vegetation withering under its heat; the fountains and pools along the path we must travel were rapidly drying up; all tending to make a journey of six hundred miles through a waste wilderness an exceedingly trying and even dangerous thing; in addition to

B

which, the people on the station had been bereft of their missionary by death, and it was highly desirable that at the earliest possible opportunity the new missionary should be at his post. As the Nisbett Bath mission station was directly in the route of the brethren proceeding to the Damara country, it was arranged that Mr. Tindall and myself should start together, leaving Mr. Haddy and family to follow in a week.

The preparations we had to make for our journey were of a very extensive and novel kind. As we were going into the interior for two years, during which time we should have no chance of making purchases, a list of all the articles that might prove necessary during that lengthened stay had to be carefully prepared. Tea, sugar, coffee, rice, &c., had to be purchased wholesale, our medicine chest had to be replenished with drugs, and many other little *et ceteras* needed attention. As our family was small, our own wants would soon have been supplied; but the wants of others had to be considered. As Her Majesty's coin is not current in those realms, we had to convert notes and gold into pins, needles, thread, buttons, handkerchiefs, shirts, trowsers, waistcoats, jackets, hats, prints, calico, powder, shot, lead, tin, and everything acceptable to the natives, in order that on our arrival we might exchange them for sheep and goats, milch cows and oxen, for the use of the mission family, and that with these articles we might pay native servants, and secure the help of the people in any kind of service we might require of them. The visiting of store after store to effect these purchases was both novel and wearisome : but having the wise counsel of our experienced friend, Mr. Tindall, we accomplished all to admiration; though, as bale after bale and parcel after parcel arrived, we began to wonder how, after all, we should be able to stow them into our one waggon, which at the same time was to serve as our house and home; and seriously to doubt whether our one team of oxen would be able to draw so much over the sandy plains and rocky mountains between Cape Town and our distant station.

We were now very curious to see the waggon in which we were to travel. We found it about thirteen feet in length, and three feet broad at the bottom, but gradually widening upwards to the top of its sloping sides. A chest behind, of large dimensions, made to suit the shape of the waggon, and a similar one in front, which served as the seat of the waggon driver, we saw would prove very convenient for the stowage of numerous loose articles; whilst on each side, at the exterior of the waggon, another smaller chest was attached for articles required during the course of every day. A light and neat framework of wood sprang from each of the high sides of the waggon, forming a cap-tent throughout the entire length. This was covered first with a well-painted sail-cloth to render it rain-proof; then, as a protection from the heat of the sun, a layer of long reed-mats was thrown over the tent from side to side, and fastened down close upon the painted cloth; and finally, a white sail-cloth, cut to shape, and neatly buttoned down on each side, served as an exterior covering to all; in addition to which a flap of the same material hung in front, and another behind, both of which could be rolled up or closely buttoned down at the convenience of the travellers. As the waggon had to be drawn by oxen, a pole was attached to the fore axle, like the pole of our English carriages; to the extremity of this pole the *trek tow*, or drawing-line, was attached; this was made of ox-hide cut into long strips or thongs, plaited together, and, when new, about two inches in diameter. As our waggons were to have long teams, the *tow* was fifty-six feet in length. The first yoke was fixed at the end of the pole, and the rest at a distance of eight feet throughout the whole length of the line; so that the team, when yoked and drawing, was of the above length. An inspection of our conveyance was, on the whole, very satisfactory; some wrong notions were corrected, and we found it by no means the clumsy vehicle which the name of waggon is apt to suggest to an English mind.

At last, after what seemed to us a somewhat long detention in Cape Town, the day arrived when the process of packing had to be commenced; a duty that required considerable skill and care, so that no space might be lost, and everything made to fit together in the most compact manner possible. When all was completed, the space left for our convenience was wofully limited. The sleeping apartment was high up in the waggon, much too near to the roof, whilst the space in front, between the stretcher and the waggon driver, was only just sufficient to *sit* at ease as we travelled. Some of our good friends were quite concerned at the discomfort which they saw we should experience, and had serious fears lest in passing over roads that slope down to one side, the waggon packed to such a height should go over. These were the reasons urged why we should leave some of our packages behind. But though not very experienced travellers, we were sufficiently awake to know that there were no shops in Namaqualand; and as everything we had would be necessary as soon as we reached the station, we thought an inconvenience of a few weeks could be better borne than one of two years; so we resolved on taking the full waggon load.

When everything else was ready, a swarthy son of the Cape came one morning, as we sat at breakfast, to say, " If you please, the oxes has strayed ;" so we had a little longer to wait. On Monday, 27th of November, however, they were brought and yoked to the waggons, and we joyfully took our leave of Cape Town for the interior, accompanied for the first stage by a number of kind friends and ministerial brethren. This was intentionally a short stage of about three miles, so that our friends, who had to return on foot, might not be inconvenienced. Salt River was the name of the place of our halt; and here, whilst the tea was being prepared in gipsy fashion, anxious to make a rapid acquisition of all knowledge likely to be useful in interior life, and knowing that wild beasts of various kinds were by no means scarce, and that even lions sometimes showed themselves in the neighbourhood of my station, I made loose my rifle for the purpose of practising upon some lifeless object, wishful to rival in accuracy of aim the chosen men of Benjamin, every one of whom " could sling stones at a hair breadth, and not miss." I thrust a piece of wood, fourteen inches long by two wide, into the sand, and took deliberate aim.   " Wait, Sir, wait, Sir," cried Aaron, the " oxes " man, and instantly rushed up and put his hat on the stick, by way of showing his confidence in my ability to miss! I begged him to remove it, promising that if he refused, I would do my best to make a hole in it. "Shoot, Sir, shoot," was the only reply. So I obeyed, and sent the ball through his hat and the wood, and out on the other side. Poor Aaron looked serious, but when I told him the holes would serve as ventilators to keep his head cool, and added a shilling by way of making amends, he appeared to be comforted; whilst I hoped after a little practice to become a thorough Benjamite. From the experiment of that hour, I inferred that since I could strike a hat, I might, in case of need, be able to slay a lion, and put away my rifle with all the satisfaction this kind of reasoning could impart. But mere trifles sometimes originate very serious reports. Five weeks afterwards I was startled by a person addressing me with, "Why, Mr. R., I understand you had a very narrow escape from killing a man on the journey." Filled with astonishment, I asked, "How so?" "Why, you were firing your rifle, we heard, and the ball passed through a man's hat!" How very natural to conclude that the man's head must have been in it, and that consequently the danger was imminent!

When our tea was ready, the whole company found seats for themselves on the grass, and partook of the refreshing beverage: after which we all united in singing a hymn; one or two of the brethren prayed, and we parted, some for the town, and others for the wilderness.

As soon as the friends were gone, the oxen were again put to the yoke, and we commenced another stage in the cool of the day. Brother Tindall's waggon, containing himself, wife, and son, an intelligent and agreeable youth of about twelve years of age, went first. Ours followed at a short distance. The first waggon was drawn by a team of sixteen red oxen, ours by a team of as many black ones; a number that at first appeared to us, strangers, unnecessarily large; but one that we afterwards found only just adequate to the task to be performed. Each waggon had its own native driver, who sat on the fore-chest, or walked by the side of his team, wielding a *whip* of enormous dimensions, the stick being about fourteen feet, and the thong of the same length, enabling him to apply the stimulus to a slinking ox at a considerable distance. The crack of these huge weapons, when wielded by a skilful hand, is quite startling to persons unaccustomed to the sound, and is more like the explosion of a rifle than the voice of a whip-lash. The best lash is made of a slender strip of the skin of an antelope, called the *koodoo*, and the smacking of the whip itself is quite an accomplishment. A blow from such a weapon, skilfully applied, has a most terrible effect. An angry or cruel driver can easily lash through the hides of his oxen, and bring the blood in streams, and I have occasionally seen some poor oxen that had been fearfully lacerated all over by the merciless drivers. It is, however, well known to the natives that missionaries never allow their oxen to be ill-treated, and therefore, by the drivers in their employ, cruelty was never attempted. In addition to a driver, we had also a leader attached to each waggon; indeed, a waggon is never properly " found " without one. A thong is attached to the outermost horn of each of the two oxen foremost in the team, and the leader, taking the middle of this thong in his hand, walks in front of the team. When the path is good, the duties of the leader are light, as he can then throw up the thong on the horns of the oxen, and seat himself by the side of the driver. But when the path is rocky, or abrupt descents into watercourses periodically crossing the path occur, intelligence and care are required in the leader, as well as in the driver, otherwise the waggon may be overturned. To complete the travelling party, another man is necessary to take charge of a few milch goats and slaughter sheep, and a few spare oxen to supply the places of any of the regular teams that may fail by the way. As Mr. Tindall and myself travelled in company, one man of this kind was sufficient for the purpose, so that five men and one Damara female servant formed the number of natives who travelled with us.

We travelled on till rather late in the day, when our oxen were allowed to graze a little; and then, with thongs around their horns, were attached to the yokes, as the latter lay upon the ground, to rest for the night. We were still on the Cape Flats, the grand outline of Table Mountain was still in view; the sound of the nine o'clock gun, fired every night at the Castle, fell heavily on our ear, and made us still feel that we were within the reach of civilised life. Whilst our men were sitting around their fire watching the boiling of the pot in which their evening meal was being prepared, we left our waggons, with Bible and hymn-book in hand, to join them, and after singing a Dutch hymn, with which they were familiar, we all knelt down under the starry heavens, and committed ourselves to the protection of the God of missions. Our men soon finished their meal, wrapped themselves up in their karosses, turned their feet towards the fire, and lay stretched out in all directions, like lines radiating from the centre to the circumference of a circle, and were soon sleeping profoundly. Our travelling apartment was closed for the night, and, though limited in its dimensions, and lacking some of the conveniences of a "fixed property," was quite as comfortable as we could have ever imagined a waggon to be. The excitement and actual labour of the day had wearied us, and " tired nature's sweet restorer, balmy sleep," was near at hand. Before the day dawned, our men were up, the oxen placed in the yoke, and we were travelling on, our morning stage over the sandy soil before we awoke ; and as the stage was rather long, and the motion of the waggon was new to us, it produced an uncomfortable sensation, analogous to the earlier developments of sea-sickness—an effect often produced on inexperienced travellers. By seven we reached the outspan place, or camping ground. Here the traveller draws up his waggon, looses his oxen from the yoke, and refreshes himself. In starting on such a journey we have a list of all the places suitable for "outspanning" between Cape Town and our station ; places where, in the proper season for travelling, we generally find both water and grass. In this long journey of six hundred miles, which, with our heavy waggons, would occupy, including necessary rests, eight weeks, we had only forty-two such places on our list, with the exact number of hours it would take our oxen to go from one stage to another; so that, day by day, we were under the necessity of pushing on to a certain point, if we had any regard for our own comfort, and that of our poor oxen.

We were now at *Baas Harrie's Fontein*, the second place on our list.   As' soon as the oxen were unyoked to graze, one man made a fire not far from the waggon, another opened the water barrel, and filled the kettle; this was put over the fire, resting on two or three large stones, which had been evidently used by travellers before for a similar purpose.   Clean new mats of native reed were spread on the grass, and all the array of a breakfast-table soon appeared in the shade of our waggons.   We sat around on our camp-stools, or reclined on the mats, as taste or convenience dictated, and heartily enjoyed our morning meal and the magnificent scenery before us.   We had passed over the lowlands of the Cape Flats, which are almost on a level with the sea, and were now on rising ground.   Table Mountain, and the other mountains of the Cape peninsula, stood out to view in all their native grandeur, whilst Cape Town, with its mass of white buildings stretching all along the base of Table and Lion Mountains, and washed by the blue waters of Table Bay, glittered resplendently in the sunshine, and formed a beautiful sight, though twenty-seven miles away.   These were noble accompaniments of the breakfast-table; but there was one drawback to its full enjoyment, viz., a too liberal supply of sand scattered by a strong wind over our bread and butter, and eggs, and into our coffee.   It was not so bad in the latter case, as, owing to its specific gravity, it soon found its way to the bottom of our cups, but in the process of mastication we found the greatest discomfort, and were obliged to withdraw to the shelter of our waggons to finish the meal. As it was our intention to maintain family prayer throughout the journey, after breakfast, our people, being summoned, seated themselves in a semi-circle upon the grass; a portion of the Dutch Scriptures was read, a hymn sung, and, as it was my turn to officiate, I resolved to make the best use of the amount of Dutch I had acquired, by endeavouring to offer prayer in that language. For a short time I proceeded with tolerable liberty, when, a suitable term failing to offer itself, I naturally resorted to my mother tongue for expression. The people, however, were pleased at the early attempt, and as it was my main object during the journey to advance in the language, and be ready for duty as soon as I should reach my station, I had no doubt of success; especially as I had diligently pursued my studies during the voyage, and intended to do so on the journey, having the advantage of two critics at hand, in Mr. Tindall and his son, both of whom were familiar with the language.

As we were not to resume our journey till the cool of the afternoon, it only remained that a few little matters should be attended to, and then the men would have some leisure. Each of the mission party would be able with comfort to read, write, and study, and the ladies to sew or converse at will. One of the men's first duties was the greasing of the wheels, which has to be done daily, when the waggons are heavily laden. To do this, one man, with a long lever placed on a suitable fulcrum, raises one side of the waggon, another draws off the wheel to near the extremity of the axle, when its point is allowed to rest

just within the nave, whilst a third smears the axle with
a brush, the axle is again slightly raised by the lever,
the wheel is pushed up into its place, the linchpin put
in, and everything is ready. This process has to be
repeated to every wheel. On this occasion, whilst one
of the front wheels of Mr. Tindall's waggon was being
greased, and Mrs. Tindall was standing on the front of
the waggon, busily washing up the breakfast things, the
wheel was drawn off too far, the man at the lever let
go his hold, and down came the waggon, the point of the
fore-axle resting on the ground. Down came poor
Mrs. Tindall too, and was sadly grazed and shaken,
whilst some of her cups and saucers were broken—a
serious matter in the wilderness, where they cannot be
replaced. Fortunately she had laid in a stock in anticipation of such accidents.

A considerable portion of the morning was spent in
endeavouring to raise the axle, and replace the wheel ;
but as we could not muster sufficient strength, we were
glad to avail ourselves of the aid of some men who
happened to be passing, and at length succeeded.

About noon we received a visit from a Boer whose
farm was near. Though living so near to Cape Town, he
was far less polished in appearance and manners than
many I have since met very far up in the interior, but
his disposition was kind and friendly. We supplied
ourselves with eggs from his house at a cheap rate, and
exchanged two of our weakly oxen for two stronger
ones, paying him the difference. At four p.m. the
wind began to blow up cool, and we commenced preparations for our next stage. The oxen in charge of one
of the men had wandered a considerable distance, and

we imagined a long time would elapse before they could be sought and found. It was not necessary, however, to dispatch another man in search, as a more ready method was at command. Our waggoner, with his huge whip, just went to the brow of the hill, turned his face in the direction in which he supposed the oxen were grazing, smacked his whip about half a dozen times, and, though he could not see them, quietly returned to the waggon, put up the whip, and proceeded to make all ready for the journey, never doubting that by the time we should be ready, the man with the oxen would be at our service. My curiosity was awakened, and I was anxiously on the look out, feeling certain that we should be detained by the non-appearance of the oxen at the proper time. I had not gazed long, however, before I saw a small dust rising from amongst the low bushes of the plain below, and, on a little minute examination, perceived indistinctly some objects moving along the plain. They proved to be our oxen. The watcher had known what time to expect the summons, he had heard the cracking of the whip, and had instantly turned with his numerous charge towards the place of our encampment. The wheel-oxen were first yoked, then the next couple, and so on to the end. Sometimes an ox will prove refractory, especially if young and untaught, but the well-trained and experienced oxen know their work, follow with alacrity, and instinctively incline the head to receive the yoke. To my unpractised eye, the black oxen composing our team looked so much alike, that it seemed impossible to distinguish one from another. Yet the driver called each ox by his name, and each answered to it. I resolved, therefore, to

extend my knowledge in this direction, especially as
these oxen were destined to be my companions in travel,
not only on this journey, but on many a future one.
Walking by the side of the team as they travelled, I
wrote down their names, and a brief description of some
peculiarities by which each might be readily distinguished, as a patch of white on the flank, the shoulder,
or knee; circular, or spreading horns; and I soon
learned a difference in the faces of the animals; as a
vicious, or a gentle, placid eye; a countenance that
was benevolent, inviting confidence, or one that was
sinister, and that taught one to be wary. In this way,
by an occasional reference to my paper, I soon became
perfectly acquainted with every ox in my team.

On the 29th we passed through Malmesbury, a picturesque little village, about forty miles from Cape
Town. The population consists almost exclusively of
Dutch residents, with their native servants. The houses
are regularly built, have a respectable appearance, and
are many of them tastefully adorned with little flower
gardens in front, enclosed by railings. The Dutch
Reformed Church, the residence of the minister, a
school for the instruction of all classes, and the public
offices, all stand on one side of the principal square of
the village. The black soil surrounding the village,
and pretty generally prevailing throughout the district,
is admirably calculated for the produce of grain, the
supply of which is so plentiful, and the quality so good,
that this division has been called " the granary of the
colony."

On Friday, December 1st, 1843, we reached the Berg
River. The river has its rise in the mountains which

enclose the vale of Draakenstein, and discharges itself on the west coast in St. Helena Bay. We were at a part of the river called Tron's Drift, at no great distance from the sea ; it was of considerable breadth, with a depth probably of eight or ten feet. There are still two or three hippopotami preserved in the deep pits of the river, which are not allowed to be shot, as no others are found south of the Orange River. Although they are extremely timid in general, only just raising the nostrils above water to breathe, and instantly sinking themselves at the least noise, these are said to be so tame, as on leaving the water to graze near the house of the Dutch Boer, who may be called their protector. Our mode of crossing was novel, viz., on a "*pont*," or floating bridge. This was drawn up close to the south bank of the river, and our waggons, one at a time, were drawn on to it by the two "after-oxen" only, assisted by men at the wheels, and taken with all its burden to the other side, towing lines being firmly attached on each side of the river, and running along both sides of the "pont" to prevent its being drifted by the stream. By these lines it was drawn towards the north shore. Our oxen were driven in, and swam over with ease. We breakfasted and dined under the shade of a large white jessamine tree ; but the day was so intensely hot, the thermometer standing at 98° in the shade, that the best shelter we could find was a very inefficient protection from the burning sun; whilst the air, as it swept over the surface of the heated hillocks of white sand, blew upon us as from an oven. We were almost overcome, till, having found a suitable spot, plunging head first into the river, I enjoyed a most blissful ablution, and felt the refreshment throughout the remainder of the day. Brother Tindall and his son, for safety, bathed in a shallow pool adjacent to the river.

December 3rd.—Our first Sabbath in the wilderness. A more than ordinary—a Sabbatic—stillness seemed to pervade nature. The sun shone in cloudless splendour; only gentle airs were stirring, and, though far from the sanctuary and the crowd of them that keep " holy day," everything seemed to invite to devotion. After breakfast all our party were assembled, and the service commenced in God's own grand temple, the ample sward of the desert spread out on every side; the sun in all 'his splendour peered down upon us through the ethereal dome above, and while in simplicity and godly sincerity we worshipped, with new feelings and in a fresh sense, we could cry, " How amiable are Thy tabernacles, O Lord of Hosts!" or as it was in the Dutch version we were using, " How *charming* are Thy dwellings," &c., a term that expressed with wonderful appropriateness the feelings with which we engaged in Divine worship in the temple of nature, and which invested our hymns of praise, our prayers, our preaching, with a new and marvellous charm of its own. Later in the day a second service was held, and there was something peculiarly spiritual in them both. They proved to be times of refreshing from the presence of the Lord. During the interval of worship suitable reading and conversation were enjoyed, and thus agreeably and profitably filled up the hours of the Sabbath. In the evening, just when the sun had dipped below the horizon, the shrill yell of a jackal fell upon our ear. It was the first sound of any beast of the wilderness we had heard, and though an insignificant animal, so sharp and shrill was the sound as to produce, for the moment, a startling effect upon the nerves. Though man has nothing to fear from the jackal, yet it has seemed to me that the yell of the South African jackal has a more thrilling effect upon the nerves than that of almost any other beast of the desert. There is a shrill and horrible twang in his cry that would be positively alarming to one unacquainted with the animal. Our sheep and goats started and ran near to the waggon for society and safety. This was *Klip Kraal,* a grass plat surrounded by a circle of trees, and a prettier place than was often to be met with.

On the next day we passed the Picket Berg, and called at the Boer's living at the road side, to deliver the "compliments" of the Rev. B. Shaw, who passed on his first journey to Little Namaqualand twenty-seven years previously; but the person occupying the house had no knowledge of our veteran missionary. His message, however, served as an introduction, and we were very kindly welcomed. It was merely a call *in transitu,* but several important questions were put in Dutch. "Who are you, pray, if I may ask?" "Where have you come from?" "Where are you going?" "Are you married?" And when I replied in the affirmative, it appeared to give great satisfaction. But when, in reply to the next question, "Has your wife come from England?" I was able to assure him that she had: "What, over the great sea?" said he. And when I answered "Yes" to that question, he seemed quite filled with admiration at the courage of any lady who should venture to accompany her husband across the mighty ocean; for the present race of Boers, who have all been born in the country, have quite a dread of the sea. The reason of his gratification at the fact that my wife had come with me from England was not difficult to divine. One or two missionaries, not of our Society, had, no doubt from philanthropic and benevolent motives, married native women. Such compacts, however, have seldom turned out well: generally speaking, they have injured the influence of the missionary with the people amongst whom he has resided. Instead of raising his partner to his own level, the natives generally supposed that he had lowered himself to theirs. Now although the loss of influence to a missionary by such a marriage would be matter of very little regret to Boers generally, one thing is certain, they and their families are strongly averse to such relationships; for whilst natives look upon a European missionary who has married one of their own people as having become one of themselves, the Boers regard the act as an implied acknowledgment that no great distance exists between the native and European, an idea that very much shocks the Boer's sense of propriety, and one that he is very anxious to keep from the view of the native, whom he too often haughtily regards as a menial only destined to do the meanest offices at his bidding. Hence the delight of our new friends at hearing that my good wife had accompanied me from England; whilst their admiration rose to its highest point when they thought of her courage in having crossed "over the great sea-water" to a foreign land. We still found in connection with this Boer's residence "beautiful gardens, orange groves, and cornfields, with an abundant supply of water," as when the venerable Barnabas Shaw passed so many years before. Upwards of a hundred and twenty families lie scattered about the neighbourhood, chiefly behind the mountain, who raise and ship a considerable quantity of grain for Cape Town through St. Helena Bay. Here let me remark, that, generally speaking, we found the Boers fairly hospitable as a race, especially if cleverly managed; but the following description, though taken from a standard work, is so overstrained, that I never saw anything approaching to it : " A stranger has only to open the door, shake hands with the master, *kiss the mistress!* seat himself, and he is then completely at home."

Wednesday, December 6th.—This morning we travelled through very deep, loose sand, with large blocks of stone ever and anon occurring in its midst. These coming unexpectedly in contact with the waggon wheel made it necessary to sit with caution, lest our heads should be brought into unpleasant collision with the tent frame of our waggon ; but what we feared even more than that was lest the pole of our waggon should be snapped off by the frequent and violent jerks it received. Before 8 a.m. we reached a place called *Het Kruis.* Here on a small grassy flat in the centre of a narrow winding valley, bounded on three sides by sandhills covered with low bushes, we outspanned till the afternoon. At one extremity of this valley rose a high and rugged mountain, black and bare, and not far from its base was the residence of a Boer. The valley, with adjoining corn and pasture lands, constituted his farm ; but though he had horses, sheep, goats, oxen, and poultry in considerable numbers, his residence

certainly cut a very sorry figure.   An air of discomfort
was everywhere apparent.   During the course of the
day we visited the Boer, conversed, read from the
Scriptures, and prayed with the family; and as they have
very seldom opportunities of this kind, all appeared to be
highly acceptable.   Being unable to resume our journey
that evening, owing to some repairs to Mr. Tindall's
waggon not being completed, whilst all of us were
taking a short walk in the dusk of the evening, the first
incident of an exciting kind occurred.   A night-adder
was, like ourselves, taking an airing, and whilst to us it
proved dangerous, to him it proved fatal.   We only
just perceived its serpentine motion in time to avoid
treading upon it, when we instinctively sprang back
and escaped a bite.   In another minute the reptile was
despatched with our walking-sticks.

On Saturday morning we arrived at the *Uitkomst.*
This has for many years been a place of rest and refreshment for missionaries of all denominations.   Mr.
Van Zyl has proved their steadfast friend for forty
years past, in consequence of which he has often exposed
himself to the derision of some of his neighbours, who
call his farm, " *een Zendeling's plaats,*" a mission station.
He was now an old man, and very ill, but his good wife
came to the waggons, and welcomed us with a mother's
affection.   The old lady seemed much struck at the
fresh and youthful appearance of myself and my wife.
I was "so handsome a young gentleman " that she could
not think I was married!   " The mistress also was so
young and handsome " that she supposed she could
only be sixteen or seventeen!!   Here we remained, at
the pressing request of our kind host and hostess, for

several days, during which time our whole party of ten persons were most hospitably entertained free of expense. On the Sabbath we held services in their house; and daily, during our stay, we enjoyed reading, singing, and prayer in the family, so that our visit proved not only a rest and refreshment to the body, but to ourselves at least, and we trust to them also, a renewal of spiritual strength. On the day previous to our departure, our waggons were replenished with an ample supply of all the good things the benevolent hearts of our friends could conceive of. Raisins, peaches, apricots, figs, lemons, oranges, a number of sweet cakes, and about thirty large loaves of both fine and coarse bread for us and our men, were supplied. In addition to which, a fat slaughter sheep, two milch goats, four live fowls, and four pigeons were presented to us; and for all this array of provisions, nothing in the shape of payment would be received; though any little present we had it in our power to bestow as an affectionate remembrance was graciously accepted and prized. Not the least valuable act of kindness on the part of Mr. Van Zyl was the promise to assist us up the long sandy steep that occurs on leaving his house, with a team of his own fresh and well-rested oxen. And as we were to start at two or three o'clock next morning, the oxen were all secured in the kraal over night; and after we had bidden adieu to our kind and bounteous friends, we retired to our waggons, that at the appointed hour we might resume our journey at the break of day.

In a letter from Mrs. R. to her sister, written from this place, she says: "I have been very agreeably disappointed in regard to this African waggon-travelling.

I thought it would be insupportably tedious and wearisome to jog on scarcely three miles an hour for weeks
together after the expeditious travelling we are used to
in England. But I find it anything but tedious. The
scenery is so constantly changing, and alternately so
grand, so beautiful, so wildly romantic, and so terribly
sublime, that it keeps the interest constantly excited.
We cannot in general see long ·before us, nor far
behind us; for, through almost the whole country which
we have as yet traversed, mountain after mountain
rises all around so as quickly to hide the road we have
passed, and to conceal what is to come. The land in
general is indeed a chaos of mountains and valleys of
every variety of form, and thrown together in every
variety of combination, so that in looking around and
before you, it seems impossible to me to conceive how
anybody can find their way to a place through such a
chaos of peaked and rugged hills."

About midnight we arrived at *Heere Logement*, "Gentleman's Lodging," extremely fatigued with long journeying through deep and heavy sand, and with the intense
heat of the day. But though the day had been so hot,
we were now quite nipped by the strong keen wind that
was blowing. Having arrived so late, and men and
oxen being jaded, we took no morning stage on
Thursday the 14th, but after breakfast went on an
expedition to the famous "Logement," or cavernous
chamber, from which the place takes its name. After
ascending a steep hill-side, thickly overgrown with bushes,
at about one hundred feet above the plain, we came to a
large cavern in the side of the rock, forming a tolerably
spacious apartment. Through a fissure in the rocky

roof a wild fig-tree sends its spreading branches, giving a pretty effect.   On one side of this cavern, full open to the daylight, the names of many travellers and missionaries were cut.   And here I spent some time chiselling my name into the hard face of the rock, a process which I found required much patience, as the rock was of granite, and the only instruments available were a hammer and an old blunt screwdriver.   I succeeded quite to my own satisfaction, considering the sorry tools at my command, and left my name, as Brother Tindall said, " in superfine London type ! "

On Saturday the 16th, we reached Ebenezer, a German mission station, situated very near the banks of the Elephant River.   The Rev. Messrs. Hahn and Lutz received us all most cordially into their house, where we remained till the following Monday.   The station had a regular row of small houses of lath and plaster, as well as a number of huts, which are very slight structures, consisting of native reed-mats, thrown over and fastened to a framework of bamboos, and of beehive shape.   The chapel, a new structure, is a really beautiful building, especially considering the difficulty of raising such a structure in such a part.   The corn-lands connected with the station are somewhat extensive, and in years when the country is flooded by the overflow of the river, so rich a deposit is left that, we were informed, in some instances they had reaped a hundredfold.   It very often happens, however, that one such year is more than counterbalanced by several years of extreme drought.   An excellent windmill has been raised on the station by Mr. Hahn, who united the duties of missionary and artisan.   Early on the

Sabbath morning a prayer-meeting was held, public service at ten, and again at three. In the afternoon service Brother Tindall and myself took part, and here my first really extempore address in the Dutch language was delivered. In vain I pleaded that I was merely a novice in the language, only six months having elapsed since I acquired the sounds of the Dutch alphabet. Yielding, however, to importunity, I made the attempt, and spoke with facility for upwards of ten minutes to the surprise of my travelling companions, and to my own satisfaction. One thing struck me, viz., the general wakefulness of the congregation, notwithstanding the extreme heat of the weather, and the drowsy period of the day. The fact is, every one in this part of the world deems it quite necessary to have a good siesta after the midday meal. We were not a little amused ourselves, after dinner, to be led into our respective apartments for the express purpose of courting "tired nature's sweet restorer, balmy sleep;" and to facilitate its approach, as soon as we had entered, the shutters from without were carefully closed to exclude the heat and splendour of the day. Very soon the whole household were in a deep sleep. After a good rest of more than an hour, the shutters were thrown open, a rap at the door was heard, a cup of hot coffee was served to each, a slight ablution in cooling water followed, the church-bell was rung, and we were all refreshed and ready for a wakeful and devout engagement in the services of the sanctuary. That the process should form part of an established system amused us; but, judging from the comfortable effects produced, we could not but think it a most rational custom, especially in the hot days of a South African summer. All hail to this part at least of German philosophy!

Monday, December 18th.—We were now entering upon a hot and, to a great extent, waterless country called the Karroo. We had just passed through the Zandveld, or sand country; now we were to traverse one where the surface was hard, and rocky, and barren. All the vessels we could devote to the purpose were therefore replenished with the soft and sweet waters of the Elephant River, every drop of which would have to be used with care, as almost all the water we should find for some time to come would be so salt as to be nearly unfit for use. The Rev. Barnabas Shaw records that some years before, the Rev. Mr. Schmelen, whilst crossing the Karroo, owing to heat, thirst, and fatigue, lost forty-five of his oxen, and in consequence was detained several weeks in this dreadful wilderness. Amidst the prayers and good wishes of our dear friends, and in firm reliance on the God of Israel, we entered upon this terrible part of the wilderness, believing that He would neither fail nor forsake us.

The following days were dreadfully hot, so that we were obliged to travel almost the whole of the nights, and rest by day.

On Tuesday, 19th, the thermometer stood at 112° in the shade. The most effectual shade we could find was underneath our waggons, where on a springbok skin spread out for a carpet I was prosecuting my studies in the Dutch language, and young Henry Tindall with notes and flute taking his first lessons in music, though the tar, melted by the heat, was dropping constantly from the wheels and other parts of the waggon where any had been applied. We were most effectually sheltered from the direct rays of the sun in this position, but the reflection from the sand made it intolerable; the atmosphere seemed like particles of fire; our poor fowls lay helplessly upon the sand in the shade, with outspread wings and open beaks, as if just on the point of expiring.

Thursday, December 21st, Midsummer-day of the southern hemisphere.—This morning we reached Zwaart Doorn Rivier, "Blackthorn River." Everywhere the sand was loose and barren, save here and there a solitary shrub. The river, so called, was a mere line of glowing sand over which the streams of periodical rains *had* flowed *some time*, but all had long since disappeared from the surface. There were some fine large blackthorn trees in the neighbourhood, which looked as if they might be umbrageous in favourable seasons, and so tastefully arranged in some places, that, but for the waste and arid appearance of all nature, one might have supposed it the site of some old park; but in general these, and others that lined the sides of the river, were so dry and withered and void of foliage, as to afford only the semblance of shade against the sun. Our men dug in various parts of the river-bed, but no water could be found, except what was nauseously salt. Yet, our supply of fresh water from the Elephant River being exhausted, we were compelled to use it. Our tea and coffee were so impregnated with the mineral that morning and evening we were literally taking saline draughts! Sick headache, feverish symptoms, and indescribable languor, were some of the distressing effects of the intense heat and salt water. The body seemed loaded at every point, and instead of the blood coursing lightly and actively through the veins, it seemed as if every vein was weighted with lead, rendering the slightest exertion intolerable.   Yet at this miserable place, owing to a domestic mishap, we were detained nearly two days, and our poor oxen suffered extremely.   Though without water for nearly three days, and almost dying of thirst, many refused the water obtained by digging in the bed of the river.   At length we found a place at some distance where better water was obtained; of this they drank scantily; but one of them, feebler than the rest, after drinking, lay down in the water to die.   Had he died there, the best water in the place would have been corrupted, and become quite unusable by any other travellers who might happen to pass that way; and as Mr. Haddy and party were to follow us in a week, we were all the more concerned to preserve it in a usable state at least for his oxen.   The only plan we could adopt was to attach the whole team to the horns of the poor animal, and draw him up the slope leading down to the water, that he might die there.   We left him in charge of the people who were living near, but, as we heard, he died soon after our departure.

On Friday evening, when the heat had somewhat abated, we resumed our journey, all being very languid and poorly, Mrs. R. especially so, on whose account we proceeded very slowly, and only a short distance that evening.   Next morning we took only a short stage, and rested again.   At noon, being in the vicinity of a periodical stream, we obtained water of a little better quality, but still quite brackish.   Having no suitable food, I went out amongst the trees with my fowling-piece, and brought home two turtle-doves for my invalid wife, this being the only " game " I found in the neighbourhood.

On Saturday evening, 23rd, we reached one of the prettiest outspan places we had yet met with, and though it was not comparable to Elim, with its " twelve wells of water, and threescore and ten palm-trees," it was a good encampment. Our waggons were drawn up, side by side, on a tolerably good grass plat, surrounded at nearly every point by shrubs and lofty trees, whilst the water was a slight improvement on that of the preceding day. As the water improved we gradually lost our distressing languors, and regained our wonted spirits, and, feeling more comfortable in health, and having a pleasant resting-place, we enjoyed a very sweet Sabbath in our sylvan retreat.

At the earliest dawn on Monday, the 25th, our first Christmas in South Africa, and our first Christmas at Midsummer, we commenced the ascent of the Khamies Berg range of mountains, at the summit of one of which our mission station, called Lily Fountain, stands, at an elevation of 5,000 feet above the level of the sea. The roads now began to be terrific, and it seemed a constant miracle that our waggons were preserved from turning over. The exertion of dragging them up a very long and rugged height, heavily laden as they were, was tremendous : and though the oxen were rested every minute or two, I feared they would not be able to get them to the top. The patient creatures stood remarkably well as long as the morning air kept tolerably cool, but as soon as the sun arose, with burning heat, they grew faint and flagged, and some lay down and refused to rise. After a tedious delay, some of our loose oxen were yoked in the place of those that had failed, and by dint of great effort we at last attained the summit, faint and exhausted by the heat, and early morning toil. It was a cheerless Christmas, and one of much physical discomfort, owing to fatigue and heat, and want of shade and water. We thought of home with its frost and snow, bright fires, snug apartments, family meetings, and the multitudes who went to the house of God with the voice of joy and singing. But there were no regrets. We had counted the cost, made a voluntary sacrifice for Christ, and were content. At our family worship appropriate portions of Scripture were read and hymns sung that day. In the evening we went another stage, and were struck with the sublimely rugged character of the mountain scenery, as our waggons travelled slowly along the winding, but steadily ascending path, crossing the points where base locked into base. The wild grandeur of the scene appeared under an ever-changing aspect; and when the night darkened in upon us, and the stars glistened in the vault above, the gigantic forms of these rugged mountains, wrapped in the nocturnal gloom, inspired the soul with profound and overwhelming awe. We thought of Sinai with its thunders and lightnings and the " voice of the trumpet exceeding loud, so that the people that were in the camp trembled ; " and of all the terribly sublime associations which its name recalls; and we could not help thinking that the actual Sinaitic range does not probably present scenes of more savage grandeur than do some of these Khamies Bergen.

Filled with awe as I gazed, I could not but feel that, though it was a small thing for me to traverse this gloom and grandeur, knowing as I did that others had gone before, and that a mission station was flourishing far in advance of my present position, the man who first threaded his way through these stupendous highlands, and established that Gospel Zion "on the top of the mountains," must have been a man of extraordinary enterprise, and the wife of that man must have been inspired by a courage higher than that of ordinary women.   Both were nerved not only with natural courage, but by that which religion imparts; a courage roused by zeal for Christ to a pitch adequate to all sights however awful, and to all occasions however trying.   Such were Barnabas Shaw, and Jane, his wife.

December 26th.—Still very bad road, steep and rugged.   In the afternoon, as we travelled over a more level part than any we had recently had, two persons were seen in the distance on horseback, travelling towards us at a swift pace.   One was Mr. Jackson, the missionary at Lily Fountain, the other Mr. Macleod, who had recently arrived there from Cape Town, and who was to accompany us to the Nisbett Bath mission station in the capacity of schoolmaster, and assistant in the work of the mission.   It was a joyful though brief interview, for soon both bade us farewell, and left us at nearly race pace, to inform Mrs. Jackson that we should be at the station that night.   As we drew near, the corn lands, in all their richness, were spread out to our view, some belonging to the natives, others for the use of the mission, and all nearly ready for the harvest. At dusk, we released our own jaded oxen from the yoke, and had two powerful teams belonging to the station to take us up the final and steep ascent. Just before reaching the mission house we travelled along the centre of a fine valley on the mountain heights, nearly a mile in length, and of considerable breadth, covered with waving corn, a sight that would have been beauteous to behold, had not the day been too far spent. What a change in the face of the country, and in the habits of the people, since the venerable Barnabas Shaw first asked leave of the old chief Haaimaap "to cultivate corn for his own use!" These Namaqua valleys, covered over with corn, and, in the poetry of Scripture, "shouting" for joy and "singing" for gladness, are literally the fruits of Gospel labour. There is now "seed for the sower, and bread for the eater."

We had now passed over nearly four hundred miles, including the windings of the road, and were all unspeakably thankful that though we had suffered much from heat, salt water, and fatigue, no serious accident had occurred to our waggons, or to ourselves, though it is no unusual thing for even the most practised drivers to overturn their waggons in these rugged mountain regions.

The mission house is a substantial stone building. In front is a grass plat, and in the centre of that a stone pillar surmounted by an excellent dial, though, as it is not exactly adapted to the latitude of the place, it is only at the hour of noon that it shows true *solar* time, which, when the equation of time is applied, gives the time by *clock*. An orchard and kitchen garden are also connected with the mission premises, and an ample supply of good water is at hand. The chapel, of stone, is a very creditable structure, and accommodates about four hundred hearers. It stands on higher ground than the mission house, and at a distance of three hundred yards from it. Wandering one day to a place called the *poort*, or " gate," an opening in the mountain top towards the west, a scene of sublime grandeur presented itself. From an elevation of five thousand feet above the sea, a perfect ocean of mountain peaks, mostly lower than the position from which we viewed them, stretched away to an immense extent, and beyond the limits of the land lay the dark blue waters of the South Atlantic, at a distance of about forty miles from the spot. Another day I stood upon the same spot once more, to see the same grand sight, but, to my amazement, the waters of the ocean had disappeared, and instead of them a white appearance, perfectly level, and apparently solid as marble, was visible. I stood bewildered for some time, as if I had seen a vision, and could in no way account for the mystery; but three or four hours afterwards a thin white mist came curling and creeping up from crag to crag and peak to peak, till the whole top of the mountain was enveloped in a haze, and everything loaded with moisture. Never having lived above the clouds before, this was to me a new phenomenon, though, as I afterwards found, familiar to the people. The seemingly solid white mass reflecting so brightly the light of the sun that fell on it from above was simply this mist covering the face of the ocean, and gathering increased density as it rose into a colder atmosphere, till the whole mountain range was encompassed with it as with a garment.

As we could now muster four mission families, including that of Mr. Macleod, we had an occasional service in English, which, being the most recent comer, it fell to my lot to conduct. On the Sabbath, in addition to the sermons in Dutch, delivered by Messrs. Jackson and Tindall, the usual watch-night services were commenced at ten p.m., by a sermon in English by myself, followed by addresses in Dutch. The building was well filled by a deeply attentive and intelligent-looking audience, when all felt the solemnity and impressiveness of the occasion. To us it was particularly interesting that, in a sanctuary on one of the highest summits of the Khamies range, five thousand feet above the sea, such scenes should be transpiring at the midnight hour. We could not help thinking of Isaiah ii. 2 : "And it shall come to pass in the last days, that the mountain of the Lord's house shall be established in the top of the mountains, and shall be exalted above the hills; and all nations shall flow unto it."   And in the agricultural tastes awakened since the Gospel came to this land, we saw a *partial* fulfilment of the fourth verse, and the *promise* of its full and universal accomplishment amongst all nations: "They shall beat their swords into ploughshares, and their spears into pruninghooks : nation shall not lift up sword against nation, neither shall they learn war any more."

On Tuesday, January 2nd, 1844, having spent a happy week with Mr. Jackson, and having had our waggons replenished with good things, we left with good heart and cheerful spirits, though in certain prospect of much to try us, the portion of country over which we had now to travel being hotter and more

D

destitute of water than any through which we had yet had to pass; almost literally, "a dry and thirsty land, where no water is." Our party, too, was increased by the addition of Mr. and Mrs. Macleod, and the sister of the latter, so that our waggons amounted to three. It was very pleasant to have additional company, but as each waggon brings with it an additional team of oxen, and an increase of men, and of human wants, we regarded the addition, on the whole, as very serious in traversing a desert where scarcely sufficient water can be found for the sustenance of a few. At the *best* season, it is an advantage to travel this part of the country with a small party; for whole parties of natives have nearly perished for thirst when passing between our two stations, Khamies Berg and Nisbett Bath, at this dreadful period of the year. To us there was no alternative. It was impossible to wait till the proper season for travelling; so, with a list of places where water might *possibly* be found, and the distance between each carefully marked down, we ventured forth, putting our whole trust in the protection of the Almighty.

At dinner, the first day, our fare was varied by the addition of a novel dish, viz., a peacock, many of which are to be shot in the neighbourhood. They are not to be compared to our English peacocks for beauty, the plumage being of a light brown, speckled. Though the flesh was good, we should hardly have esteemed it one of the highest luxuries, notwithstanding the opinions of Roman emperors and modern epicures.

In descending the mountains to the plains that lay between us and the Orange River, the roads were fearfully steep, and obstructed by huge rocks and stones, so that if our waggons had not been very strongly built, and very carefully driven, they must have been riven to pieces. My wife, in writing home, says of this part of the journey: "The road we had to pass the two first days is the most terrific among all the terrific roads of this wild country." On the Wednesday afternoon we prepared to encounter the notorious Pieter's Kloof, a pass through the mountains, unrivalled for the confusion and the chaotic appearance of its rocky masses. One would imagine that in ages immemorially remote, immense upheaving forces had driven up the granitic crusts of our globe, tumbling over all the superincumbent strata into the wildest disorder, and burying whatever soil there was beneath the inverted strata in the mighty overthrow. The whole scene on every side was calculated to produce an abiding feeling of awe; the grey, aged, and naked appearance of the rocks made one feel as if a sight of chaos was vouchsafed, before God spake order out of confusion, and made our earth a fit habitation for man. It looked a fit abode for tigers, and every raving beast of prey. Soil was scarcely to be seen anywhere, so strewn was every part with loose rock and stone. Vegetation scarcely existed, save here and there a solitary shrub, a euphorbia, a sunburnt aloe, and very occasionally a *koker boom*, or quiver-tree, of light spongy wood, out of which the Bushmen make quivers for their arrows.

Of all the spots on earth, this must at least take rank as one of the most savagely naked, wild, and desolate, anywhere to be found. In this dreary spot we were detained four days and nights, through the breaking down of Mr. Macleod's waggon in passing over the rugged road. A messenger was instantly despatched on horseback to Mr. Jackson (who was a good smith), and with very acceptable promptness he soon appeared on horseback, accompanied by one or two men skilled in the art of Vulcan, with tools and iron to repair the breach. We all felt much indebted to Mr. Jackson, who with his men worked unceasingly most of the night. After putting us in travelling trim, he returned to his station, and we might have resumed our journey had it not been Saturday; but as the waggon had to be repacked, and we could reach no water until very late, we resolved to spend the Sabbath in the kloof, though it was intensely hot, and the water nauseously saline. During the day we were visited by a few people who had got to know of our accident, and with these we held two services, endeavouring to make the best use of the circumstances in which we were placed.

From this time the weather was insufferably hot, and water very scarce and brackish, whilst we had sand and dust in abundance. Sometimes we were almost stifled in our waggons by the clouds of fine impalpable dust in which we were enveloped, and which found its way through every crevice. Even our best closed boxes were no proof against this most insinuating pest.

On Saturday, January 13th, we reached Quick Fountain, where we halted for the Sabbath. We enjoyed the usual Sabbath services with our people, notwithstanding the melting process through which we were passing; and in the afternoon my curiosity to behold a veritable Bushman in a state of wild nature was satisfied. He was short, lean, nude, save a narrow strip of leather round the waist, which served the purpose of a hunger belt. Attached to this was a small skin pouch, a receptacle for any little valuables he might pick up in the wilderness. His only weapons were a bow and poisoned arrows. His sole companion a dog, gaunt and meagre as himself. In his hand he held something burnt black as a cinder, which, on examining more closely, we found to be the head of a jackal. He had captured and made a meal off the animal, and this head, thrown into the embers and roasted black, was a delicious morsel reserved for the next meal. He had, however, something else in prospect, for he had shot a poisoned arrow into an ostrich, and was deliberately following on the track of the wounded bird. He was in no hurry, and though he had lost sight of his game, he knew it would only run a certain distance, and then, from the smart of the wound, aggravated by the poison, lie down and perhaps die. His practised eye would trace its course unfailingly over the country, and he knew that by-and-by he would secure the prize. He asked for tobacco, but we had none to give, and after awhile he went his solitary way into the depths of the wilderness, a real child of nature. At this place we lost two of our oxen, one of which, on going down to the water, drank, and lay down to die.

On the Monday, January 15th, whilst our waggons were standing outspanned in the open plain, several Bushmen came up, bringing with them a donkey that had strayed from the party of a trader (Mr. Morris, whom we knew) who had gone to the northward several weeks before. During this time they had taken charge of the animal, and now, hearing that we should meet with Mr.

Morris on arriving at our station, honestly delivered up
their charge. This act might put to the blush the conduct
of many living in civilised lands and bearing the name
of Christians ; as, if they had chosen to keep the animal
and use him for their own purposes, no means existed
for proving their dishonesty, or bringing them to
punishment. We did not fail to remunerate them with
what proved to them some very valuable presents.
Unfortunately, however, the day after, the ass escaped
from the Damara lad who had charge of him, and
made his way back in the direction of his old friends.

After a day of intense heat and exhausting travel,
during which our oxen had no water, we reached
Gezelschap Plat Klip, where water is generally to be
found, and where we felt almost sure of meeting with
some. Before they were unloosed from the yoke, the
poor oxen, recognising the place where they had
often quenched their thirst before, were bellowing
piteously for water, and as soon as they were set at
liberty, they made for the spot where they had often
found it, but where none was to be found now. It was
distressing to witness the disappointment of the poor
animals ; and their loud bellowings, which I had never
before heard during the whole journey, produced a
more painful effect on my feelings than anything had
done for a long time. No alternative remained but to
get a hasty tea, and push on again in the cool of the
night ; and whilst we partook of the refreshing draught,
we were glad to see our poor oxen, unable to eat for
thirst, lying down around us, and gathering a little
strength for the great effort they were soon to make.
From the eminence on which our waggons were drawn

up, an immense plain, covered with a long tufted grass withered almost to whiteness, spread out in ample extent, bounded on the north by the Gariepine Walls, all empurpled in the light of the setting sun.   These mountains, of massive grandeur, exhibited a magnificent spectacle; and to us the view was not only magnificent, but delightful, because we knew that along the base of those mountains the waters of the Orange River were flowing to the ocean.   To reach those mountains before the heat of the next day was an absolute necessity, and the consummation we devoutly wished; but whether our oxen, faint with thirst and with the labour of the day, would be able to draw our waggons over that ample plain of loose, sandy soil, a work of ten hours of hard straining in the yoke, was very doubtful.   It seemed much more likely that they would fail utterly by the way, and leave us at a standstill in the middle of the fiery plain all next day.   But we were compelled to try, and our hope lay in the coolness of the night air, and the good providence of our God.   As soon, therefore, as tea was over, everything was "made fast," and the oxen yoked in.   In a few minutes we had descended from the edge of the plateau where we had rested, and were in the plain.   Providentially a refreshing air, cool by comparison with the glow of the day, was stirring over the plain, so that, to our delight, the poor oxen pulled with more than ordinary vigour. The monotonous, low, grinding sound of the wheels, as they turned on the sandy soil, soothed us into an hour or two's refreshing sleep, in spite of the resolution to keep watch during the night, so that midnight arrived almost unawares.   We now spanned out in the midst of the plain for two hours, for the sake of resting the men and oxen. A fire soon blazed cheerily, and the supper of our waggoners was boiling in the pot; when suddenly a mishap occurred that might have proved very serious. The long grass near the men's fire, so dry as to be almost always near the point of ignition, was seized by the flame, which, wafted by the night breeze, spread rapidly towards the waggons, all of which were drawn up side by side, very near to each other. In our waggon was a quantity of gunpowder, an annual present from the Colonial Government to the chief of our station; so that, in case of an explosion, our waggons must have been shivered to pieces, whilst some of our party must almost certainly have been struck and killed by the flying fragments. All felt the danger, and ran instantly to the waggons to make loose the spades. These were energetically plied in throwing the loose soil on the approaching flames, and at the same time beating down the burning grass; and just when the grass growing under the wheels of my waggon took fire, we conquered the flames, and our peril was past. The real magnitude of the danger was seen more distinctly when it was past than at the time; and the gratitude for our deliverance was greater when we had time to consider all it might have involved, than immediately after the excitement of the occurrence.

At about half-past two a.m. our journey was resumed, and after tediously travelling for several hours, on a morning of suffocating heat, the breeze having dropped, we found ourselves winding through the bases of some of the outer and solitary mountains, not very far from the river. At length the foliage of the trees growing close to the banks of the stream came in sight, when Mr. Tindall, his son, myself, and Mr. Macleod, hurried down before the waggons, all perfectly bathed in perspiration, anxious to catch the first sight of the river, and hoping to find it sufficiently low for us to cross without delay. To our great disappointment it was now full, and presented a noble stream of five hundred yards in breadth, and twenty or thirty feet in depth, with a very rapid current towards the South Atlantic. We were obliged to make up our minds to remain at least a week at the river, even if we should succeed in speedily obtaining the aid of native swimmers. Fortunately, some living in the vicinity of the river soon appeared, and offered their services at a reasonable rate. Away they went with axe in hand to seek among the trees lining the river banks suitable poles for the construction of a raft; and as our waggon was first to be put across, whilst we were busy unloading it and placing its contents together on the sand, Brother Tindall and Co. brought a large supply of branches of the willow and other trees, and formed a booth around and above our luggage, and this sylvan retreat formed the abode of myself and my wife for nearly the whole of the week following, the other brethren occupying their waggons until obliged to adopt a similar habitation to our own.

The swimmers having collected a good quantity of wood, and long strips of the bark of the mimosa tree for lashing the poles together, the making of the raft commenced. A number of poles of willow wood, mostly young trees that had been used for a similar purpose before, and which they had found thrown up

on the bank, were placed side by side, and then bound
firmly to cross pieces near each end with strips of
bark, which, when swollen by immersion in the water,
holds more firmly than rope, without any danger of
slipping. Several layers of poles were placed on these,
and all firmly bound together, till a raft sufficiently
buoyant was formed. It was about ten feet in length
by five or six in breadth. But attached to the front
were two light poles, extending six or eight feet beyond
the body of the raft, and looking very much like a pair
of shafts. When it was sufficiently weighted, resolving
to accompany them, I surmounted the whole myself.
The best swimmers now grasped the projecting shafts
with one hand, the others ranged along each side did
the same, and the word of command being given,
away we launched into the deep, the swimmers grasping the float with one hand, and swimming with
the other and their feet, thus propelling the clumsy
and waterlogged craft as rapidly as their strength would
allow; but so heavy was the labour, that they puffed
and blowed, shouted and groaned, quite enough to
make even a strong man nervous; and before reaching
mid-stream some began to rest on the float, making it
tip to an alarming depth, first on one side and then on the
other. At one time they all ceased swimming together,
resting for a few moments on the float as they continued
immersed in the water, which so nearly submerged the
whole concern, that, though on the top of a box, I
stood nearly knee deep in water. Thinking my friends
on shore would take alarm at our position, I drew out
my pocket-handkerchief, and displayed it to the breeze
by way of conveying the assurance that, notwithstanding

the apparent peril of my situation, I was not quite
bereft of all presence of mind.   After resting a little,
our swimmers struck out afresh, and before long we
gained the northern shore, and I trod the soil of Great
Namaqualand, of which the Ky Gariep, the native
name for the Orange River, is the southern boun-
dary.   Owing to the force of the current, we had
drifted half a mile or more down the stream, so that
the point of debarkation was much lower down than
the point from which we had started on the south side.

When the heavy boxes, all of which were saturated
with water, had been conveyed high up the bank, the tedious process of unbinding the raft and separating it into
its component parts had to be commenced.   Each man
then shouldered a pole which he was to bear, or rather
which was to bear him, back to the other side.   But a
painful task had first to be performed.   As the current
had drifted us so far down the stream, of course in
getting back to our waggons on the opposite side the
force of the current had to be allowed for, and we all
had to go nearly a mile along the north bank before we
could take to the water.   This was no trifle; the day was
intensely hot, this being the very hottest period of the
year, and the neighbourhood of the Orange River one
of the hottest regions of the world.   The light, dusty
sand, absolutely destitute of grass or of any vegetation
to bind it together, is so loose, that at every step one
sinks ankle deep, and every particle is like a particle of
fire.   Yet our swimmers, fresh from the water, had no
other alternative than to pass through the fiery ordeal.
After standing awhile beneath the scanty shade of a
mimosa, with poles ready shouldered, away they bounded,

one after another, light as the antelope, to the next tree, where they would stand another moment beneath the imperfect shade, lifting first one foot off the ground, then the other, as a temporary relief from the burning heat. In this way, the whole party, nude as Adamites, reached the place where we were to start for the other side. How the poor fellows could stand the trial surpassed my comprehension, for though I was well clad in light apparel, suited to the weather, and had stout English shoes, my feet burned most painfully, and with the heat generally I felt almost knocked up. Being now assembled amongst the trees at the water side, the men prepared their " river horses " for mounting ; *i.e.*, each man, taking the pole he carried, inserted a peg of wood in a hole bored for the purpose about three feet from the upper end ; then, striding across the pole, just as a little boy rides a walking-stick, and grasping the peg with his left hand to prevent the pole rolling, he launched forth, swimming with his right hand and his feet.

Being unused to this mode of swimming, and not knowing whether I should succeed in managing such a concern, I resolved to swim in English fashion, though being already somewhat exhausted I had some misgivings as to whether my strength would suffice to cross a stream so broad, with a current so rapid. For some distance, therefore, I kept near the swimmers on their " blocks," occasionally taking the peg with my left hand as a relief, till, finding my strength hold out much better than I had anticipated, I went away on my own responsibility, to the admiration of the natives, who shouted one to another in combined Dutch and Namaqua : " Look, look, look at the Englishman ! " I suppose it seemed a venture to them, for I never saw a native swim that stream except with the aid of a log of willow; and on reaching the southern shore, I was surprised to feel so little fatigue. Still the native mode, when acquired, must be a great saving of strength, the support of the " block " being so great as to enable the swimmer to rest, without danger, whenever he grows weary. One of these *anthropopotami*, with the support of his block, brought all my clothes, formed into a bundle, on the top of his head, with my broad-brimmed Manilla hat surmounting that as naturally as possible, but presenting a spectacle sufficiently grotesque to excite the amusement of all the party.

During the absence of the swimmers, our own men, acting as cooks, were busily engaged in preparing dinner, as after their exertion they required both food and rest. Decently attired, they assembled for the meal, of which they partook heartily, requiring that it should be supplemented by tea. Then followed a lounge or a *siesta* among the sylvan shades of the river, which to us, impatient as we were to get away, seemed of unconscionable length. " Never while away time " was a maxim with which they had no sympathy; and accustomed to the rapid modes of transit adopted in our own country, we found our patience severely taxed by the dilatoriness of the natives the very first day. The conveyance of three loaded rafts a day to the other side of the river seemed to us a very small amount of work; and as our three waggons, with their loads, would require twelve such trips, we saw that four days would be consumed in the transit alone. I had made a trial of the river, however, and could understand better than those who had not, that the crossing of such a stream six times a day, which of course three loads involves, was no trifle, especially taking into account the loading and unloading, and travelling a mile up the north bank to return again, as necessitated by the current. In fact, a little consideration showed that for men not naturally strong and muscular, and frequently underfed, the tax on flesh and blood must have been very severe. There was no prospect of expediting matters if left in native hands, so the brethren Tindall, Macleod, and myself, resolved on making a raft of our own. It was to be made in *no time*, to be worked with oars, and, in short, we were going to show the natives science! A good place for making and launching this raft was found about three hundred yards lower down the river, and with adze and auger my two brethren were soon manfully at work; but the exertion of swimming on the previous day, and the extreme heat, rendered me so languid and feverish that I could scarcely sit erect to observe them. Five or six good-sized trees of willow, a very buoyant wood, were obtained and shaped by the adze; these were laid side by side and pegged by wooden pegs to a cross-piece at each end. Another layer and cross-piece, pegged as before, seemed sufficient for buoyancy. An upright was then fixed on each side, hollowed out at the top, as rowlocks for the oar.

This simple affair we imagined was to do wonders. It was duly christened *The Experiment*, and launched. We were soon on board, Mr. Tindall taking the " bow oar " on the shore side, and myself the other, whilst Mr. Macleod stood astern to preserve the balance. Our first object was to row our raft up the river side to the place where our waggons were standing; but as the current was very strong against us, we found this hard work.   As we had to stand to row, and had no rail thrown round to serve the purpose of a bulwark, in case of a slip, we were in danger of going overboard. Before long an accident occurred.   Mr. T., rowing the bow oar, missed his stroke, and, finding himself going, instinctively grasped my cravat, and took me backwards with him into the stream.   Fortunately we were not far from the shore, and fell into water only breast deep; and though well drenched, we soon scrambled on board again ; and the water at this season generally being of a temperature of ninety degrees, we suffered nothing, and were only laughed at.   We could not but feel thankful, however, that we had not gone over on the other side, where the water was out of our depth.   As it was becoming dark, and we were weary, we moored our barque to a tree for the night, and went home to sup and slumber, hoping next morning to complete the task we had left unfinished.

Next morning, refreshed by rest, and strengthened by a good breakfast, we set to work in high spirits, and got our raft much better up against the current, till, all three of us happening to get to one side, our frail vessel turned bodily over.   I was entirely submerged, and under the raft.   Mr. Macleod managed to scramble upon the inverted concern, and was stretched full length where the keel ought to have been; whilst Mr. Tindall was holding on, as he said, "where best he could." We were none of us entirely out of our depth, however, so that we sustained no injury.   But to the non-swimmers these accidents were rather alarming, and Mr. Macleod, by this last immersion, got his courage so much cooled, that he resolved to have nothing more to do with *The Experiment*, regarding it as a " dead failure." Mr. Tindall and myself, reluctant to give up our attempts, thought there would be no harm in another trial, and as the rowing had proved a bad speculation, we converted our oars into poles for pushing our craft up the stream. This answered pretty well at first, till another mishap occurred. The moment before I had found the bottom at a depth of about five feet, but on next dipping the pole, owing to the unevenness of the bed of the river, no bottom was to be found, and, overbalancing myself, in I fell ! I was in fact out of my depth, and, had I not been able to swim, must almost certainly have been drowned. A few strokes, however, brought me to shore, and on turning to look after my companion, I saw him safely on board the raft, but in a rather awkward predicament, for, having only one oar, and being utterly unable to manage the raft alone, the current had carried him farther out towards mid-stream, and was rapidly drifting him down towards the sea.

Rather bewildered for the moment as to my best course of action, and thinking that at least a few words of consolation might be acceptable, I shouted : " Don't be alarmed, Brother Tindall, you are sure to come out *somewhere!* " But our best intentions are sometimes misunderstood, for Mr. Tindall afterwards told me that at those words his heart sank within him, thinking it a proof that I was abandoning him to his fate. Though I had no suspicion of his discouragement, I swam to his aid, met with a very cordial reception on board, and, after mutual consultation as to the best mode of action, soon succeeded in nearing the shore; and then in disgust we finally abandoned *The Experiment*, and resigned ourselves as pacifically as possible to the slow but sure mode adopted by the natives. Though our wives were not fully aware of the danger to which we were exposed, as the thick trees on the river-bank, which is sixteen or twenty feet above the river, interposed between us and the place where our waggons were standing, they were very much relieved when our experiments ceased, and on calm reflection we all saw reason for much gratitude that no serious accident had occurred, especially as neither of my brethren was able to swim. Though our failure did not facilitate our departure from the river, it was no cause of delay, as the natives were busily engaged in conveying our things to the other side all the time, and under our own inspection. No doubt they were greatly amused to find that in their own way they could do better than we. A boat would have been of immense service, and this we could have managed perfectly; so we resolved, as soon as we could communicate with Cape Town, we would make a stir by way of obtaining such a convenience—a point that was gained on my next visit.

Not only were we anxious to get away from the river for the purpose of saving time, but also on account of the extreme discomfort of the place. The heat is excessive, 120° in the shade; vegetation there is none, save the trees by the river; the light dusty sand burns like fire, running the quicksilver of a thermometer thrust into it at half-past two in the afternoon up to 159° ;* and to increase the discomfort, every afternoon winds of extreme violence set in from the west, blowing clouds of light dust that seemed to envelope the tops of the mountains, many of which are two or three thousand feet above the level of the river; whilst, setting into our skin, constantly bathed in perspiration, it produced an extremely unpleasant sensation.   Mr. Bell, the Surveyor-General of the Cape Colony, says, in his Report on Little Namaqualand, in 1855: " I saw Namaqualand at the best time of the year, and its aspect, even then, was far from inviting. The sandy flats and rugged mountains in the south present a general character of wild sterility; but it is in the northern tracts, bordering on the Orange River, where its desert assumes its most appalling appearance. Twenty-four years of occasional travel have led me over most parts of Southern Africa. I have been in the Kallihari deserts and across a considerable portion of the Island of Ascension, and therefore ought to know what a wilderness is; but until I saw the country near the banks of the Orange River, in Namaqualand, I had no adequate idea of utter desolation." Through this part of the country we had been travelling for a fortnight, and now that we were in its " most appalling " neighbourhood, no one will wonder we were anxious to depart.

It was to me a great delight when my waggon was separated into its elementary parts, and wheels and lower parts placed on the float for transit; and as now many small articles were loose on the northern shore, and I was wishful to have them under my own protection during the night, I accompanied the cargo this

* Lectures of Sir John Herschel.

time, not in the capacity of a passenger, but of a swimmer, assisting to propel the raft.   On nearing the northern shore I left the raft and men, and swam down the stream with the rapid current.   But I had scarcely left when a long-armed swimmer came in pursuit, cheered on by the shouts of his companions, " Catch the Englishman, catch the Englishman!"   He could not succeed, however, and the Englishman gained the ground first.   I had found the value of this art to a missionary before, and now I gathered that the natives thought all the more of a man able to help himself in this respect.   In the evening another raft, containing the last remnant of my property, and incomparably the most valuable of all, my good wife, seated on her Neptunian car, was put through the river.   It required some nerve, as it was so dark as to make it needful to keep a fire burning on the shore she had left, and also one on that where I stood, to guide the swimmers to the right spot.   Her heart had not failed her, and with light step she bounded from the raft to join me on the soil of Great Namaqualand.   Our boxes, and other baggage, lay upon the beach, our waggon was lying in pieces around, all our friends were on the other side of the river, even the swimmers had returned to sup and sleep; and all alone, with the exception of one elderly man named Tonnis, we spent the night beneath the sylvan shades on the bank of the stream.   Tonnis aided us in drawing our waggon-sail for a roof over a temporary support, and then with mattresses on the sand we reposed for the night.   Serpents and scorpions may have been there, and for aught we can tell they may have made a passage over us, whilst we slept; nothing was more likely than that a wolf or tiger should come down from the mountains to the river side to drink after the heat of the day; but nothing harmed us. We had "hearkened unto" Him who had called us to that spot, and into those circumstances, and He made us to dwell safely. Adam and Eve, in the bowers of Paradise, were not safer under the immediate guard of heaven's angels than were we beneath the bowers of the Ky Gariep!

By Thursday morning, the 25th of January, our whole party were safely landed on the north side of the river. The last scene of interest was the passage of the river by our draught-oxen. Till now they had been in charge of two men, but in the afternoon they were brought to the river-side, when after a few shouts from the men of " trek, loop," and a sharp crack of the huge whip, led cautiously by the old oxen, they all readily took the water and swam through. They seemed to swim deeply, as the whole body was submerged, and nothing but their horns and faces were visible, the latter thrown up horizontally on the surface of the water. They all landed safely, but one wilder than the rest took the water again, and when we saw him in the middle of the river, borne along by the current, and turning round and round like a drowning cat, we almost gave him up for lost. At last making for the other side he reached it in safety, and we were obliged to send two swimmers over to escort him back. Having repacked our waggons, and paid the swimmers for their services, as soon as the glowing heat of the day began to abate, the oxen were put to the yoke, and, just fresh from the river, looked as if their coats had been polished for the occasion. Away we went on what were now some of the last stages of the journey, with light hearts, having the trees of the river on our right, and the rugged " walls " of the Ky Gariep, *i.e.*, the Great River, as the natives call it, on our left, till, coming to a natural opening at their base, we turned and took our proper course northward. Next morning we reached Zand Fontein, where a son of the chief soon made his appearance, mounted on horseback, and bringing the pleasing intelligence, that his father and a number of his principal men were approaching.

Before long the whole cavalcade appeared, descending the slope of a hill, all mounted in true African style, on oxback, the chief, by way of distinction, riding a milk-white ox. On coming up to our encampment they dismounted, and after we had shaken hands with the chief, our whole party had to pass through the same ceremony with every one of the chief's company. A few inquiries were made with respect to the affairs of the station, when the chief and his men considerately withdrew from our waggons to the shade of some camel-thorn trees to pass the heat of the day. Having heard of our arrival at the Orange River, they were coming to " swim us " through, a kindness which we fully appreciated, though they came too late. As they had sent on a man with slaughter sheep for their consumption on the journey, one was soon killed; but as the means for cooking were limited, and the party large, the cooking and eating process was kept up pretty nearly the whole time they remained with us. As they are passionately fond of tea, we sent them a small supply, and after we had refreshed ourselves by partaking of the same beverage, we again made preparations for the start; but as eight-and-forty oxen had to be caught, drawn out and yoked to our three waggons, and upwards of thirty of the chief's company to be bridled and saddled, this occupied some time, and occasioned no small dust and bustle.   At length we were in motion. Evening soon fell, and "the stars appeared."   It was a brilliant night.   Not the fragment of a cloud was visible on the blue arch of heaven.   The finest stars and constellations were up; and the northern heavens immediately in front of our waggons were remarkably rich and full, being at their very best at this season of the year.   The proof was most demonstrative that we had passed from the northern into the southern hemisphere.

During this, one of the last stages of our journey, we experienced a marvellous exhilaration.   Our circumstances were new and interesting.   We had met with some of the people with whom we were to live, and were now nearing our mission home.   If we looked below, the earth appeared barren and blasted; the rocks were eaten into by age and atmospheric influences, and were baked brown by the fiery rays of the sun; but whilst everything below was forbidding, the heavens, those magnificent heavens, "declared the glory of God, and the firmament showed His handiwork."   We appreciated the scene.   Our hearts were filled with devotion, and they naturally found expression in song.   The tune chosen was that sweet and devotional one, "Byzantium:" the hymn—

> "Eternal Wisdom! Thee we praise,
>   Thee the creation sings;

> With Thy loved Name, rocks, hills, and seas,
>   And Heaven's high palace rings.
>
> Thy Hand, how wide it spreads the sky !
>   How glorious to behold !
> Tinged with a blue of heavenly dye,
>   And starred with sparkling gold."

These verses we sang ; and as we sang the oxmen of the chief's company crowded around the waggon, eager to catch every sound, and in their eagerness came so close that the feet of their oxen were in danger of getting under the wheels of our waggon.   Thus we went on our way to our wilderness " Zion with singing, and with everlasting joy upon our heads."   The whole of this night was spent in travelling, with the exception of a rest of two hours, just after midnight; and about seven a.m., from a rising in the road, we looked down upon the station, still a couple of miles distant.   To hearts less enthusiastic the scene was calculated to depress rather than cheer.   A dreary-looking plain was spread out to view, and in the centre of that stood the lone mission·· house and chapel side by side in the midst of a seeming wilderness; for though a few native huts were on the station, they were too small to be seen at that distance. The only verdant spot was the missionary garden to the right of the station, and that was beautifully verdant, with green fig trees and other produce, kept green by daily irrigation from the fountain.   All immediately around us was uninviting.   We were now travelling over a hard, undulating—surface, strewn with loose stones, with rocks, brown and calcined, jutting through here and there.   Large vultures were slowly wheeling in circles far over head, whilst others were perched on the rocks around us, a wild and barren scene.   No trace of vegetation was visible, save here and there a shrivelled tuft of grass, white as the driest hay, and a few aloes of stunted growth in the crevices of the rocks. At eight in the morning, on Saturday, the 27th of January, 1844, our waggons drew up in front of the mission premises, and we felt that the goal towards which we had been almost incessantly travelling, both by sea and by land, for twenty wearisome weeks, was at last attained.

CHAPTER II.

GREAT Namaqualand lies north of the Orange River, between 23° and 28° 30′ of south latitude. It is bounded on the west by the South Atlantic, north by Damara-land, east by the Kallihari Desert, and south by the Orange River. The southern portions at least are a vast elevated table-land, about two thousand feet above the level of the sea. The Nisbett Bath Mission Station " is situated on a plain so elevated that the peaks of mountains that appear lofty at the side of the Orange River, only emerge here a few hundred feet above the surface of the plain, and the barometer only rises to about twenty-six inches." The *plains* of Great Namaqualand, which are the principal feature of the country, are of vast extent, and are many of them covered with a long grass about three feet in height, which, when in seed, and waving in the wind, reminds one of a field of oats. This is commonly known as the Towa or Bushman grass, probably because the plains in Bushmanland, on the south of the Orange River, are mostly covered with it, and because of the important use the Bushman makes of its seed as an article of food. This grass seems adapted by Providence to the hot and dry nature of the country, for it is exceedingly durable, and even after a drought of two or even three years' continuance, it stands erect and waving in the breeze, though white and withered. It must be exceedingly nutritious, for, even after long droughts, the oxen that roam over the plains, only coming every second day to drink at the fountain on the station, are mostly in excellent condition, and sometimes rolling in fat, when the sheep and milch cows that have to feed nearer home are poor and lean in the extreme. This grass formed the only forage for our horses, when on journeys of a hundred and sixty miles from home; but it was strong food, and enabled them to effect their journeys with great energy and spirit. It grows in tufts, the roots of which are three or four inches in diameter, separated from each other by the intervening soil. There is another grass, of a sour kind, growing not in tufts, but in separate stems, like wheat, but reaching a height of only eight or nine inches. This grass, after exposure to the sun's heat for a few weeks, crumbles into dust and utterly perishes. In many parts low shrubs variegate the plain; but except in the neighbourhood of a periodical river, trees are so extremely scarce, that if one affording tolerable shade should happen to occur in a plain over which the traveller passes, he will not fail to mark the exact spot, so that in travelling the same region again, he may know where to find relief by the way.

It sometimes happens, however, that in the distance the traveller espies a winding line of trees exhibiting a green appearance, in refreshing contrast with the grey and barren aspect of all around. These indicate the course of a *periodical stream*, of which there are many in Great Namaqualand; though, unfortunately, they run only for a few hours once in the year, perhaps, or even less frequently, so that generally, instead of the flowing stream, they only exhibit beds of glowing sand to the bloodshot eye of the thirsty traveller. The only stream throughout the whole country that flows perennially is the Orange River. Including its windings, it is about one thousand miles in length from its source to the ocean. Rather to the eastward it has some fine falls. Of this part Mr. Moffat says : " The Orange River here presents the appearance of a plain, miles in breadth, entirely covered with mimosa trees, among which the many branches of the river run, and then tumble over the precipices, raising clouds of mist, when there is any volume of water." But though a constant stream, it can scarcely be said to *water the country;* for its bed lies so much below the general level of the land, that it is rather the great drain of the country through which it has its course. Its banks are generally margined with trees, among which are the willow, the *Acacia detinens,* the rozyntje-boom, the dabby, the ebony, and some others. Several sorts of fish abound in its waters, some, as the natives informed me, of four and a half feet in length, and among the rest the flathead, mentioned by Burchell. The hippopotamus was once very numerous, but their number has been much thinned since firearms were introduced. Though five hundred yards wide at the part with which I am acquainted, in the winter season it is generally low, and at certain fords the traveller can drive his team and waggon through ; in the summer it is generally full, and it is then a formidable stream.

Of *fountains* there are exceedingly few, there being only eight or ten in a country thousands of square miles in extent, one of the strongest being the one on the Nisbett Bath Station, which has a temperature of 102° to 105°. This stream I never saw sensibly diminish in the volume of water it supplies, even during droughts of the longest continuance. The depressions in different parts of the country, however, form *natural reservoirs*, of various dimensions, which are replenished by the thunder-rains, and afford a supply both to the wild animals, and also to the flocks and herds of the people, till, by absorption on the one hand, and by evaporation on the other, the waters disappear. "The soil," says Mr. Moffat, "contiguous to the fountains, is generally so impregnated with saltpetre, as to crackle under the feet like hoar-frost," which is particularly true of that near the fountain of Nisbett Bath.

The *geological* character of the country must be left to the scientific and practical geologist ; but in general it may be remarked that the abundance of granite, gneiss, quartz, mica and talc schists, and clay slate, show it to belong to the earliest formation of rock. And, as Mr. Moffat remarks: "Quartz is so abundantly scattered, reflecting such a glare of light from the rays of the sun, that the traveller, if exposed at noon-day, can scarcely allow his eyelids to be sufficiently open to enable him to keep the course he wishes to pursue." This being the character of the district, the soil, such as it is, being almost exclusively a granitic sand, is merely the wearing down, during the course of ages, of the rocks around, or immediately below.

The *mountains*, in some parts, run along in low ranges, and, in others, attain a considerable height, as the Karas Bergen, near the centre of the country, which rise to an elevation of three thousand feet above the elevated table-land on which they stand. Several mountain peaks, of a remarkable kind, occur near to, or within sight of, the mission station. There is one about fifteen miles to the east, known as the Zwart Kop, and several farther off in the plains to the south-east, known as the Zwart Kopjes, all of which are quite black; " but whether," says Mr. Backhouse, " they be entirely mica or contain tin, is an interesting question." But the great characteristic of the country is not its mountains, but its vast and ample plains.

The *botany* of such a country cannot be expected to be rich. A few aloes, growing out of the crevices of the rocks, and euphorbias here and there are to be seen ; and once a striking flower of rather large size arrested my attention, which proved to be a carrion-flower, " with square, succulent, leafless stems, and flowers resembling star-fish." The odour is that of putrid meat, but the plant " has an insipid yet cool and watery taste, and is used by the natives for the purpose of quenching thirst." These are the chief plants that arrested my attention ; whilst the principal trees are the mimosa, the camel-thorn, the wild ebony, the yellow tree, and the koker, or quiver tree. " The acacias," says Mr. Burchell, " present some remarkable species. *Acacia vera*, and *Acacia Capensis*, are often loaded with large lumps of very good and clear gum, and they have so great a resemblance to the true acacia of the ancients, or the tree which yields the gum arabic, as to have been considered the same species. Wherever these trees are wounded the gum exudes; and it is probable that a large crop might thus be annually obtained without destroying them. If a computation could be made of the quantity that might be obtained from those trees only which skirt the Gariep and its branches, amounting to a line of wood (reckoning both sides) of more than two thousand miles, it would be found that the supply thus obtained would be more than equal to the whole consumption of Britain."

The *Acacia giraffæ*, or camel-thorn tree, Mr. Burchell describes as a remarkable species, "having thick brown thorns, and an oval pod, of a solid mealy substance within, and which never opens, as those of other acacias. The head of the tree is thick and spreading, and of a highly peculiar form, which distinguishes it at a great distance. Its wood is excessively hard and heavy, of a dark or reddish brown colour. It is called the camel-thorn tree, because the camelopard browses chiefly on it; and it is one of the largest trees in these regions." However long the wood may be dried, the texture is so hard and close that it sinks in water like a stone.

Of the *Acacia detinens*, he says: "The largest shrubs were nearly five feet high, a plant quite new to me, but well known to the people by the name of Haakedoorn (Hook-thorn).   I was preparing to cut some specimens, when, though proceeding with the utmost caution, a small twig caught hold of one sleeve. While trying to disengage myself with the other hand, both arms were seized by these rapacious thorns, and the more I tried to extricate myself the more entangled I became; till at last it seized hold of my hat also, and convinced me that there was no possibility of getting free but by main force, and at the expense of tearing all my clothes.   I therefore called for help, and two of my men came and relieved me by cutting off the troublesome branches. In revenge for this ill-treatment, I determined to give to the tree a name which should serve to caution future travellers against venturing within its clutches." It is known to the natives not only as the Haakedoorn, but quite as much by the name the Wacht-een-beetje-doorn, or the *Wait-a-bit-thorn!*

Its *birds* are the ostrich, which is to be frequently seen on the plains; vultures, circling high in the air, sometimes at such an elevation as scarcely to be visible, but ready to swoop down with the rapidity of lightning upon anything that may attract their unrivalled scent or keener vision. Crows are numerous, on the look out for all sorts of offal, and very destructive to weak and sickly lambs, whose eyes they pick out and feed upon under the protection of a scout, perched upon a tree near at hand, ready to give the alarm as soon as an enemy is in sight. A very remarkable bird inhabiting the country, and making its nest in the mimosas and camel-thorn trees, is the republican bird, or social grosbeak. A roof, like that of a thatched house, is built over many branches of the tree, and the nests are entered from beneath, as a protection against serpents, the roof projecting some distance beyond the entrance to the nearest nest. There are many entrances, and regular streets, with nests on each side, at about two inches from each other. From five to eight hundred birds are sometimes found congregated together in one community; and sometimes the trees have been known to give way under the weight of the birds and their dwelling. The wood pigeon and partridge are numerous, and frequent pools and fountains to drink at regular hours, the latter about seven a.m., and the former about five p.m. Ducks and geese are in good number near the pits and pools in the bed of the periodical rivers.

South Africa is remarkable for its *quadrupeds*. In no part of the globe is there so large a number, and some are of the largest dimensions. But elephants, rhinoceri, camelopards, indeed all the larger animals, have retired from this part of Great Namaqualand, and have gone considerably to the northward, so that they are never seen now; but leopards and panthers, wolves, jackals, and the hunting hyæna, or wild dog, as the natives call it, are still numerous, and this latter is the most destructive animal that infests the country. It hunts in regular packs, attacks and devours everything that comes in its way, and very few even of the swiftest animals escape from its pursuit; for, when hunting any of the antelope species, they have relays of the pack stationed in certain parts of the plain; towards these they chase their game, and party after party take up the chase, fresh and ready, when the others are weary, chasing the animal in a vast circle, till, wearied out by their relentless pursuit, it falls a victim to their voracity. Oxen in presence of a pack standing with their hind quarters in the centre of a circle present an array of horns too formidable for even such an enemy to attack; but oxen weak and sickly, and that become separated from the herd, are easily surrounded, and in a few hours devoured. Even vigorous oxen are sometimes stealthily approached in their sleep, and suffer the loss of their tails, in whole or in part, as I have often seen.* Fortunately hyænas seem to have a very intelligent dread of fire-arms, and do not appear again for a long time after a few of their number have been shot. Zebras, quaggas, or the wild ass; the eland, the gemsbok, the springbok, and other species of the deer or antelope, are numerous; and the springbok, after the rains have fallen and the young grass appears, unscared by the prevalence of fire-arms, still frequent the country in vast numbers. When they abound, *lions* may be looked for; indeed, then all the beasts of prey are specially alive and on the *qui vive*, " seeking their meat from God." The muishond, or ichneumon, a small animal, closely resembling the weasel, has a natural antipathy to the serpent race, and attacks them with great ingenuity and courage. The natives, who are keen observers, say it has been seen preparing for such a conflict by providing for itself a singular shield. Biting a hole in the centre of a dried cake of cow dung, it has been seen to thrust its head through the hole, thus carrying it as a shield of defence, and at the same time as a foil, by which to distract the attention of the reptile, when, avoiding the deadly stroke of the envenomed fangs, it adroitly seizes the serpent by the throat and destroys it. If a hollow bone should be the only means available, it has been known to thrust its head through that, and, with this remarkable armour, attack and destroy the enemy. The ferret, the squirrel, the porcupine, the hare, abound

---

* " A young officer of my acquaintance," says Mr. Backhouse, " was lately crossing the Great Fish River at the ford called Trumpeter's Drift. When in the track, in the bush, a pack of these animals fell upon his dog; while they were devouring it, he escaped, under the conviction that had not their attention been temporarily occupied with his dog, himself and his horse would have been in great danger."

F

in different parts of the country. The *ophidia* are of great variety, and in general very deadly. The yellow snake, the yellow-spotted, which are the South African cobra, the puff-adder, the horned snake, which is only about twelve or fourteen inches in length, though it has very large fangs in proportion, and is extremely venomous, and the spūg slang, a black snake which has the remarkable faculty of spitting its poison, as its name denotes, are numerous.

The *climate of Great Namaqualand* is, for the largest portion of the year, one of intense heat, far surpassing anything the latitude of the place might lead one to expect, owing chiefly to the rocky and sandy nature of the country, the absence of large vegetable growths, and the extreme scarcity of water : in addition to which the rays of an almost vertical sun, in December and January, and the reflection of the heat from bare rock and sand glistening with quartz, mica, and talc, render the temperature almost insufferable. The wind blowing from the north and east over immense tracts of country, having so heated a surface, comes like blasts from a furnace ; and if, on the hottest days, between one and three in the afternoon, a door facing that quarter be opened and the head exposed, it seems almost enough to strike one dead, such is the intenseness of the glow. On days like these, doors and windows are carefully closed from about ten in the morning till the day begins to decline. By this means the temperature of the air in the house is kept twenty degrees lower than that of the air outside in the shade. But though the heated air is kept out by closing up doors and windows, the want of a free circulation makes the oppression within almost unbearable ;

and sometimes, rather than forego the relief which some action in the atmosphere would impart, we have thrown open the door or window, when, the outer air rushing in, the quicksilver might be seen to run up the tube of the thermometer like a thing of life. The natives give way to such weather, and yield themselves up to regular *siestas* of two or three hours' duration in the day, and to rouse a sleeping Namaqua under such circumstances would be almost worse than sacrilege. The dogs of the village imitate the example of their masters; the world seems wrapped in slumber, scarcely a sound being heard save the hum of the beetle on the wing; nothing living seems astir, but on every side the incessant flicker of the intensely rarefied atmosphere near its contact with the burning earth is distinctly to be seen. High up, however, far away, in the blue vault above, the vulture may be seen sweeping in circles over the village, on the look-out for anything acceptable.

On such days I have sometimes been compelled to travel, and have seen the ostrich standing in the plains with open beak, and with its small wings lifted from its sides, distressed with the heat, and instinctively exposing itself to any breath of air that might happen to stir across the country. And after a long stage, when we had out-spanned and made the oxen fast to the yoke, to prevent their wandering too far in search of water, so hot has the ground been that they could not endure to stand, but have alternately lifted their feet to allow the air to circulate around them, till from sheer necessity we have been obliged to resume the journey, or to order them to be liberated from the yoke. Trying as is the heat by day, the climate might be more tolerable to an European if the nights were even comparatively cool. But for many months it almost constantly happens that when the heavens are bright with glorious constellations and we look for cool refreshment, everything around us still glows, and sleep is impossible. Often have I gone to the room below, in which my thermometer hung, when at one or two o'clock in the morning I have read it off at from 93° to 96°, though the window had been wide open for the whole night. On such occasions, as the only mode of getting a little rest, I have carried a sofa mattress outside the house, and, with nothing warmer than light trousers and a brown holland coat, have cast myself down on it and slept till daylight.

The day of rain is of all days the greatest for this region, and awakens a joy which no Englishman, who has resided only in his native country, is able to realise. In December a few showers are hoped for, rather than calculated upon, and again about April or May, though it not unfrequently happens that these hopes are disappointed. A steady continuous rain, unaccompanied with thunder and lightning, is of very rare occurrence. The blessing of rain almost invariably comes attended by terrors. " His lightnings " enlighten the whole heavens, flashing up in huge sheets all around and from below the horizon, for several evenings before a drop of rain falls, and the morning dawns cloudless and brilliant as before. Day by day the heavy thunder-clouds gather again, and pile themselves one upon another in the north-eastern quarter of the heavens like a huge electric battery, keeping us waiting expectantly for days together, but gathering in intensity for the grand display. At length the whole heavens are covered with dark and massive clouds. The lightnings dart in zigzag lines across the sky; chain lightning, forked lightning, sometimes fireballs, come from the clouds and split up into zigzag fragments, flying in all directions; and yet not a drop of rain falls. The thunders are first heard muttering from afar; then rumbling and rolling louder and louder in their approach; and at length they crack and crash and utter one continuous roar, till the earth seems to quail beneath the mighty reverberations. Then down comes the rain in floods upon the hot and steaming ground. By these rains the face of the earth is "renewed," and the grass grows and flowers spring where an Englishman would imagine they had never sprung before, and with a rapidity that is amazing. The soil is warm, the rain warm, and everything springs as in a hothouse.

Owing to the excess of electricity, hail is not an infrequent accompaniment of the storms of summer. Once in the month of December a storm broke over the station which made havoc of all the gardens. The hail was as large as marbles and broke many panes of glass in our house, and would have destroyed the whole, had we not prevented the possibility by throwing open the casement windows. The thunder and lightning were grand in the extreme, and the floods of rain which succeeded to the hail were such as to deluge the entire place. Streams of twenty or thirty feet in breadth ploughed up the stony ground, and poured along in careering waves before and behind the mission premises. The thermometer, which was standing at 110° in the shade before the storm began, was in half an hour reduced to 68°. The regret caused by the devastations of the storm was, however, greatly diminished by the hope that, in a week or two, the new grass would furnish more milk for the people than their gardens would have supplied food.

When these storms occur in the dead of the night, they are enough to strike awe into the depths of the soul. The natives of a whole village will sometimes rise in the dead of the night and light their fires, as some mitigation of the terrible glare of the lightning.

The winter winds from the south are often very keen, and are felt peculiarly sharp after the enfeebling effects of the intense heat of summer. Once I saw the thermometer down to 30°, and brought in as a novelty for my wife to see, and as a remembrancer of the winters of our native land, a mug that had been left out during the night, full of ice! Such a degree of cold does not often happen, and is of very short duration, so that before the constitution can derive any benefit from it, the heat sets in again, and the frame is relaxed as before. Days of cold and days of great heat often alternate even in mid-winter, and are extremely trying to any constitution.

The most prevalent winds are from the west and north-west. The north-east bring over great storms. Continuous rains for a day or two, whenever they do occur, are brought by an east wind. The keen winter winds are from the south, and rain never falls while they last.

The climate is on the whole very salubrious, owing to the dryness of the atmosphere; and if at any time fever prevails, it is generally after the rains. The most prevalent complaint from which the people suffer is inflammation of the eyes, occasioned by the intense glare of the sun and the want of habitual cleanliness. That which is the most difficult to be borne by an European is the great heat, occasioning an almost perpetual languor, and so diminishing the strength as to render all exertion intolerable.

"The entire country, extending in some places hundreds of miles on each side of the Orange River, and from where it empties itself into the Atlantic, to beyond the twenty-fourth degree of east longitude, appears to have the same character for dearth and barrenness." "It is rare," continues Mr. Moffat, "that rains to any extent or in any quantity fall in those regions. Extreme droughts continue for years together. The fountains are exceedingly few and precarious, and latterly many of these have been dried up altogether."

The inhabitants of Great Namaqualand belong to the Hottentot family. At the period when the Cape was first discovered by Bartholomew Diaz, and also when colonised by the Dutch, the whole of what is now designated the Colony was inhabited by Hottentots proper, whose origin and history continue involved in profound mystery. They resemble none of the other tribes of South Africa on the east or west coasts; but by many they have been thought in physical appearance to bear a striking resemblance to the Egyptian or to the Chinese races. Barrow thought that "in their colour, and the construction of their features, they approach nearer to the latter people than to any other nation." I have myself been very much struck with this resemblance. Referring to the notion of their Egyptian origin, Mr.

Moffat says : " It may not be considered chimerical to suppose that when the sons of Ham entered Africa by Egypt and by the Red Sea, the Hottentot progenitors took the lead, and gradually advanced in proportion as they were urged forward by an increasing population in their rear, until they reached the southern extremity of the continent. Research may yet prove that that remarkable people originally came from Egypt." Arrested on the east by the bold and warlike Kaffirs, they were impelled westward and southward where no powerful enemy occupied the country, and where they were found by the Dutch two hundred and thirty years ago dwelling on what is now the site of Cape Town, and on the other lands of the Colony. Thence, many of them, before the arrival of the Dutch settlers, " stretched out into Great Namaqualand, along the western division of the Colony, till, checked by a barren country, they became located in their present abode. Another division proceeding eastward settled along the banks of the Orange River. Thus they became separated into three great divisions—the Hottentots of the Colony; the Korannas, inhabiting the banks of the Orange River; and the Great Namaquas," whose country has been described.

The inhabitants of Great Namaqualand are divided into about a dozen tribes, each under the rule of its own chieftain.

The 'Kami 'Nuka, or Bondelzwaarts, are the most important, influential, and, as it is thought, the most populous tribe in the country. Nisbett Bath is the seat of government, and the residence of the chief. It is situated about sixty miles north of the Orange River.

The people are, generally speaking, in good circumstances, whilst the most wealthy among them are possessed of large flocks and herds, of horses and waggons, and are better armed with European weapons than any other tribe of Namaquas.

At a distance of about eighty miles to the eastward are the Afrikaners. Amongst these people the Rev. R. Moffat spent the first years of his missionary life, until the London Missionary Society withdrew its labours from that part of the field. Christian Afrikaner, the chief, was converted through the instrumentality of his ministry, and died in the faith of the Lord Jesus.

To the north-east, in the region of the Fish River, reside the 'Karakikooika, or people of William Fransman. But a portion of this tribe is located, by permission, in the territory of the 'Kami 'Nuka, at a distance of about one hundred and twenty miles from Nisbett Bath. This affords them the opportunity of enjoying the religious services of the Wesleyan Mission. About three hundred of the people of the tribe are located in this place, which is called Nieuwe Fontein, or New Fountain, whilst the chief and his council reside with the largest portion of the tribe near the Fish River.

To the north of Nieuwe Fontein, and one hundred and eighty miles from Nisbett Bath, is Klip Fontein, where the tribe called the 'Khabobika, or the Velschoen Draagers, reside. The chief is Hendrik Hendriks, a man of scarcely middle age at the time I first met with him; yet a man of some notoriety. It is a somewhat populous tribe, and the people have a good supply of flocks and herds, horses and waggons, and, considering their distance in the interior, a considerable number of guns for hunting purposes.

These were the tribes with which I came most frequently in contact in connection with the work of the mission ; and as all belong to the same family, and have the same manners and customs, personal features, and national characteristics, a description of the people of my own circuit, which included the four tribes above-mentioned, will serve for the whole race.

In *personal appearance* the Namaquas are of the ordinary height, generally slight, with small hands and feet, and for want of muscular exercise the upper limbs are undeveloped, though, being great pedestrians, the lower limbs are strong and muscular. The countenance is not such as would strike the Circassian race as one of beauty, the cheek-bones being high, the lips thick, the nose depressed, the eyes wide apart, the hair black and crisp, growing in tufts at a distance from each other, " having the appearance and feel of a hard shoebrush." The complexion is a light yellowish brown, though many áre nearly as white as an European, often having a tinge of colour in the cheek. Their eyes are of a deep chestnut, and their teeth beautifully white. The limbs are generally well-proportioned and delicate, and it is very rarely that a corpulent or deformed person is to be seen. " Many of the women, when quite young, might serve as perfect models of the human figure, so exquisite is their form ; their hands and feet are small and delicate, and they move in an easy and graceful manner. Their charms, however, are quickly dissipated," when they enter on the married life and become the mothers of families. Then their whole appearance undergoes a complete change. On the faces of many of our converted Namaquas there was a beautiful expression, such as is produced by holiness within; and despite the inelegance of the separate features, an interesting expression was worn by the faces of some who had not come under the benign influence of religion.

As to *disposition*, the Great Namaquas are mild and gentle, and withal cautious in their first intercourse with strangers. The eye scans the countenance of the stranger with a sort of questioning look, and, unless assured of the character of the man beforehand, even the saluting hand is held out with timidity. Though many of them had taken the trouble to come from far beyond the station to meet and welcome us on our arrival, and though their confidence in the missionary was greater than that reposed in any other stranger, we could not fail to perceive unmistakable signs of a natural wariness of disposition. It is only an open, straightforward, and kindly disposition that can win their confidence, and even then it is somewhat slow in rising to the point of comfort. When, however, their confidence is once secured, their attachment is firm and loyal. Before the Gospel was introduced into the country, many acts of *cruelty* were perpetrated; parents who had become aged and infirm, and who required more attention than formerly, were sometimes taken by the children to a lone spot, supplied with a small amount of provisions, and left to die, or to become the prey of wild beasts. Cases of this kind are recorded by the Rev. R. Moffat, who spent a short period in this region, and also by the Rev. Edward Cook. Arbitrary and avaricious chieftains, too, would often *make* an occasion against a man of wealth, and, under the semblance of just punishment for some crime, victimise the subject to increase their own wealth. But notwithstanding these, and many things of a similar kind, it does not appear that they were *nationally* a cruel people, even before the introduction of the Gospel. It was not in every case a cruel disposition, but the lack of food, that suggested the dire expedient of leaving the aged with scanty provision. In some, deep cunning, deceit, and a trace of treachery are found, but these instances do not justify us in calling such qualities characteristics of the nation.

They are not a *warlike race.* True, they have often been engaged in internecine conflicts among themselves, and in predatory incursions on neighbouring tribes; but these do not appear to have arisen so much from a love of war for its own sake, as from the overmastering vice of cupidity, and from a conviction that European weapons had placed them in a superior position to the enemy. That they are not destitute of courage is evident from the manner in which they hunt the wild beasts of their country, when they often display a coolness and courage worthy of any people. As soldiers, " a corps of five hundred Hottentots had been formed into a regiment in the Dutch service, prior to the British attack on the settlement at the Cape in 1795, and they are said to have acted with more spirit on that occasion than any other part of the troops." This regiment was afterwards adopted into the British service by Sir James Craig, and additional numbers enlisted into it; " and better soldiers," said he, " are not trained from the lower orders of any country." The testimony this officer gives as to their general excellence, their sobriety, and intelligent attention to every part of their duty as soldiers, is very high. It is true that this is said of the Hottentots of the colony, but I feel quite convinced that the independent tribes of Great Namaquas would not be found inferior in these respects, if placed in similar circumstances.

With regard to their *intellectual* powers, much of a degrading nature has been said by men of infidel principles who never knew them, and who have disgraced themselves by reckless theorising. The old slander of Gibbon that the Hottentot race were "the connecting link between the rational and irrational creation" has been disproved a hundred times; yet in much more recent times it has been revived by some gentlemen of the Anthropological Society, as if it had never been exploded. It is not worth while to proceed to a formal disproof of the unworthy assertion. Those who have laboured amongst and know them, claim to be as fully able to form a correct opinion respecting them as their traducers, and their universal testimony is precisely the opposite of that of such men. What would any of these gentlemen, Gibbon included, have been, had the desert been their home, had they been left as destitute of instruction and of the means of intellectual development as the tribes of South Africa in their natural and unchristianised state? And what would many of these natives—have been with the same advantages of training as they enjoyed? To affirm, therefore, that owing to some physical defect in their organisation they are *incapable* of "a high degree of civilisation, of an elevated knowledge, and an intelligent piety," is to affirm what requires to be proved; a position unworthy of men of science.

The testimony of the Rev. Henry Tindall, who, as the son of a missionary, spent seven years of his boyhood, and three of his youth, and subsequently many years of his maturer life, as a missionary among the Great and Little Namaquas, is to the following effect: " Much of their talent is latent; they have little to rouse their dormant energies.   Many of them possess a strong inventive and mechanical genius, and, if they had means and opportunities of developing their faculties, would become adepts in any branch to which their attention might be directed.   The principal elements of greatness in which they appear to be deficient are diligence and perseverance; they are proverbial for their sloth and strong aversion to hard labour.   But this is only evinced with reference to such works and engagements as are foreign to their education and habits.   None will surpass them in the performance of any task to which they have been accustomed; they will bear the greatest fatigue and hardship, and endure the severest privations to fulfil their purpose.   As their knowledge and inter-. course with the civilised world advances, and as they become sensible of new wants, and find new occupations inviting their energies, and offering an ample reward for diligent toil, they are seen to rouse themselves from their native apathy, and evince a desire to emulate the attainments of others, and to rank as men among those who have often denied them the dignity of the name."

They are a pastoral people. The description Joseph gave of his brethren is applicable to them, for " the men are shepherds, for their trade hath been to feed cattle."   Their sheep and cattle constitute almost their only wealth, and from them they derive their chief support.   Could they regularly cultivate their lands and gather in and live on the produce, that would give them some additional occupation, and prevent those terrible straits to which they are often driven by hunger, and make them a settled people.   Had they only suffi- cient rain, I doubt not agriculture might be pursued; for, when looking upon the vast plains of Great Nama- qualand, covered with the strong and high *towa*, or Bushman grass, waving like cornfields to the breeze, and capable of sustaining millions of grazing cattle, I have often asked myself the question, What is there to prevent this from becoming a land of abundance of bread?   But instantly the fact has presented itself that the land is one of drought—drought of long continu- ance, and of heat insufferable, such as utterly to dis- hearten all attempt at cultivating the ground.   All that can be done is to cultivate a few gardens near fountains from which they can be irrigated morning and evening.

The *milk and flesh* of their flocks and herds are the natural and almost the only reliable supply of provisions they have.   "Honey from the rock" is sometimes brought home at the expense of getting the head and face so swollen by the stings of the enraged bees, that the aggressor, unable to find the path, has to be led home, the swollen face and forehead meeting so com- pletely, that it is impossible to see where the eyes of the sufferer are.   Occasionally an esculent root is met with in the plains and dug up for use; the animals of the plains are hunted—antelopes of every kind, the zebra, quagga, ostrich, &c.; ant-heaps are broken open, their stores ransacked, and large quantities of grass- seed carried off to be boiled in milk and made a very agreeable dish.   The plains are also wandered over in search of nests of the ostrich, and great is the prize when one full of sound eggs is found; for these, beaten up in milk and lightly boiled, are a delicious and nourishing diet.   Children climb the thorn trees and pick off the gum to allay the cravings of hunger, tightening their hunger-belts whenever the pinch of famine becomes intolerable; and sometimes, driven to necessity, they gather together the dogs of the village, gaunt and meagre as themselves, and go on a hunting expedition of their own, and, for want of more delectable game, they send them into the holes of the rocks, turn out the jackals, and run them down, returning home in triumph, not contenting themselves with the tail of the fox as *our* red-coated gentlemen do, but bringing the veritable animal, and rejoicing that by their own exertions they have obtained something to eat! Or fires are made under the bushes on which the locusts have ranged themselves side by side, as thick as they can stand, when, paralysed by the cold of the night and unable to fly till the sun has warmed them, they fall down scorched and maimed, are gathered at leisure, fried and eaten.   But whatever is gathered in this way, the community principle, with regard to food, very largely prevails.   In this particular they have " all things in common."   If game is brought home, a whole village collects about the house of the possessor till it is all consumed; and so with everything else.   In this way their ordinary supplies are considerably supplemented, and they are preserved from absolute starvation in times of famine.   Milk of all kinds is used—the milk of cows, sheep, and goats.   When milk abounds, everything flourishes; the people rapidly improve and soon appear in good condition; the dogs, sharing in their owners' abundance, soon change their gaunt and hungry appearance, and grow bold and saucy. For months together the people will live exclusively upon this diet, so true is it that milk contains in itself all the elements of support. The milk, however, is not generally taken sweet: if used in this state, it would be too heavy and constipating. It is therefore put into a duly "seasoned" calabash, where in a very short time it becomes "thick," and slightly acidified, in which state it is light, wholesome, and nourishing to those who are accustomed to it.

Even the wealthy very seldom slaughter of their flocks and herds when milk is abundant. When milk is scarce, their only staple food is flesh. But the well-to-do are never lavish or wasteful, and even the wealthy are frugal and sometimes niggardly, and will show astonishing powers of endurance rather than take the life of sheep, goat, or ox. Perhaps the great reason why they show so much chariness is the knowledge of the fact that, whatever is slaughtered, whether sheep or ox, the whole neighbourhood will expect a share, so that the man himself and his family will derive scarcely any more benefit than any other household of the village. Yet he can hardly refuse, because of the custom that prevails. And when his neighbour slaughters in his turn, he waits upon him, and expects a portion. Yet this community principle operates injuriously, and in times of great drought none slaughter without absolute necessity; for this custom, whilst it benefits the needy, has a tendency to strip the wealthy, to deprive his family of ordinary comforts, and to make the whole nation feel the evils of poverty and hunger. The notion has obtained in some quarters that the natives are voracious eaters; but this is only true under certain circumstances, as, for example, in times of famine and after long abstinence from food. Then, of course, the demands of nature are ample and must be met; but when they obtain food at regular seasons, they eat no more than we do; whilst in times of scarcity their powers of endurance are amazing.

The original native *dress* is seldom seen now, except by those who travel beyond the mission stations and their outposts; for on the mission stations it is never seen at all. In some respects it seems ill-adapted to the purposes they have in view. "A belt cut from the skin of some animal is fastened round the body of the man, to which is attached a curious bag in front, tastefully made of the skin of a jackal with the fur outside, which is black in the centre and yellow at the margins. Behind-hangs a triangular piece of dried skin with the broad part downwards to flap and cool the body. A sheepskin in winter is all the addition that is ever made; it is worn with the wool inwards or outwards according to the weather, and serves at night for a bed and bedding. The female wears a long fringe attached to the belt in front, made of a skin cut into thin strips, and variously ornamented with shells, metal buttons, glass beads, and other trinkets. The whole of the body she covers with a sheepskin which reaches down to the calf of her leg." The people of the mission stations would be utterly ashamed to appear in such a dress, and never do so; they are in general well clothed, either in dresses carefully prepared by a process of tanning with which they are familiar and by which they make the skin as soft and supple as cloth, or in moleskins and cotton prints of English manufacture. The men connected with the mission have universally adopted the practice of converting prepared sheepskins into jackets and trousers, and since the art of sewing has been taught to the girls in the mission schools, they have succeeded in making a very creditable appearance.

The *government* is by the chief and his *raad*, or council, who are nominated in the first instance by the chief, though, should he wish to introduce an unacceptable member, the raadsmen have a right to object. They constitute a legislative and executive body ; and, in fact, they hold the responsible power of the nation in their own hands. The " succession " is hereditary, the eldest son succeeding to the chieftainship.*

The *occupations* of Namaqua life are at best but slight. Their principal business consists in looking after their flocks and herds ; but even this is light, and only employs a small portion of the population. The younger members of the family, or Damara servants, generally take the sheep and goats to the pasturage in the morning, and bring them home in the evening, leaving the rest at leisure. As to the cows, they are mostly driven to the pasturage and left to graze till the attraction of the young calves, tied up at the village, brings them home, when as much milk as is required for family purposes is taken, and the remainder left for the calves. The oxen, which are only occasionally required for riding, or for draught, require no care in

* *Lectures* by Rev. H. Tindall.

herding; they take a drink at the fountain, go to the plains and rove at large, returning about every other day to drink, resting at the village during the remainder of the day, and then in the cool of the night slowly proceeding to the plains as before.

The same is the case with the horses. Many of them range on the vast grassy plains twenty miles or more from home, keeping generally to some favourite pasture ground ; yet they are bound as by a chain to the station, the fountain there being the only place at which they can drink for many miles around. No anxiety is felt by their owner if he should see nothing of them for weeks in succession ; and if at any time they are wanted, the question is simply asked of the first neighbour he meets, " When did you last see my horses at the fountain ?"   If on the preceding day, he knows that they will come again on the morrow, sets a watch, and when they approach they are immediately driven into a kraal or enclosure before they drink ;—for, if first permitted to drink, they would probably decamp to the plains without affording another chance to those on the look-out to catch them ;—those wanted are taken, and the rest set at liberty. Or should they not come to the fountain, as sometimes happens after rain has fallen, and they can drink on the plains, their resort is generally known, and one man mounted can drive home a troop to the station—a feat sometimes accomplished on foot. When the mission horses were required for a journey, my man would take a bridle in his hand, start very early, walk over towards a low mountain range where they usually resorted, drive them up among the rocks, catch " Jack," the most quiet, mount him, and drive home the rest. Ranging so much at large, and only partially trained, some of them were very wild and spirited.   On one occasion a troop of horses had been brought into an enclosure near the mission house, from which we wished to select three for a journey I was about to take.   For this purpose the troop was gently driven up to one corner of the enclosure, where men were quietly standing to bridle those wanted.   A little excitement occurred, when one of the most timid animals broke through the cordon of men standing in the rear, in spite of our efforts to prevent it; another instantly followed, dashed against me with his chest, and struck me to the ground, turning me completely over, my feet being for a moment in the air; the whole troop followed, galloping either over or close by me.   But, though in the midst of their clattering hoofs, none trod on or kicked me, nor did I suffer the slightest injury; the only inconvenience felt on rising to my feet being extreme giddiness for a few moments, owing to the sudden concussion and whirl.   The first thing I noticed, as soon as I could perceive anything, was a young urchin describing the scene to his mother : " O mamma, there stood Mynheer with his head on the ground, and his feet in the air ! "

The *home occupations* of the men are also light.   They make the wooden and other utensils of the family, and their milk bowls, which are made of the soft willow wood of the Orange River, and are sometimes carved on the exterior very tastefully.   Attention to their guns affords them a little occupation.   These weapons are not of the best kind, many being the " brown Bess " so long since discarded by our troops, and all having the old flint and lock, which they prefer to the percussion locks and caps, simply because they can easily supply a lost flint, whereas it is not so easy to supply nipples for the locks, or percussion caps for the nipples. They are delighted with the rapid and sure action of the percussion guns, for, as they say, it takes so long for the powder to burn in the pan of the old-fashioned lock before it reaches the charge and explodes it, that meantime the hand may waver and the aim be interfered with ; whereas, no sooner is the trigger of a percussion rifle touched than " the ball is out ! " When the guns they use first come into their possession, they almost always fire very incorrectly ; consequently the first act of the native is to find out the fault of his weapon. He sets up a mark on the side of a bank, so that he may dig out and recast his bullets ; so placing himself as to be rested at every point, when he fires a number of shots. Perhaps all go on one side of the mark. He takes the gun home, and sets to work with file and hammer, and shifts the sight. Thus he tries, and tries again, till the weapon fires straight. Or perhaps the balls fly in *the line* of the object, but invariably go either above or below it. The sight is then filed down, or a higher one introduced, as may be necessary, till at length his instrument fires true. Some, however, can never be got quite right, but, knowing the error, he allows for it in practice. A man thus acquainted with the peculiarity of his gun, is a formidable enemy to the game of the wilderness.

A little smithing to their waggons affords some employment, and as in that intensely dry climate the woodwork shrinks rapidly, their attention is constantly required. The more heavy and difficult work of shortening the bands of the wheels is, however, chiefly performed by the more intelligent Bastaards, who have learned it from the Dutch, and who often do the work with some degree of skill. Small patches of garden-ground are cultivated by some of the people, where pumpkins, maize, the tobacco plant, and the fig-tree, are the principal things raised. But owing to the scarcity of suitable ground, and of water to irrigate, very little can be done in this way, and in most parts of the country nothing at all.

The women make the reed mats, and build the houses, which consist of a skeleton frame of light sticks, the ends of which are placed in holes dug in a circle. The upper ends of these sticks are bent over and tied together in the centre, until a framework for the light structure is completed. A long mat is then placed edgewise on the ground, and tied to these bamboo sticks. Other mats are placed higher up, and tied in a similar manner; and one or two additional mats tied down to the bamboos form the roofing. The preparation of sheep and goat skins, in order to make articles of dress, affords further employment for both sexes. Their shoes are made of prepared goat-skin for the upper leathers, and the soles of the thick part of the hide of the ox, the eland, camelopard, or rhinoceros, which latter is exceedingly durable.

But their great occupation, after attention to their flocks and herds, is the *chase.* This is not undertaken for sport, but of necessity, as a means of maintenance. It is sometimes followed on foot. A man takes his gun and walks to a spot where with telescopic glance his eye can sweep the country. Should anything be sufficiently near, he looks for the covert of shrubs, trees, or the sandy bed of a river, taking care, if possible, to keep to the lee-side, lest the wary animal should sniff up the scent, and decamp. Along this covert he stealthily creeps, often on hands and knees, till opposite the game : then his head is quietly raised, his gun noiselessly laid along, deliberate aim is taken, the weapon fired, and the game secured. The solitary huntsman is sometimes so fortunate as to discover the nest of an ostrich, with twenty or thirty large eggs in it; and knowing that before long the bird will return, he conceals himself in the nearest bush, fires as it passes, or whilst sitting upon the nest, and thus secures a double prize. When a native is so fortunate as to possess a horse, he takes his gun and rides to the plains, when whatever first offers is followed. It is, however, only the larger game that is thus hunted. The zebra is not so swift as a good horse, but has great powers of endurance; it is by dint, therefore, of hard riding, from the moment the chase is commenced, that he is overtaken; but unless shot at once, both horse and rider might be severely injured by the savage biting and kicking of this impracticable animal. Some animals are approached slowly till they take alarm and begin to run; the huntsman rides coolly after, and continues the chase, mostly at an easy canter, occasionally breathing his horse, till the poor chased animal, wearied out by alarm and continued running, is overtaken. This is sometimes a perilous occupation. Some animals when driven up are exceedingly fierce, and have terrible weapons of defence.

In this part of Namaqualand, the ostrich is frequently hunted in this way. It is not attempted, however, in winter, nor on cool days, for then "she scorneth the horse and his rider." On the hottest days in summer, when scarcely any air is stirring, the huntsman ventures forth on his distressing chase, and not by the fleetness of his horse, but by long-continued running, exhausts the endurance of the giant bird, which, overcome by heat and fatigue, at length lies down. The huntsman rides up, and with a stroke on its head from the thick end of his riding whip kills it: the best feathers are plucked, the parts of the bird fit for food fastened to the saddle, and the prize is borne back to the village. But this is dreadful work, and the lives of both man and horse are seriously imperilled by such a chase. On one of these fearfully hot days an ostrich passed near a village I had gone to visit. A man saddled his horse and went in pursuit, and in three or four hours returned nearly dead, whilst the poor horse, when the saddle and bridle were removed, stood with his legs stretched out, and his head hanging down nearly to his hoofs, overstrained and exhausted to the last degree. Sometimes hunting parties are got up, when nearly all the men of a village will leave in their waggons, with their ammunition and hunting horses, trusting to the success of the expedition for subsistence while absent. In this way large sections of country are partially invested, animals of all descriptions brought within a comparatively limited space, and large quantities shot. The flesh is then cut into thin slices, sprinkled with salt, and dried in the shade and wind; and after several weeks passed in the plains the huntsmen return with their waggons loaded with the dried flesh of the quagga, zebra, and various kinds of antelopes, affording subsistence to a whole village for a considerable time.

Wild beasts are chased when they become troublesome or dangerous. If a wolf, leopard, or panther is known to frequent a particular spot, a party of men is soon formed, and the obnoxious animal destroyed; but so rapid and catlike are the motions of the leopard, that it is necessary to hunt him with great wariness, otherwise his teeth and claws are sure to be buried in the flesh of some of the huntsmen. When pursued, it sometimes takes refuge in a tree, which it climbs with great facility, and from whence it often springs upon its pursuers; and the rapidity and uncertainty of its motions render it difficult to shoot with a rifle. The panther is a considerably larger and more powerful animal than the leopard, whilst the *ocelli*, or rounded marks, on the panther are larger and more distinctly formed than those of the leopard; otherwise they do not much differ from each other. It is very fierce, and is regarded as one of the most untameable of the feline tribe, and is to South Africa what the tiger is to India. The wild dog, or hunting hyæna, is an exceedingly ferocious animal, and hunts its prey in packs. When the Great Namaquas hunt this animal, a party of men ride out in search of its lair, where it is generally found sleeping. In the hottest part of the day they are driven up from the plains by the horsemen over the rocky and burning ground, and their feet become scorched and worn by the chase, when the huntsman rides up, and, at close quarters, fires. In this way large numbers are shot, and before long the rest leave that part of the country.

The lion once roamed over the plains around the Nisbett Bath Station, and was rather frequently seen; but of late years, owing to the introduction of powder and lead, and the system of extermination adopted, they have become somewhat rare in that neighbourhood. They still occasionally appear; and during one year of my residence we heard of nine, though not more than two or three were known to be together at one time. When the footmarks of these noble animals are first observed, the person who discovers them proceeds immediately to inform the chief. Several others, experienced men, are sent as soon as possible, in company with the guide, to examine and to follow on the *spoor* or *trail* for a short distance. If there are indications of the spoor being recent, and becoming fresher the farther they advance, the men hasten back to report to the chief. The horses are collected from the plain, a party of fourteen or fifteen men is formed, and then, proceeding to the spot where the footprints are visible, they carefully follow upon it, sometimes for days, till at length they come in sight of the animals. At first they often run, taking different directions, till one, finding himself the object of attention, becomes chafed, and takes up a position, generally with a tree or rock immediately behind him.' The men dismount, deliver their horses in charge to one or two others, and approach, getting as near as possible. Perhaps the monster roars and makes a bound or two in the direction of the party; but, if a firm front is shown, returns to his position, and again roars, waving his stiffened tail majestically from side to side. To make sure of their aim the men advance, if possible, to within fifty yards, and then sit down upon the ground in the form of a semicircle. The captain of the party orders a certain man to fire; deliberate aim is taken. The head is always aimed at, as a ball through the brain produces instant death;

whereas a ball has been known to go through the heart, and yet afterwards the lion has killed a man. When the men are calm and true to each other, the danger is not great; but if any prove cowardly, and flee, the peril is extreme.

Marriage amongst these tribes, as amongst all people, is an affair of importance. A youth is smitten by the beauty or other attractions of some young female, and, generally through the medium of a friend, reveals his passion. If accepted, and the match is consented to by the parents, the chief, and his councillors, who must all be consulted, an early day is fixed (for long courtships are not approved of), the young people assemble at the house of the parents of the bridegroom, an ox is slaughtered, a feast held amidst great merriment, and the ceremony is accomplished. This is marriage *à la mode* where the tribes live in their unevangelised state. But on mission stations, after preliminary arrangements are made, the missionary is informed, the banns are published- on three successive Sundays, and the parties are united according to the rites of the Christian Church. A little training, however, is necessary before the ceremony has to come off; and even after such instruction has been given, we sometimes find a dull bridegroom has to be prompted to duty by his brighter bride; who, should his responses linger, instructs him, "You must say Yes." The usual time for the performance of the marriage ceremony was at the close of the week-day morning service. On one occasion, when the bridegroom alone was present, lest there should be any mistake, he was privately asked, "Where's the young woman?" "*Oodaha,*" *Ik weet niet!*

" I don't know," was the immediate reply. Several started off to make inquiries; one or two pursued a waggon proceeding to the plains to collect firewood, when lo! there was the lady, never for a moment imagining that her presence could be at all needed at the ceremony. She was instantly brought back in breathless haste, one article of suitable attire was borrowed of one, another of another; and just when the morning service was closing, the bride was brought in, duly " adorned for her husband ;" the marriage was celebrated, and the innocent pair were made happy. It is only fair to state, however, in extenuation of the little mistake, that these were not residents of the station, but, in company with their parents, had travelled on oxback nearly one hundred and fifty miles to the station to be married.

Their mode of life is necessarily nomadic, wandering wherever grass and water are to be found for their flocks and herds; though all their wanderings are limited to a certain distance from the mission station; to which as many as can do so return after the rains have fallen and the grass has grown. The same must be said as to several outposts, where, in general, they live, as long as grass and water continue; but from which they wander to graze off unused territory, as long as there is grass and water; and to which outpost they return as soon as practicable. At the station, the chief and the missionary are generally resident; hence that is the seat of principal attraction to the natives; but as all cannot reside there, it is necessary to have several outposts, at each of which, if practicable, a native assistant is stationed, and to which places the natives can return as soon as their wanderings to other places in the vicinity cease. These wanderings are often a great detriment to them religiously and intellectually, as congregations and schools are thereby very much thinned, and regular plans of instruction very much interfered with. But they are unavoidable in such a climate.

The language of the Great Namaquas is remarkable for its strange clicking sounds, which abound, so that not many words are found without their peculiar click, or clicks. These clicks cannot be adequately represented by any combination of letters, so as to acquire the sounds from a book. The only way in which this can be done is *vivá voce*. Moreover, they occur so frequently, and form such an important part in the root of many words, that they are an essential element in the language, and could not be dispensed with unless it were entirely reconstructed. The construction of the language is regular and beautiful.

The Great Namaquas are very fond of music, but their instruments, like those of the other tribes of the Hottentot family, are few and simple. They have a kind of *guitar*, with three strings stretched over a piece of hollow wood, having a longish handle. Another, called the *goura*, consists of a sinew twisted on a small cord, and fastened to a hollow stick. At one end there is a small peg to bring the string to a proper degree of tension, and at the other a piece of quill fixed into the stick, to which the mouth is applied, and tones are produced by breathing. The *trommel pot* is a milk bowl, over which a piece of skin is tightly stretched, and is used as a drum at their public dances. Reeds of several feet in length are likewise made use of as *flutes*.   But missionaries at the present day scarcely ever see them; for the people themselves are so conscious of their utterly imperfect character, and of the impossibility of making them produce any really *musical* sounds, that they seem ashamed even to allow them to be seen. Their *love* of music, however, is very great, and I have witnessed effects produced by the congregational singing on the mission station such as I have never seen elsewhere, and such as never could be produced except upon a people remarkably sensitive to harmonious sounds.   After my removal to Cape Town, being visited by a native, I took him into the parlour and played him a tune on a small seraphine.   His head dropped, his bosom began to heave with irrepressible emotion, and I was obliged to stop, or he would have fallen over in a faint, as I had very often seen the Great Namaquas do under the congregational singing, especially strangers, who had come from far, and who attended the services for the first time.

Their religious ideas were exceedingly few.   Peter Kolben, an early Dutch writer who lived in 1716, asserts of the Hottentots of the Cape that, in his time, they believed in a deity whom they described as " an excellent man who does ill to no one, and lives far beyond the moon; but they regarded him as too remote to be worshipped.   When the moon is at the full, they make sacrifices to her," he adds, " accompanied by prayer for favourable seasons, with dancing, leaping, and violent grimaces.   They had also a malignant divinity, little, deformed, and ill-natured, to whom they offered sacrifices by way of softening his temper." But modern travellers and missionaries find none of these usages remaining, either among the Hottentots of the colony, or the Namaquas.

Amongst the latter the original traditions seem to have become almost, if not entirely, extinct. One day, when I was questioning David Afrikaner, a man of remarkable intelligence, as to the ideas prevailing amongst the Namaquas respecting God; "Ah, Sir," said he, " we knew nothing about Him, and we thought nothing about Him; we had our sheep, our goats, and our oxen, and these were all we thought about or cared for." The fact that terms exist in the Great Namaqua language denoting God, spirits, and an evil one, would seem to imply that they were not altogether without *ideas* on such subjects; but they appear to have been so faint as to be practically valueless. There was no sense of responsibility, and no "fear of God before their eyes." "And what were your ideas as to a future state?" "We had none," said he. "Had you no traditions on the subject?" "Well, yes, there was this tradition, of which our old men used to tell us. ' On a certain occasion the moon sent a hare with a message to mankind to say that as she died and lived again, so after death man would live again. The hare came and told them, "After death you will live no more." On returning to the moon, the moon said, "Well, what sort of a message have you taken to mankind?" "I've told them," said the hare, "that after death they will live no more." "Then," said the moon, flying into a great passion, "why have you taken such a false message to mankind?" and snatching up a hatchet that was at hand, she fetched the hare such a blow on the upper lip, as cleft it in two ; and that's the reason why, when you see a hare, it has a cloven lip. The hare in return flew into the face of the moon, and scratched it so violently, that that's the reason why you see all those dark marks on the face of the full moon.' Hence they concluded that because the hare brought a wrong message their doom was sealed; that when they died, they died like a dog, and there was an end of them. Whenever they saw a hare, they said, ' See, there goes the hare : if it had brought us a right message, then after death we should have lived again ; but it brought us a wrong message, and now after death we shall live no more.' For this reason," said David, " we always regarded the hare as an accursed thing, and we would never eat its flesh. But now," said the old man, his eyes glistening with delight as he spoke, " now that life and immortality are brought to light by the Gospel, we don't care for the old tradition, but we catch the hare as often as we can, and we eat him too ! "

This was the only tradition I ever heard of as having prevailed amongst them in early times, and the only one with which David Afrikaner was acquainted ; whilst he knew of no single practice that could be interpreted into an act of religious worship. The Rev. Henry Tindall says : " They do not seem, before they became acquainted with the first principles of Christianity, to have been in the habit of observing any rites or ceremonies of a religious character, or to have had any idea of responsibility to a higher Being. I believe that the superstitious tales which have been gleaned from them by travellers and advanced by them as religious records, are regarded by the natives themselves in the light of fables, which are either narrated for amusement, or intended," as some of the allusions indicate, " to illustrate the habits and characteristics of wild animals."

" In their native state they appear to have had more confidence in witchcraft than in religion," says Mr. Tindall; and even to this day many, amongst whom the lingerings of superstition are still found, regard all sickness, calamities, and especially death as traceable to some enemy who is supposed to hold the fatal charm. The practice of medicine is now almost exclusively exercised by the wizard doctor, and though as a matter of course he often fails to restore the patient, occasionally the recuperative powers of nature bring him through despite the wizard's treatment; hence the native is confirmed in the belief of his accusations, and of the success of his art. He sometimes applies his mouth to the seat of pain, and makes a hollow moaning, at the same time adroitly dropping small sticks or little pieces of sheep's bones upon the spot without being observed, which he pretends to have extracted from the part affected, and exhibits as the cause of the disease. After such manifest sources of pain and uneasiness are removed, amendment is supposed to follow.

Before closing this chapter, I must not omit to refer to the Bushman people. The Bushmen are found interspersed among all the tribes of Great Namaqualand, and they may be said to stand in such a relation to the tribes generally, as the gipsies of this country do to the townspeople. " They appear," says Rev. H. Tindall, " to have sprung from poor Hottentots, who by war, or some other calamity, had been deprived of their cattle, and were necessitated to break up their communities, and range the desert for support in isolated groups."

"The agreement of the Bushman dialect with the Hottentot in its structure and general principles, is an additional proof that they undoubtedly belong to the same race, and have only been separated by the force of such circumstances as those we have alluded to. Bushmen are to be met with in the most unlikely spots: in the mountain cavern, on the rugged hill, on the solitary plain, in the wild and shady retirement of the streamless river-bed, where it seems utterly impossible for any human being to subsist, where no water flows to quench his thirst, where no flocks roam, and no cultivated ground yields its fruits to satisfy his craving appetite, and where no human voice awakens or charms the emotions of his soul, this sorry and pitiable specimen of humanity may be seen; the juice of the wild melon, or the moisture of some succulent root, or the sap of the mimosa bark, his only drink; the bulbs and roots of the earth, the reptiles of the rocks, the courser of the plain, his food; and monotonous solitude his only companionship. He is in every sense of the word a wild man. He has no religion, no laws, no government, no recognised authority, no patrimony, no fixed abode."

And yet in this debased condition, sunk to the lowest depths of which we can conceive, his natural intelligence and sagacity render him immeasurably superior to the irrational creatures, and enable him to some extent to press them into his service, and make even the fiercest of them to contribute to his maintenance in the dreary and desert land of his abode. When his usual source of supply fails him, viz., the chase, he has recourse to

honey, roots, the larvæ of ants, gum, and reptiles, the
head of which latter he strikes off, and makes use of the
rest. A swarm of locusts is hailed by him with delight ;
he follows its course for days, and by firing the bushes
on which they settle at night, gathers and lays up a
store for many days. Even then his resources are not
exhausted, as will appear from the following account,
which I received from David Afrikaner, who I believe
was, on his mother's side, of Bushman descent, and from
whom I have yet several letters in which he speaks of
himself as " David Afrikaner, the old Bushman."

In many parts of Great Namaqualand where lions
abound, said David, the Bushman and the lion sometimes meet each other in the open plain, where there is
neither rock nor shrub to serve as a hiding-place, and
where no tree stands, by ascending which the Bushman
might seek to escape. If there should yet be some distance between them, the Bushman will quietly walk off
at right angles to the lion, without appearing to see him,
and as if without any intention to avoid him. Without
showing any signs of fear, he walks to the right or to
the left, in a sort of sauntering, indifferent manner ;
and the lion, observing no token of fear, nor of defence
or defiance, will seldom follow him. The escapes of the
Bushman are sometimes very marvellous. The lion and
he seem to regard each other as in some sense companions in the desert country over which both roam,
and though sometimes the latter is destroyed by the
savage and mighty foe to which he is exposed, his frequent exemption from destruction is no doubt attributable to that fear and dread of man which are still
" upon the beasts of the field." Something is no doubt

due to the naturally magnanimous and generous nature of the lion, which sometimes displays itself when he is roused neither by defiance nor attack. And further, the exemption of the Bushman is very much owing to the marvellous coolness he possesses, and in which he has been trained from infancy by the desert life he leads. Sometimes an escape from an actual meeting cannot be effected, and all the self-possession the Bushman can command is requisite. The lion meets him with a subdued growl, eyeing him up and down with savage keenness, whilst he stands perfectly motionless, and seemingly fearless. In a gentle voice, he talks to the lion: "*Ons moet malkander geen kwaad doen: ons arbeid op dezelfde vlakte:*" "We must not hurt each other; we labour on the same plain." A subdued growl follows, and finding there is nothing to quarrel with, the lion perhaps leaves him and walks away.

Very often, continued David, the Bushman will make his hut within sight of a pool, or other water, frequented by lions, so that he can always see when one comes to drink. If, after one has drunk, he return from the water by the same path by which he came to it, then the Bushman knows that he has got something, that he has been gorging himself till an irresistible thirst has been excited, and that he is returning to finish his meal. After waiting awhile he ventures forth, following upon the spoor of the lion, till at length he comes within sight of the ferocious beast, who is too busy to notice the noiseless approach of his follower. The Bushman looks for a place of concealment, either a rock or a shrub, when, stepping forth for a moment, he utters a loud, startling cry, "Hi!" and returns to his concealment. Tho lion lifts his head grandly, and looks towards the quarter from which the sound appeared to come; but seeing nothing, he resumes his feast. Again the Bushman steps forth and shouts, "Hi, hi," and again retreats behind his concealment. Again the lion lifts his head, and with stretched-out neck looks in all directions; but as all is again silent, and nothing visible, he tears away at the carcase as before. The Bushman, fearing that sufficient will not be left for himself, once more steps forth and hurriedly, and in angry tone, shouts, "Hi, hi, hi," returning to his secrecy as before. This time, the lion begins to show symptoms of alarm; "he thinks there's a plot," said David, " and there he stands with his forepaw on the carcase, and his head erect, looking around, till his fears get the better of him; at length he is fairly cowed, and, dropping his tail between his legs, he walks away in a direction opposite to that from which the sound came." As soon as it is prudent, the Bushman runs up and carries off as much as he can of what his provider has left behind. Thus "He who giveth to the beast his food," forgets not the poor Bushman, but often provides for his wants through the instrumentality of one of the most powerful, and most to be feared, denizens of the wilderness.

For this reason the Bushman is very reluctant to have him destroyed. If perchance any traveller should come into the vicinity of the water with cattle, the Bushman will warn him, and entreat him to move on to a safe distance. "There is a lion about here," says he; "keep your oxen off; *you must not injure him; he is our dog;*" meaning, he catches what it would be difficult for us to catch, and provides us with food. He regards the visit of men with guns with anxiety, lest they should shoot "his dog," which to him would be an irreparable loss.

Sometimes he learns a lesson from the baboon. He knows that the baboon will eat nothing that is bitter or nauseous, and that whatever is eaten by it will be edible to himself. When, therefore, he is pressed by hunger, he seeks out places where roots have been scratched out of the ground by the baboon; and as the creature will eat only the root, breaking off and casting away the stalks and leaves, he picks up the first of these he can find, and taking them in his hand, as an index to the root, he narrowly observes as he traverses the plains and crevices of the mountains, till he finds others like them, when he digs up the bulb and eats, or puts it in his wallet against a time of need. One lesson learned of the baboon in this way is never forgotten.

Yet another auxiliary he finds in the birds of the air. He sallies forth to the open country, or to a nook in a mountain. With his piercing eye he scans the earth and the heavens in succession. In the dim distance he spies as a speck in the high heavens a vulture, or other bird of prey, wheeling round in circles in the air, and, like himself, scanning the surface of the earth for food. He watches the bird narrowly, following it with his eye, till perhaps, taking a few larger circles in its descent, it alights. Leaving his haunt, he runs with the fleetness of a hare to the spot, scares away the vulture, and if anything is to be obtained, secures the prize for himself. The birds, being frequently deprived of their morsel in this way, become exceedingly crafty, so that it is only by a great deal of ingenuity and skill in manœuvring, that the Bushman is able to ascertain where the spoil is.   Should any animal have been killed by a lion, tiger, or other wild beast, the vulture is the first to discover it.   But should it perceive a human being near, it will not descend, or hover over the spot, but fly off, "till he thinks," said David, "his human enemy will have been tricked into a departure." But the Bushman waits; for when he sees the vulture flying straight away, he regards it only as a feint to "put him off the scent;" he knows the bird will return, and he is patient, meantime carefully concealing himself from its view.   If the bird should weary him by long delay, he resorts to another expedient.   He sits down, makes a small fire, and then covers it up with green sticks, or dry grass, so as to make a smoke.   He then leaves his fire, and removes to some distance to a place of concealment from which to continue his observations.   The bird is now deceived.   Seeing no one, and supposing the Bushman is at a distance where the smoke of his fire ascends, it swoops down unsuspectingly, and thus reveals the place where the treasure lies; and almost before it can commence the feast the Bushman rushes out, and by shouts drives away the bird, takes his own share of the spoil, and leaves the remnant to the discoverer.

Sad indeed is it to think of the small numbers of the Bushmen as compared with what they once were, and of their scattered condition, and the melancholy nature of the life to which they have been reduced, since men from *civilised* lands first settled on their shores, less than two hundred and fifty years ago.   At that time they were very numerous, drinking at their own fountains, killing their own game, and enjoying the patrimony bequeathed by their fathers; but driven from their home by the remorseless advance of the white man, oppressed, tyrannised over, and enslaved, wronged and plundered in every way by his all-grasping cupidity, what wonder that the Bushmen should be inspired with an intense hatred to their white oppressors, and become " the pirates of the desert," as a means of maintaining their existence?

" I have traversed those regions in which, according to the testimony of the farmers, thousands once dwelt; but now, alas, scarcely a family is to be seen! It is impossible to look over these now uninhabited plains and mountain glens without feeling the deepest melancholy; while the winds, moaning in the vale, seem to echo back the sound, ' Where are they?' In this more enlightened age the farmers cannot refer to the melancholy history of that unfortunate race without feelings of regret; while it is but justice to add, that many of them made strenuous efforts, and collected thousands of cattle and sheep, which they presented to the neighbouring Bushmen, hoping to induce them to settle, and live by breeding cattle; but these efforts always failed. It was too late; past sufferings, and past offences on both sides, had produced a spirit of hatred so universal, that it was of no avail to pacify one party, while thousands were thirsting for revenge and plunder."*

The weapons of the Bushmen are few and simple, but terribly effective. They consist almost exclusively of the bow and arrows; the latter are poisoned. And as they are very skilful archers, having been accustomed

* Rev. R. Moffat.

to the bow from their childhood, their weapons are
very much dreaded. A Hottentot belonging to the
travelling party of the Rev. J. Campbell was shot by
a Bushman in the back of the neck. Everything was
done to mitigate the pain, but the poor fellow suffered
extremely ; his whole body was greatly swollen, particularly about the head and throat. A Bushman in the
company said in the morning, that the sufferer would
die at the going down of the sun ; " and," says Mr.
Campbell, " the sun had not dipped below the horizon
five minutes before he breathed his last."

Deep as were the wrongs inflicted upon the Bushman
in the times of the first European settlers, since the
Colony came into the possession of the British, it is a
relief to find that the missionary societies have not
entirely overlooked this poor afflicted race. The London
Missionary Society, especially, has sought to make some
reparation and amends by imparting to them the blessings of Christianity.

Nothing less than a philanthropy of the noblest character could have rendered either missionary societies
or missionaries willing to undertake missions exclusively to Bushmen ; for at best few only could be
gathered on one spot ; and, from the wildness of their
character and habits, ultimate failure might almost
have been anticipated, even by the most sanguine. It
appears to me that the best, and perhaps the only, way
of gaining any permanent influence for good over the
Bushman is through the instrumentality of native con-
verts, against whom the prejudices and suspicions he
entertains towards the white man have no existence.
These, by showing kindness, as I am sure many of

them do, by employing them to take care of their
sheep and goats, and remunerating them by the payment
of a few for themselves, may inspire confidence ; and
by bringing them under the influence of the truth on
the mission station, or at its outposts, and gathering
their children into the schools, may succeed in gradually
enlightening their minds, and perhaps, eventually, bring
them to settle amongst the people of the country, and to
submit to the restraints of law and order, at the same
time leaving them a considerable measure of liberty to
hunt and roam over the plains in accordance with
their wild tastes and habits ; till, in the course of
generations, *for the process must necessarily be slow*, they
become incorporated with the tribes, Christianised and
civilised.

CHAPTER III.

HARD AT WORK.

SUCH was the country, and such were the people amongst whom our mission had to be prosecuted. It was not, however, a new mission that had to be established, other messengers of salvation having preceded us in that region, a brief reference to whose labours shall be made before proceeding to detail our own.

St. Paul exclaims, "O the depth of the riches both of the wisdom and knowledge of God! How unsearchable are His judgments, and His ways past finding out!" And to the Christian, perhaps, no mystery is deeper than that from the foundation of the world so many nations and tribes of men should have been suffered "to walk in their own ways," and remain unvisited by the Gospel of the grace of God. Down to the year 1806, the natives in this part of the African continent were allowed to continue more literally without God and without hope than heathen nations generally are, having nothing that could be called a religious system, and only a few fragmentary traditions of the crudest character. To this uninviting region the two brothers, Abraham and Christian Albrecht, fearlessly directed their steps, traversing the desert at the most trying season of the year, suffering much from want of water and provisions, " being never in their lives so perplexed as to what they should eat or drink, and rejoicing when they could get a draught of brack or saltish water." They were the first heralds of salvation who sounded out the word of the Lord amongst the Great Namaquas. These noble men were missionaries in connection with the London Missionary Society.

At a place called Warm Bath, the brothers resolved to establish their mission ; for, though the soil on the station is sandy and rocky, and is covered with a saline incrustation that crackles under the feet, the presence of a strong thermal fountain, from which the place derives its name, as well as smaller springs of cool water, renders it a place of value and importance in such a country. In addition to the liberal supply of water, ample plains of grass stretch away to the south and east, where any number of cattle may find sustenance ; whilst the sheep and goats of the inhabitants find pasture among the shrubs and bushes that line the banks of the Droog Rivier, *i.e.*, the Dry River, a periodical stream that passes through the station. The Warm Bath, therefore, though by no means, in some respects, a good station, was the best that could be found, and for this reason it was fixed upon by the missionaries. Their first experiences were of a chequered character, successes and discouragements alternating with each other, till, owing to the debilitating effects of the climate, the health of the elder brother failed, and he was compelled to leave the station for the colony. There he died in the Lord about ten weeks after he had taken his leave of Great Namaqualand.

The mission was then continued for a time by Christian, the younger brother, who immediately after the death of Abraham had proceeded to Cape Town, where he remained only a short time, and then returned to the station with his newly-married wife, an accomplished lady of Rotterdam, thoroughly imbued with the missionary spirit; but shortly after resuming his labours, owing to a quarrel between the Bondelzwaarts, the tribe with whom he resided, and Jager Afrikaner, the chief of a neighbouring tribe, all their hopeful prospects were suddenly blighted. An attack from Afrikaner, a man of great daring, heading a people of equally desperáte character, was hourly expected, and as he vowed vengeance on the mission, the mission family, as well as the people of the station, were kept in continual alarm, and at length the missionary and people abandoned the place. On the arrival of Afrikaner, his followers, finding the station forsaken, "commenced a rigid search for any articles which might have been concealed for safety in the earth. One of the chieftain's attendants strayed to the burial ground, about a mile to the north of the station, where a few mounds distinguished it from 'the surrounding waste as the place of the dead. Stepping over that which he supposed was a newly-closed grave, he heard, to his surprise, a mysterious sound vibrate beneath." This proceeded from Mrs. Albrecht's piano, which had been buried in the dry sand previous to their hasty flight from the station, but which was now brought to light again by the ruthless marauders, who kept the wire, wrapping it round their wrists and ankles for ornament, but destroyed the wood-work. The native huts and mission premises were fired, "the light of Divine truth which had just been enkindled in those gloomy regions was extinguished for a season, and a peaceful Zion reduced to a heap of ruins." This disastrous event appears to have taken place about 1811. The mission was resumed at Pella, on the south side of the Orange River, and here they were joined by about five hundred of the Warm Bath people. Whilst at this place, Mr. Albrecht "had the ineffable joy of making peace with Afrikaner, and seeing the standard of the Prince of Peace reared in the very village of the man who once 'breathed out threatenings and slaughter' against not only his fellow heathen, but against the saints of the Most High."* But Mr. C. Albrecht was soon to rest from his labours; for, being under the necessity of going to Cape Town for medical advice, he suddenly expired, in about 1813, "leaving behind him a bright testimony of zeal, love, and self-denial seldom equalled."

In 1825 the Rev. William Threlfall, accompanied by two pious natives, travelled through the country in order to ascertain the practicability of commencing a Wesleyan mission in Great Namaqualand; but, falling into the hands of a treacherous guide, they were led to a party of Bushmen, who, moved by cupidity, and a desire for plunder, fell upon them in the darkness of the night and murdered the whole party.

In August, 1826, the chief of the Bondelzwaarts made a personal application to the Rev. R. Haddy, then at the Khamies Berg Station, for a missionary, but was unsuccessful. In August, 1830, he visited Cape Town for the same purpose, and had an interview with the governor. But neither did he succeed at this time. In the year 1832, however, a missionary meet-

* Rev. R. Moffat.

ing was held in the Wesleyan chapel at Simon's Town, near Cape Town, presided over by Josiah Nisbett, Esq., of the Madras Civil Service, who was so much affected by the statements then made respecting the earnest desire of the people of Warm Bath for the Gospel, that he promised at the meeting to give £200 towards the establishment of a mission among them. And in case this sum should not prove a sufficient inducement to the Missionary Committee to undertake the work, he said he would give another hundred; "and should I fall short in any way," said he, "while remaining at the Cape, I will dispose of my carriage and horses; for I had rather part with these, and trudge on foot, than that Great Namaqualand should remain without the Gospel."

The Rev. E. Cook, who was present at the meeting, at once offered to go, if the Missionary Committee would appoint him. They accepted the offer of Mr. Nisbett, and in 1834 Mr. Cook commenced his labours amongst the Bondelzwaarts, in the very country where the blood of William Threlfall, and his native companions, was mingled with the sands of the desert. From the period of Mr. Cook's arrival the name of Warm Bath was discontinued, and the name of Nisbett Bath substituted, in honour of the gentleman who so liberally contributed to its formation. Mr. Cook, after eight years of laborious and successful labour (during a portion of which time he had the valuable assistance of Mr. Joseph Tindall), was compelled to leave the mission in failing health; and, whilst journeying to Cape Town, expired in his travelling waggon on the banks of the Orange River.

When the intelligence of Mr. Cook's death arrived

in England, the writer was steadily pursuing his ministerial duties in the south-west of this country. For three years he had already been engaged in the home work; but having expressed a preference for the mission field, when first offering for the ministry, he was holding himself in readiness for any application that might be forwarded from the Missionary Committee. In the month of June such an application arrived, and in the following month the Conference was held, at which he was appointed to South Africa.

On 27th of January, 1844, after travelling for nine weeks and a half by sea, and eight weeks and five days through the wilderness, as already detailed, we reached our distant station. It was a perfect delight to us all when our poor jaded oxen were for the last time loosened from the yoke, and we watched them slowly moving to the fountain at which they had often drunk, and then to the well-known plains, where most of them had spent the days of their bovine infancy and childhood, to enjoy a long vacation after the ceaseless toil of their late journey.

As was natural, we felt some degree of curiosity before reaching the station to know what sort of a habitation we should find on our arrival, a curiosity which was not altogether satisfied by the descriptions of Brother Tindall, who had spent several years there. We were gratified, therefore, on finding a good-sized substantial erection, eighty-four feet in length, by twenty-two in breadth, with upper rooms and thickly thatched roof. The houses were built of stone, the walls very thick, and plastered outside. The doors and window-frames were painted green, and a neat stuccoed wall, with gates,

enclosing a space in front, made the general appearance
of the premises very agreeable, especially in such a
land, and after so long a confinement to our travelling-
waggons. The newer and larger building was to be
occupied by myself and wife, the other by Mr. Macleod,
the schoolmaster, and his young family. The chapel at
the back of the mission house, with a passage only a
few feet broad intervening, was also built of stone, and
capable of holding a congregation of four or five hundred
persons.

As to the scenery, there was little in view from
the mission premises that could be dignified with
the name. Immediately in front was barren soil of
rock and sand intermixed; a little further forward a
mass of gneiss rock, and another of mica schist; further
still a perfect chaos of loose granite rocks, with sunburnt aloes rooted in their crevices, and creeping lizards
for their tenants; and through this chaos of rocks a
small footpath leading to the only spot of living green
in the neighbourhood, viz., the mission garden, which,
despite long drought and intense heat, was made to
flourish by daily irrigation. Extending the view in the
same direction, the eye met nothing but barren sand
and loose stone, with here and there hillocks of quartz-
ose rock, till, beyond, and stretching away into the
southern horizon, was an extensive plain of long grass,
parched whiter than hay by drought and heat, yet
standing erect, and waving in the wind. A little to
the west of south, and about twenty miles from the
station, in full and distinct view, a low range of mountains stretched away. The view to the north was even
less attractive. At the distance of a mile, two broad-

based, cone-shaped hills of basaltic rock, and altogether destitute of soil, formed the background of the station; whilst between them wound the bed of the Dry River, whose course is marked out by trees and bushes growing along its sides, and tending towards the south-west as far as the eye could trace it. To the west the ground gradually swelled so as to obstruct the view; and though to the east the country was more open, no object of an attractive kind presented itself. Two camel-thorn trees, with a very scant supply of foliage, at upwards of a hundred yards from the front of our house, another in a yard at the west end, and one more, the largest of all, at the distance of another hundred yards from that, were all the station could boast, save the thin line of trees and bushes along the sides of the river-bed. True, at the distance of seven hundred yards from the front of our dwelling, the green fig trees, and a pomegranate tree, were very beautiful to look upon, by contrast with the barrenness all around; but, with the exceptions named, the eye might scan the whole country for miles, and not mark another tree, and scarcely a shrub.

The first thing to be done, after a little rest, was the removal of our stores from our waggons to an upper room, entered by a door at the east end of the house. With the aid of the natives, whom we found very clever in the management of heavy packages, this was soon accomplished. Before this was finished, the announcement was made that a cavalcade was approaching, and, on looking out, upwards of fifty men, mounted on oxen, were seen, marching like a line of cavalry towards the centre of the station. These having dismounted, all came to the house to shake us by the hand, and welcome

us to the country.   Some of them had come upwards of
a hundred and thirty miles, and had travelled two days
and nights.   As soon as they heard of our arrival at the
Orange River, they set out, like their forerunners, to
assist us through, but like them they were too late.   It
was very cheering, however, to have so substantial a
proof of their regard for those who were to minister
to them the Word of Life.

On reaching the station, the absence of a native
population, and the lone mission premises, was a scene
calculated to repel the goings forth of feeling we had
already experienced towards our home, and the people of
our charge, and drive all back again into the fountain of
the heart.   It seemed an almost stunning fact that we
should have ploughed the waters of the ocean for so
many weeks, and that for nearly as many more we
should have traversed the burning plains and rugged
mountains of the wilderness, to reach what on our
arrival proved an almost unpeopled station.   We had
often been told by Mr. Tindall during the journey what
we must expect ; but we were slow to comprehend and
realise his statements.   Sorrow, deep and sad, would
certainly have filled our hearts on arriving, to behold
that desolate scene, had we not once more been told
that for three years the heavens had given no rain of
any value, and consequently the people had been scattered in all directions where they could obtain grass
and water for their flocks and herds.   We were informed, moreover, that after rain had fallen in sufficient quantity, the people would flock to the station,
and the deathly silence of the village give place to
scenes of animation and sounds of life.   We were

glad to believe it, and already we had the promise of that happier state of things in the parties that had come to greet our arrival and to enjoy the Sabbath services.

Just as the sun arose on the Sabbath morning, sounds sweet and heavenly fell upon our ears and woke us from our slumbers. The natives had assembled at their usual prayer meeting, and, waked by their divine songs, we felt something of the calm and heavenliness our first parent felt when he first woke to life in Paradise, possessed of a perfect happiness springing from a full sense of the Divine complacency. It was one of those spiritually blissful seasons we sometimes experience on earth, and that most forcibly remind us of the bliss awaiting the people of God in heaven. At half-past eight the bell was rung, the people waiting for the summons were soon assembled, and nearly filled the chapel. I had not yet conducted a full service in Dutch, but as for the previous six months I had made diligent application, and had, several times, made successful experiments on a small scale, I felt quite disposed to make the trial now. The preliminary portions of the service being past, the text was announced (Rom. v. 1): "Therefore being justified by faith, we have peace with God through our Lord Jesus Christ:" and I preached, in Methodist fashion, an extempore sermon; for, never having read a sermon before, I could not be persuaded to begin now, when, if ever, it might be deemed excusable, as I was preaching for the first time in a foreign tongue. When the service was closed, I received the congratulations of our missionary party at the ease with which the language was wielded, and I was quite inclined to feel gratified and thankful.   It is not pretended that the idiom was very correct, but the sermon was distinctly understood by the native interpreter, and by him translated into Namaqua for the benefit of those who only knew that tongue.   In the afternoon the Sabbath school was held, though at present a very small one, at the close of which the station bell was again rung, when Brother Tindall conducted the service.   In the evening, whilst the natives were holding a prayer meeting in the chapel, I preached in English to seven of our own party, and the families of Messrs. Dixon and Morris, two Christian traders to the country.   This service was held in the mission house; and thus our first Sabbath in Great Namaqualand was brought to a close.   To us it was one of new and deep interest and spiritual profit.

To many it will appear singular that the Dutch language should be employed in conducting services amongst the Namaquas; but the circumstance is explained by the fact of the Colony of the Cape of Good Hope having first been settled by the Dutch, upwards of two hundred and twenty-five years ago.   The Dutch boers, or farmers, as the word denotes, gradually went further and further into the country, employing many of the natives in their service.   These rapidly acquired a knowledge of their masters' language, and by degrees it spread from them to others of their countrymen around.   When, therefore, missionaries first proceeded to Great Namaqualand, it was not difficult to find a Namaqua able to speak Dutch; hence, as soon as the missionary had himself acquired that language, a door of access was opened, through the medium of an interpreter, to the tribes far beyond.

From the first, missionaries have always preached in those regions in Dutch, and this is the language that for upwards of seventy years has been taught in the mission schools of that part; so that large numbers of natives, for a thousand miles to the north of Cape Town, have become acquainted with it; in addition to which many descendants of the Dutch and native race, called by the uncouth name of Bastaards, born in the Colony, where Dutch is the only language they have been accustomed to speak, settle down with the natives on the mission stations, so that in nearly all the mission congregations of Namaqualand there are a number who understand only Dutch, while there are others who understand only Namaqua. This renders an interpreter absolutely necessary, so that both parts of the congregation may share in the benefit of the service.

When the missionary is careful to prepare his interpreter for each service by previous conversation, and by giving him the outline and substance of his intended address, and questioning him as to his knowledge of the meaning of any unusual word he may have to introduce, no serious error will occur; an evil which is also the less likely to happen in a congregation where many know both languages just as well as, and sometimes better than, the interpreter himself. When a missionary continues to utter several sentences together, he runs the risk of having his instruction marred, as it is only few Namaqua heads that can carry much matter safely. But when the ideas are clearly and concisely put, and the interpreter is taught to deliver them in a similar way, it has often struck me as a very impressive mode of teaching; the matter being more condensed than when we speak in our mother tongue, and the momentary rest between the delivery of each sentence being a positive benefit to minds untrained and slow of perception.

On the following day some novel duties had to be performed. As soon as the daily morning service, which was regularly held at eight o'clock, was finished, the natives came to the mission house to make purchases of various articles, which were to be paid for, not by Her Majesty's "coin current," but by the produce of the country. Here I may state that at the district meeting I was directed to purchase a flock of sheep and goats for the use of the mission family, this being the only way of obtaining a supply of provisions. The direction sounded somewhat startling to one, nearly the whole of whose life had been spent in London, and in pursuits the most opposite that can be conceived to those now indicated. One customer, perhaps, wanted a clasp knife and a shirt, for which he would promise to pay a slaughter sheep; another wanted a Dutch hymn-book, for which he would pay a similar price; another a handkerchief, for which a lamb or kid just weaned would be promised; another a fustian jacket and trowsers, for a young ox, or heifer two years old. But as we only required a few slaughter sheep, and one or two milch cows, for present use, the largest number of what was purchased consisted of ewe lambs and goats, and heifers and young oxen of two or three years old, this being the most economical way of procuring a flock for the Society, and of replenishing our team of draught oxen, as that might be necessary. During the day, upwards of one hundred animals,

great and small, were purchased. Of the flesh of this
flock we were to eat, and of their milk to drink, as
long as we remained in that country; and on leaving,
to hand over the whole of the surplus to my successor.
The bartering process was by no means difficult, as
the price of every article purchased by the natives, and
of every animal received in payment, was well known
by both parties; so that not a moment was lost in unpleasant altercation; but as the natives were all
strangers to us, only on a visit from afar, and in
general gave a promise instead of a *bonâ fide* animal,
the work was rendered rather tedious by having to take
down the name of the purchaser, the article purchased,
and the animal promised. In giving credit so extensively, we were very much guided by Brother Tindall's
knowledge of the people, and the recommendations he
gave; and though to us it seemed a risk, punctual if
not very prompt payment showed him to be a very safe
guide, and the natives very trusty purchasers; whilst,
in the quality of the animals sent, the people showed
very great honour.

On the Wednesday following, the whole party, who
had come a considerable distance to meet the new missionary, and to attend the Sabbath services, took leave
of us for their distant homes, so that the station was
left with not many native residents. The school class
and daily service were still kept up, though, necessarily,
few attended; and we new comers were sometimes
ready to think that because there were only few on our
arrival, they would always continue so.

Towards the end of the week we were all in excitement once more. The Rev. R. Haddy, who had been

appointed to the Damara mission, was reported to have crossed the Orange River, and to be near our station. On the Saturday evening, just after tea, the two waggons, with their long teams of oxen, were seen descending the hill towards " the Bath," as the mission station was generally called. Soon they were with us, having had, like ourselves, an exceedingly hot and trying journey.

On the Sabbath we all took part in the services of the day, our congregations being again increased by the arrival of many of our people from the outposts to spend the Sabbath, and enjoy the services. In the evening, as before, I again preached in English.

As the Rev. Messrs. Haddy and Tindall would be under the necessity of remaining at Nisbett Bath until the rains should fall, one of the first steps was to arrange the part we should respectively take in conducting the services : and as there was a daily morning service, two evening services during the week, and a public prayer meeting, besides the full services of the Sabbath, and an English service to the mission families on the Sabbath evening, we all found congenial occupation.

Very soon after we had reached Nisbett Bath we received a visit from David Afrikaner, a son of the notorious Afrikaner, who, a few years previously, was the terror of the country. David is now, and has been for several years past, a native assistant at Blyde-verwacht, the chief residence of that portion of the Afrikaner tribe which separated from Jonker Afrikaner when he went with all his people to Damaraland, and commenced a series of freebooting expeditions against the inhabitants of that country. David is regarded as the father of his people, and is one of the most intelligent and useful men in the circuit. Titus Afrikaner, his elder brother, once renowned for his dauntless courage and for his deeds of violence, resides with him at the same place; but is now an old man. In the expression of David's countenance there are no indications of a warlike spirit, but, on the contrary, those of a peaceable and retiring disposition. In his person he was rather below the ordinary height, well nourished generally, and his face plump for a Namaqua, his eyes large and remarkably intelligent; and as a natural orator he was particularly effective. One Sunday morning, during his visit, he acted as interpreter to Mr. Haddy, and at the conclusion of the service engaged in prayer, when sighs and tears were wrung from nearly the whole congregation, so that the chapel was a very Bochim; and many were compelled to leave, that they might give expression to their feelings.

The long-continued drought which had produced so sad a famine in the land, and which seemed to threaten destruction to multitudes, unless speedily terminated, filled us with anxiety, and led us publicly to observe a season of special prayer for rain. We remembered the Lord God of Elijah; and we believed that " the effectual fervent prayer of a righteous man " still " availeth much." Encouraged by the success of the prophet when he prayed for rain, we too prayed, in faith, and hope, and patience, for an abundant outpouring, that the famine might be stayed, the earth bring forth her fruit, and that with a replenished pasturage the people might be able to return to the station, and come under the influence of the teachings of the sanctuary. And very soon the Lord graciously answered the prayers of His people, according to the promise, " Before they call, I will answer; and while they are yet speaking, I will hear."

After having spent several weeks together on the station, the brethren Haddy and Tindall, and myself, resolved on a visit to some of the people of William Fransman's tribe, who were living about one hundred and twenty miles to the north-east of the " Bath," intending to call at one or two other outposts on the way.

On Wednesday, March 13th, 1844, we started from home, and, to our great joy, the same evening we had rain in abundance, thunder muttering from afar, becoming more and more distinct as it approached, till it burst in crashing peals all around us, and lightning magnificent in the extreme. At first, the path lay to the north of the " Bath," where we found the country interspersed with shrubs and trees already putting out green foliage, whilst the grass was growing in numberless little tufts, and the aspect of nature already changing, though so few days had elapsed since the first rains fell.

14th.—We travelled from half-past two a.m. till seven, when we took breakfast near the side of a periodical river, where the water from the late rains was standing in pools, but, owing to the saline nature of the soil, more salt than any we met with on our journey from Cape Town to our station. Towards evening, whilst passing over a barren stony part of the country, a remarkable flower attracted the attention of Mr. John Haddy and myself. We found it to be a carrion flower, the only one we had seen since entering the country. This genus is described in Murray's *Encyclopædia of Geography*, as " highly curious, with square, succulent, leafless stems, and flowers resembling starfish. They derive their appellation from their abominable odour, which so much resembles that of putrid meat, that insects are deceived by it, and deposit upon them their eggs, which are hatched by the heat of the sun, when the larvæ perish for want of animal food. The stem has an insipid, yet cool and watery taste, and is used by the natives for the purpose of quenching thirst; for which purpose it would seem Providence has designed it, by placing it only in hot and arid tracts of country." To the purpose of quenching thirst our men now applied it, cutting away the rind, and eating the inner part of the stem. The same evening we reached a place called *Wortel*, one of the outposts of the station, to which many of our people frequently resort. There were only a few families resident on the place; but on the summons being given, they gladly assembled in their temporary chapel, and we held a refreshing service with them. Here we remained for the night.

Friday, 15th.—Having obtained one of our members to act as a guide to the next outpost, we resumed our journey in drenching rain,—of all temporal gifts the most acceptable heaven could bestow. In our own country we often found it to be a plague and a vexation, but in a hot, dry, and thirsty land like this, its arrival is a source of unspeakable joy, for it is literally life from the dead. Never were we disposed with such fulness of gratitude to praise God, and to say with the old Rabbi of Magdala: " Thousands of thousands and millions of millions are bound to praise Thy name, O our King, for every drop Thou causest to descend upon us, because Thou renderest good to the wicked." "He sendeth rain on the just and on the unjust." This morning it fell in such abundance, that in several places on the road the oxen had to wade through it several inches in depth.

Soon after starting, an accident nearly happened, that might have proved serious. The goat we had purchased for slaughter, had been made fast on the foot-board in front of the waggon, but had succeeded in getting partially loose. On leaning over to secure it, the waggon descended the steep bank of a river-bed, when the waggon-chest, on which I was leaning, was jolted out of its place, and had not Mr. Haddy seized me by the ankle, I should, in all probability, soon have been under the wheels; as it was, the only damage done was to the chest, which was very much injured by the waggon-wheels going over it. In the afternoon, whilst travelling over an extensive plain, a shout was raised that a serpent was near. At the moment I was walking by the side of the waggon, exercising myself with the large whip. With this I followed the reptile, which was escaping to a bush, on reaching which it glided into a hole in the ground, which, however, was not sufficiently large to admit its whole body. About four inches of the tail still remained outside, to which I made the lash of the whip fast, but so firmly did it hold that it was impossible to draw it out by this means. I therefore handed the stock of the whip to Mr. Tindall, when, taking the tail of the reptile in my right hand, I drew it out so far as to make room for the left, then with both hands I drew it two feet further, when, letting loose, I sprang back, and as the tail was still attached to the lash, it was drawn out as easily as a fish from the water. Unable to escape, and fierce with its unwonted treatment, its eyes glistened and protruded as if they would start from the head, whilst the tongue was incessantly darted forth. The contents of a fowling-piece quickly despatched the dangerous reptile. The enmity to the serpent race is no mere fancy, but a reality; and I made the resolution to bruise the head of every serpent that I could, in the conviction that every serpent destroyed was, probably, a human life saved. This was a yellow serpent with a few black spots on the body; it was five feet in length, and not quite so thick as my wrist. The act of taking such a serpent by the tail was extremely perilous, and cannot be justified, and I have always regarded it as a very great mercy that I was not made to pay the penalty of my life. In the course of half an hour afterwards we destroyed a *cerastes*, or horned snake, so exactly of the colour of the sand, that, but for its motion, it could scarcely have been perceived.

Saturday, 16th.—About sunset this evening we reached 'Amas, another of the outposts of the mission. Here Job Witbooi, the native assistant, has charge of the people, and receives a slight remuneration, for maintaining the services and exercising a general supervision during the absence of the missionary. Here, too, we have a school on week-days conducted by one of the natives. One of my first duties on arrival was to pay the allowance granted to these agents. Payment it cannot be called, as articles of clothing, to the value of three pounds, are all the assistant receives, whilst the schoolmaster receives articles of much less value than that. What is given is scarcely more than a mere acknowledgment for services rendered, and would not be sufficient to retain them at their posts were it not that the grace of God influences their hearts, and makes them willing to do good for the satisfaction it affords; in addition to which, the fact of their position being regarded as an honourable one, both by themselves and their countrymen, may have some weight in attaching them to the service of the mission. During the course of the evening we held service, upwards of one hundred being present, this being, with the exception of a few young children, and those who were obliged to remain to take care of them, the whole population of the village. We soon after retired to rest in our waggon amidst the roar of mighty thunders, and the glare of the most extraordinary lightnings I ever witnessed.

17th, Sabbath.—Some of the natives from surrounding parts, having had messages sent on the previous day to inform them of our arrival, came early this morning to enjoy the services, so that we had a considerable congregation. Mr. Haddy preached in the morning; in the afternoon I met the members of society, and afterwards preached. The people were deeply attentive, and some were much affected at both services, as well as in the class meeting. Many of the countenances bore a look of bright intelligence, that contrasted very favourably with the appearance of afternoon congregations in some parts of our own country. To the people it appeared to be a season of perfect jubilation; they seemed greatly delighted at the presence of three missionaries, a sight upon which they had never before looked. And to ourselves it was a day of great "refreshing from the presence of the Lord."

Monday.—This morning we held service again and resumed our journey. During the morning's stage our guide narrowly escaped treading on a large yellow serpent, nearly a foot longer than that we had shot three days before. Mr. John Haddy, hearing the alarm given, sprang from the waggon and ran to the spot where the serpent was, and nearly trod upon it before perceiving his danger. The reptile, being alarmed, and bent merely on escape, made no attempt to defend itself, but took refuge in a bush. Driven from that, it made towards an acacia tree, which it ascended, not by coiling itself round the trunk, but, maintaining a perpendicular position, it worked its way slowly upwards by a slightly serpentine movement. As the only mode of reaching it was by a gun, one was fetched from the waggon, when it was shot among the branches. The frequency with which we met with these dangerous creatures had the effect of making us keep our eyes wide open when we walked, a duty highly advisable in all lands, but in this, where danger so constantly beset our path, absolutely necessary. A little further on the road, a steenbok, a small but beautiful antelope, sprang up from beneath a shrub, being startled by our approach, and bounded off with great grace. Its flesh is esteemed a great delicacy.

In the afternoon the weather rapidly changed, and we had one of the most gloomy and winterly storms that can be imagined, and quite extraordinary in this fiery land. The winds howled, the day became dark an hour before sunset, the rains fell and deluged the country, the thunders rolled over each other in heavy moaning sounds, except now and then, when we were electrified by a sharp rattling volley of heaven's grand artillery fired right over our heads. The vivid lightning opened out in broad sheets, darted in long streams, came in the shape of fireballs which split up into zigzag fragments flying in all directions from their centre, or glimmered incessantly all round the horizon, especially to the north and east, whilst towards the south and west the display was comparatively trifling, from which we inferred that no storm was raging and, probably, little rain falling at the Bath. Once or twice we lost our way, but eventually got into the right path. It was densely dark when we outspanned, and our men had great difficulty in getting a fire. At length they succeeded, and whilst we were standing around watching for the boiling of the kettle, we were surprised to hear a gun discharged in the distance, three or four times in succession; for what purpose we could only imagine, but the sound was ominous in such a place.

19th.—At half-past four a.m. we resumed our journey, and during the day reached the most distant outpost, called *Nieuwe Fontein.* Here we found Johannes Gagup, our native teacher, and about two hundred of William Fransman's tribe settled with him. The people had selected a small valley for their abode, a portion of which was enclosed as garden-ground; and under cultivation, whilst their small houses of reed mats were pitched in different parts of the valley, just as the fancy of the owners had dictated. There were a considerable number of members present, all of whom were met by Mr. Tindall and myself, who spent some time in endeavouring to ascertain the religious condition of each. Whilst some appeared to be in a satisfactory state, on the whole, there did not seem to be much depth in their Christian experience; which is not to be wondered at, considering their opportunities, and the necessity they are under of being confined almost exclusively to the spiritual instruction of their native teacher; for these, belonging to another tribe, never can settle on the mission station and receive the same instruction as those who have that privilege. Some had fallen into sin, and discipline had to be enforced; but, notwithstanding some drawbacks, it was delightful to find so many under a real religious influence, sincerely endeavouring to walk according to the Gospel. For want of a chapel, Mr. Tindall and myself assembled the members in two large circles under the shade of some large mimosa trees, thus investing our class-meetings with an air of romance quite new to me. At night, again, the heavens gathered blackness, the rain fell heavily, and the lightnings flashed and the thunders rolled with fearful grandeur. We could not but feel that our waggon, having so much iron about it, was scarcely a refuge, and that we were entirely dependent upon the God of the storm for protection.

Wednesday, 20th.—This morning the water was running in rills down the slopes of the small valley, though the storm had ceased, the clouds disappeared, and the sun was shining in full splendour. As the morning advanced, and the ground dried under the warmth of the sun, the signal was again given for the people to assemble, as we intended returning in the afternoon.

The horn of an antelope (the koodoo) was taken by an adept in the art, and blown with a strong, steady stream of breath. This produced a low, monotonous sound, which soon found its way to the extremity of the village; and as the voice of the trumpet sounded long, and waxed louder and louder, the population were seen tending towards the trees beneath the shade of which the service was to be held. The congregation was good, the whole of the inhabitants being there, save those who had gone to the pasturage with their sheep and goats, and one left in some of the houses where there were sick to tend, or where there was a little provision to guard against the depredations of those inveterate robbers, their dogs. We were much interested with our visit, and the people were much cheered, and will feel the beneficial stimulus far longer than those whose privileges abound, and who are always depending on excitements from without to preserve them in vital energy. After a simple repast of roast mutton, bread, and water, eaten beneath the shade of a mimosa tree, we bade them farewell, and turned our faces homeward for our journey of one hundred and twenty miles.

The river Ky' Kaap, which was a mere river bed when we crossed it two days before, was now, owing to the recent rains, a broad stream with strong current. When we passed before, the silence of death reigned; now the rocks and river were alive with geese and other wild water-fowl.

On the next morning early, as we travelled, we saw in the distance a number of wild animals that we could not distinctly make out. "What if they should be an army of lions?" said Mr. Haddy. As we neared them they turned out to be something more tolerable, being nothing more than a number of harmless and beautiful springboks, one of the most elegant of the antelope species.

On Saturday, March 23rd, after hard travelling, we reached the mission house again, unfeignedly thankful for our own preservation, and for that of our families during our absence. Although for a week in succession, when on the journey, we had storms of thunder and lightning, and frequent rains, only a few showers had fallen in the immediate vicinity of the station; but on the day of our departure, the 13th, a lightning stroke severed off the principal limb of a large mimosa tree standing very near the west end of the mission house, when two young men, standing at the open door of the kitchen, narrowly escaped, one of them being struck to the kitchen floor.

Hitherto the four mission families had been good company for each other. But now the rains having fallen, and the pools by the way having been filled, the Brethren Haddy and Tindall recommenced their journey to Damaraland, having in prospect a distance of six hundred miles.

About this time charges of a startling nature were brought against one of our people, the chief's principal counsellor, and the interpreter usually employed by the missionaries; charges of gross immorality, committed when the station was left without a missionary. The sin was now brought to light, and proved by decisive evidence. It was to me more distressing than I can express, for I felt it necessary, in order to make a suitable impression on his own mind, and on the minds of the people, as to the enormity of the sin, to impose a severe penalty, that of expulsion from membership with the church. Feeling my responsibility to the Great Head of the Church, I could not conscientiously modify the sentence. To my unspeakable joy, it soon appeared that the effect on his own mind was most salutary, and that his conduct was that of a true mourner. On the Sunday following, instead of taking his usual position by the side of the missionary, or of venturing to mingle with the congregation as an ordinary hearer, he seated himself in the farthest part of the building, apart from every one else, his appearance indicating deep dejection and penitential distress. At half-past six a.m., on the Monday following, he came with a broken heart to acknowledge his guilt. His eyes were swollen and red with weeping, and an expression of grief was deeply depicted on his countenance. He said that since his expulsion he had not been able either to eat or sleep; that he very much wished to confess his crime on the Sunday night, for he was wretched, and felt that he could have no rest till he had done so. Previous to the Sunday services he said he had resolved to leave the place, and take his family to some distance from the station, but he was much affected by the services of the day; and on entering the chapel, he said, " the place seemed so holy, and the society so holy," that he was ashamed to be there, and had, through a deep sense of his unworthiness, gone to a distant part of the chapel. He added, that under the preaching his feelings were more than he could bear; and he had come to the determination not to leave the place, but to remain and prove the reality of his penitence. "And," said he, "were I to depart from the station, I should deprive all my family of the benefit of the instructions of the missionary; and I feel God would require their souls at my hand." He "went softly" about the village, with sorrowful countenance and dejected mien, thus humbling himself in the sight of men, as well as of God. Though his fall has been awfully deep, and I have thought of it with weeping, yet now that I see the depth of his repentance I am filled with comfort and am "exceeding joyful," because I hope his present excision from the church may have a sanctifying effect and may result in the salvation of his soul, as well as lead to more watchfulness and diligence on the part of the members generally. The punishment seems to have brought home to him the full sense of his guilt; and sometimes he was so distressed that, fearing lest he should be "swallowed up of overmuch sorrow," I felt it needful to administer words of solace, pointing him to the Lamb of God as the sacrifice for sin, and cheering him with the hope, in due season, of readmission into the church. This man was always afterwards a source of joy to me, and a faithful and attached friend.

Messrs. Haddy and Tindall being now on their journey to Damaraland, the entire responsibility of the services, which they had hitherto shared, now devolved upon myself, still a novice in the language, and all the other affairs of the station required constant attention. Each morning throughout the week the station bell was rung for service, when the congregation at once assembled; a hymn was sung, followed by the reading and exposition of a portion of Scripture and prayer. The service

was little more than half an hour in length, and
might be regarded as a sort of family prayer for the
whole population.   Shortly after this service had closed
the bell again .rang for school, which assembled at
nine o'clock and continued till near twelve, when,
during the prevalence of drought, and almost of famine,
that afflicted the land for three months after our arrival,
Mr. Macleod observed that, immediately on being
liberated from school, the children all ran to the bed of
the Droog River, instead of to their homes; and on
inquiry he learned that they ran thither to ascend the
acacia and other trees, that they might pick off the gum
exuding from them, and endeavour to satisfy the
cravings of hunger; for at that time this was all they
had as the mid-day meal.   School was again held from
two till four, and was always commenced with a hymn
and prayer.   On several afternoons of the week a sewing
school for girls was held by Mrs. Macleod, assisted by
Mrs. Ridsdale.   Nearly every evening in the week was
occupied with preaching, prayer meeting, or class
meetings; whilst on the Sabbath a prayer meeting at
sunrise, preaching at nine, Sunday school and preaching in the afternoon, and prayer meeting at night, fully
occupied the day.

In order to render the daily morning service as
interesting and instructive as possible, I commenced
the regular reading of the New Testament, accompanied
with expository remarks where necessary, and bringing
home its teachings to the heart and conscience as occasion offered.   When the subject was a miracle or
other incident, it was rendered as vivid as I could make
it, in order to arrest attention, and a few words were

added by way of inculcating the lessons to be learned. On commencing an Epistle, the writer, those to whom he wrote, the place of their abode, and the circumstances in which they were placed at the time, were all mentioned, and often referred to in the course of the reading, to keep them distinctly before the mind; and in this way all the teaching of a doctrinal, experimental, and practical character contained in the New Testament was brought successively before them to their great profit and delight. By degrees they increased in their attendance, and at length gathered in large numbers, manifesting the deepest interest in all that was said.

In order to make the school as attractive as possible, at certain intervals the children were put through various evolutions, and illustrations by means of the black board and chalk were given, which tended to break the monotony of school instruction as usually practised at that date. The consequence was that nearly every child in the place was constantly at school.

Although the people were exceedingly fond of music, the congregational singing was extremely bad, many old tunes being scarcely recognisable as sung by the natives. In order, as far as practicable, to remedy this, I announced that henceforth, on two evenings of the week, we should devote an hour or two to learning new tunes. I found it utterly useless to attempt to correct the old ones, which would have been as impossible as to turn the course of the Orange River in time of flood. Their bad habits of twisting and twirling were so immovably fixed, that, after repeated attempts and failures, finding that the old tunes would only prove a source of continual vexation, I felt convinced that the

only way to succeed was by introducing new tunes altogether.   As they were very anxious to learn, "the
service of song" became very popular, and when many
were located on the station, the chapel was much too
small for those who wished to attend.   On these occasions the name of the new tune was announced, for as
their horses and oxen all had names, so, I told them, had
all our tunes.   Under my direction the whole congregation would first pronounce it syllable by syllable, and
then at full length.   I used then to play it on my flute,
pointing out the peculiarities occurring in any part, the
people meantime listening with attention.   I would
then lay aside the flute, and myself, and Mr. Macleod,
and our wives, would sing it through a few times,
directing attention to any prolonged or to any quicker
notes or other peculiarity.   After this the whole congregation would make their first attempt under our
guidance, and at any hitch that occurred they were
instantly stopped, the error pointed out, and illustrated
where it could be, when all began again.   The process
was sometimes tedious, and it required considerable
patience and perseverance to continue the practising
evenings, as I did, for nearly two years; but at length
a large number of excellent tunes were correctly
acquired, and sung often with such thrilling effect that
the tears have involuntarily flowed from the eyes of
preacher and people, and a softening emotion has been
produced that was an admirable preparation for the minis-
tration and hearing of the word.   The effect on all who
came to the station from afar was wonderful.   As if absolutely overpowered, the head would drop, irrepressible
sobs find vent, the bosom heave heavily, and in many

instances they would sink down on the floor in a swoon; yet this occasioned little disturbance to the service, for our people, who had become familiar with such occurrences, would quietly bear them to the outside of the building, and lay them down, when, by exposure to the air, they would in time recover themselves.

The people now began gradually to come to the station from the distant outposts, so that our congregations were visibly increased Sabbath after Sabbath; the grass gathered strength, and grew in places which once seemed as if none had been since the creation; flowers bloomed on every hand, "thanksgiving" was felt in our hearts, "and the voice of melody" was on our lips. We were in hopes of soon seeing a large number of the tribe collected together upon the place, and brought under the blessed influences of the Gospel; and it appeared as if the chief, often a source of sore trouble and anxiety to my predecessor, was quite disposed to help forward the interests of the mission, and to retain the people under the influence of the principal station as long as possible; in order to which, he sent messengers in all directions to say that when they came to the Bath, they could only be allowed to bring as many milch cows and slaughter sheep as were necessary, leaving the rest of their flocks and herds at their cattle-posts; a direction the reasonableness of which was at once seen by the people. By this means the grazing in the neighbourhood of the station was rendered available for a long time.

One Sunday during the services the congregation showed an unusual earnestness of attention, and on the next day I was gratified to find that some had been beneficially impressed with the truths preached. At the Monday evening class meeting I was thankful to see deep feeling manifest itself in some of the members, who could not repress their sobs and tears.

On May 17th, 1844, I started about sunrise for Blydeverwachting, the residence of a portion of the Afrikaner tribe. This was my first journey on horseback to any of the outposts. Three horses were necessary, viz., one for the missionary, one for his guide, and another to carry our karosses or mantles, and whatever we should require during the journey. Among our requisites were included a small supply of tea and sugar, slices of bread baked hard and crisp to keep it from spoiling, some well-cooked mutton, a tin drinking mug, and a small copper kettle. My good wife felt something of her solitude, though she found an estimable neighbour in Mrs. Macleod, the wife of our schoolmaster; and in some notes of the parting, made as soon as I was gone, she says, " I continued looking after you yesterday morning till the rising sun dazzled, and the tears dimmed my eyes, so that I could see you no longer."

Soon after leaving the station a large herd of springboks appeared, playing their innocent gambols, and occasionally bounding six or eight feet perpendicularly into the air with astonishing lightness and agility. A few miles further on we saw another herd, grazing and lying at rest, two or three only leaving the others to take an inquisitive look at us, after which they bounded across our path, some distance in front, to get on our lee side, when, snuffing up the scent of the travellers, they scampered back to the herd; the elegance of their marking, and the grace of their motions, filling me with admiration. When we had travelled about eighteen miles, and were in a vast plain, covered with long Bushman grass, two full-grown ostriches were seen some distance ahead of us, running swiftly from north to south. At the same time four others, running as swiftly from the south towards the north, met them just in the line of our path, which lay from west to east. On meeting, all ran with surprising swiftness to our left again, wheeled about, and stood at no great distance gazing at us, and affording us a good opportunity of gazing at them in return. "Now, Jacob," said I to the man who accompanied me, "away." We gave our horses the bridle, and, needing no other stimulus, they stretched themselves out like racers over the plain; but the giant birds "lifted themselves on high;" their short wings vibrated like paddles at their sides, their long legs moved with amazing velocity, and, "scorning the horse and his rider," they soon left us far behind. The weather being cool, and it being within a month of mid-winter in this hemisphere, the ostrich is at its fleetest and strongest, and is never hunted in this way at this season. Another incident almost immediately occurred. "Jack," the horse ridden by my man, trod on the tail of a puff adder, and escaped a bite only by the rapidity of his motion. The man with the pack horse being in front of me, I saw "Jack's" hoof go on the tail, and the reptile open its jaws to strike with its fangs, but, being in a smart canter at the time, the horse escaped. We dismounted, however, and killed the dangerous reptile, which, though as to its general appearance sufficiently repulsive, proved, on a nearer inspection, to be really beautiful, the ground colouring being a soft velvet black, exquisitely marked with faint zigzag streaks of white and green. Just after sunset, or about five p.m., having reached the Aam's River, we resolved to take up our lodgings for the night at the foot of a large camel-thorn tree. Jacob soon made a fire and put on our small travelling-kettle, which served the purpose of tea-pot as well; and although the tea was served in primitive style, it was, perhaps, as much enjoyed after our ride of fifty miles, as if served in the halls of princes.

As the evening advanced all was made ready for the night. Our karosses were loosened from the pack-saddle and spread upon the sand; our saddles, propped up at the low end by a stone, formed our pillow; and then having commended ourselves to the protection of the Almighty, we wrapped our karosses round us in this region of tigers and other wild beasts, without any weapons, but without the least alarm. It was only half-past seven when we lay down, but soon my man, weary with the journey, was fast asleep. But being unused to such early hours, I lay wakeful till past ten o'clock, scarcely able to realise that I was passing the first night I had ever slept without a shelter in the wilds of Africa beneath a camel-thorn tree, with the sand for my bed, my saddle for my pillow, and wild beasts and serpents for my neighbours; and that I was doing this with entire freedom from any kind of apprehension, and from any degree of discomfort. For a long time, without a sound to break the profound silence, as I lay with my feet to the south, I watched the stars as they appeared slowly to move from east to west, from branch to branch of the camel-thorn tree, the branch immediately above serving as my meridian line, till unconsciously a wake-less slumber stole over me, from which I was only roused by my man bringing our horses early next morning. With Jacob's pillow, O that I had had Jacob's dream !

As the weather was cool, we first breakfasted beneath our tree, and then resumed our journey. Just at starting a large black snake, six feet in length, slowly crossed our path, and whilst we were seeking for stones it made for a small acacia tree, which it ascended slowly. As there were no missiles at hand, there we were obliged to leave it, our only weapons being our samboks, or riding whips, which were altogether un-suitable. Shortly after this we killed a *cerastes*, or horned snake. For the last fourteen miles our path lay parallel with a range of mountains to our left, which continue running on in an easterly direction till they lock into another range, running across from north to south. In a valley near the point of junction of these two ranges lies Blydeverwachting. The noble range with table top rising precipitously at the back of the village, and the equally fine mountain scenery on the left, the unusually large mimosas that stand here and there, and the winding line of shrubs and trees that margin the course of a periodical river running along the base of the mountains from north to south, unite to give a more striking and picturesque appearance to this place than is possessed by any other in the circuit. David Afrikaner was the first to offer his salutation, many others followed, and by all we were most joyfully welcomed.

David is a son of old Afrikaner, who had no other name till baptized by the Rev. Mr. Ebner, of the London

Missionary Society, when he was called Adam Afrikaner. He had many sons, a list of whom, according to their age, I obtained from one of them in 1846. Six of these sons were living, and were in this place at the time of my visit. Most of them were truly converted men, and the rest were members of the church, though not so prominent in their religious character, or in their position in the church, as the others. But what a mighty change has the Gospel effected in this family! At one time they were the terror of this part of South Africa, robbery and plunder being the order of the day; now they are bringing forth "the peaceable fruits of righteousness," and peace has for many years prevailed among these tribes, who were at one time always engaged in predatory warfare. David was now the native teacher to his own people, having been appointed by the Rev. Mr. Cook. Mr. Cook says of him in his journal, "He is a very interesting and, I trust, a truly pious man; a striking instance of the power of grace. He has been kept in the fear of God amidst a band of robbers and murderers for nearly twenty years, without any one to give him counsel and encouragement." From a statement he sent me in writing, it appears that he had learnt to read writing from a letter he had seen written by a Dutch Boer, and which had become his own, by studiously copying the letters till they became perfectly familiar. I am now in possession of several letters addressed by him to myself, and also an account of a portion of his life, in which latter he has ruled lines for himself, and written with great neatness, and with the letters, both capitals and small, exceedingly well formed.

From this account he appears to have heard the Word,

in the first instance, from some person who had fled to that part of the country, and whom he calls a refugee. "Afterwards," says he, "this man went to the Bushmen, by whom he was murdered. But though I heard the Word from him, I gave no serious attention to it." He next heard the Word of God from Mr. Albrecht. "But," he adds, "though I heard the Word from Mr. Albrecht, I did not trouble myself about it. Still I had a love for the school." Mr. Albrecht, who, it appears, was for a short time with the Afrikaners, then left them for Warm Bath, to reside among the Bondelzwaarts. This was a great loss and disappointment to David, and "when the missionaries left us, then I began to pray, and languished to hear the Word, where the Word was not to be had." It appears that even whilst he was without a missionary the Spirit of the Lord was strongly striving with him; "for," says he, "I felt that I was a sinner; but that God had a great love for sinners, and that Jesus Christ had died for me through the same love. I looked upon myself as perishing without God. I began to wrestle with my sins, and I longed to hear the Word; but I did not hear the Word, for I had no missionary. But afterwards I felt that I was delivered from my sins. Then I had a longing desire to be baptized and to stand steadfast. Then I met with Rev. Mr. Ebner; at that time I was called Hendrik, the godless name" (alluding to his being still a heathen). "Then was I baptized, and rejoiced to be baptized in His name; then was I called David. After this Mr. Ebner and Mr. Moffat left us." And poor David was left alone to struggle with sin in himself, and sin all around, amidst plunderings and fightings with the neighbouring tribes, without any human guide or counsel; yet by the help of almighty grace he and a few others kept the lamp of God alive during all those dreary years that elapsed between the removal of the London Missionary Society's missionaries and the establishment of the Wesleyan Mission, upwards of twenty years. As soon as David heard of this latter joyful event, he opened communications with Mr. Cook, my predecessor, by whom Blydeverwachting was taken up as an outpost of the Nisbett Bath Circuit, and a monthly visit to the Afrikaners established, to the great joy of David and others who were like-minded.

Having arrived about two p.m., the remaining part of the day was spent in conversing with David on the state of the people generally, and in conducting a service in the evening with all on the place. The next day was the Sabbath, when I was awaked by the songs of our people at their usual morning prayer meeting. In the morning I preached from Matt. xviii. 20 to a large congregation, for the intelligence of my arrival had been conveyed by horsemen to the people in the neighbouring places, and they had come in considerable numbers to attend the services of the day. A deep and solemn attention was given, and many were much affected. In the afternoon I met all the members in class, forty-five in number, several of whom wept much; and as the children of the Sunday school had not yet left, I paid them a brief visit. At night again the people assembled in great force, when I preached from Amos iv. 12.

On the Monday, we again held service at about eight o'clock, and as the weather happened to be rather wet, and it would be unsafe to sleep on the ground, we determined on riding to the Bath, a distance of seventy-eight miles, that same day. Our horses, braced by the cold weather, seemed to rejoice in the journey; and as we cantered along at a smart pace, about an hour after leaving, a cry of warning was raised by my guide, " Stop ! stop ! there lies a spitting serpent !" and there he lay in a rut on my right, but just in advance of my horse, with raised head, glistening eyes, and tongue darting out. I reined my horse out of the path to the left, and both of us dismounting, we resolved on killing the reptile. Fleeing to a euphorbia, it coiled itself round the root, when a stone, thrown with vio-lence by my man, nearly severed it in two. Thinking it must be killed, on approaching to untwist and measure it, my man cried, " Stop, Sir, the head's yet alive ;" and so I found, for, when within three or four yards, it angrily separated the stems of the bush with its head, and ejected its poison at me ; but being weakened by the wound it had received, the venom fell at my feet. This, I believe, is the only serpent that has the faculty of ejecting its poison. It is regarded by the natives as very deadly. Were the ejected poison to fall on a fresh cut, so as to mingle with the blood, and to be taken up into the circulation, it would no doubt prove fatal; though, were it to fall on the unabraded skin of the hand, or other part of the body, I suppose no injurious effect would follow, if it were at once removed. The man con-tinued throwing till a stone struck its raised head, when it fell dead at once. Untwisting and laying it out full length, I found it rather more than five feet in length.

An hour afterwards, as we rode along, I saw a large yellow snake in a bush close to the left-hand side of the path, its head flattened, and hissing angrily; but my horse was so near that I had no time to pull up, and in the next moment my foot in the left stirrup passed close above its angry head. The danger over, I called to the man, who was in advance, and once more we dismounted, with true enmity in our hearts, to bruise the serpent's head. The reptile disentangled itself from the bush, and was coursing its way over the sand, when a stone hurled by Jacob struck the ground and covered it with a shower of sand. The reptile, turning to face us, rose proudly into an erect position, with not more than a foot of its tail on the ground, scowling and hissing as it slowly advanced. But having no weapon, and missiles being very scarce, we kept at a few yards' distance; when, turning, and taking to the ground again, to our mortification it glided into a hole beneath some bushes, and so escaped unscathed.

All went well on the journey till within about thirty miles of home, when, the sun being set, the night darkened so rapidly that we lost all trace of our way. The waggon path is, in general, well marked and indented; but we had now reached a part of the road where the soil was hard and gravelly, and where the heaviest waggon left no trace behind. We dismounted, went on our hands and knees, and felt the ground, to discover any indentations of waggon wheels, but found none. We then mounted again, journeying, as we thought, in the general direction of home, till our horses got entangled in bushes, and stumbled into holes, or against the sides of hillocks, in such a way as to convince us that we were altogether wrong. After fumbling about for a tedious time in vain, we had to make up our minds to spend

the long night, with ten hours of darkness, on the plain.
Many things conspired to make this disagreeable. We
had seen and killed so many dangerous serpents on our
journey out and home, that it was not pleasant to think
of lying on the plain at all; the fresh spoor or foot-
marks of a tiger we had also passed but two hours
previously, and we were not wishful to fall in with such
company, especially as one of our class-leaders at
Blydeverwachting had been seized by one of these fierce
beasts, two or three weeks previously, and severely
bitten in the back, narrowly escaping with his life:
added to which, we were wet with the rain that had
fallen, our karosses were wet, the long grass and the
ground were also wet. But as there was no alternative,
we made loose and spread our karosses; then, kneeling
down, I commended myself and guide to the preservation of our ever-present God, and lay down, rather to
pass the hours of darkness that remained than to sleep.

Sleep, indeed, it was almost impossible to get in
consequence of the wet and cold, in addition to which,
ever and anon, the shrill yell of the jackal would rend
the silence of the desert, sometimes near at hand,
answered by others far distant over the plains. At
intervals during the night the heavy howl of the wolf
was heard, though afar. For two or three hours in
succession the profoundest silence reigned over the vast
desert, a silence so oppressive that it seemed as if by its
very weight it would press one into the earth. After
such a silence dreary was it indeed to hear a muffled,
melancholy, ghostly moan, come floating on the air of
the desert; and then, after a momentary pause, another
—and yet another, each weaker and weaker, just like

the gradually failing groans of dying ghosts! Another interval of intense silence elapsed, and then the same dismal sounds, the same in number, and of diminishing intensity, as before, were repeated. Curiosity could brook no further delay, so breaking the silence myself, "Jacob," said I, "what *is* that?" "O," said he, "that's the ostrich : it makes that noise to frighten the jackals away from its young !" That anything earthly could produce so dismal a sound seemed incredible ; but the explanation was satisfactory, and I was relieved.

At length, after ten long hours of darkness, the day began to break, and at the earliest possible moment the man was despatched for the horses, and following upon their hoof-marks in the sand as rapidly as the feeble light would allow, he soon found and brought them. Stiff and cold with our long night's lodging in the wet grass, we mounted our steeds, found the path about a mile to the left, sped away with cheerful hearts, reached home at about nine, and forgot the troubles of the past in the pleasure of their rehearsal.

I found on my arrival that the services on the station had been regularly maintained by Mr. Macleod, and that all was in a satisfactory state. Things around the "metropolis," as we playfully called it, gradually assumed an improved appearance, the grass gathering strength day by day, and the resident population steadily increasing. Every week parties of people from distant places visited the station, expressly for the purpose of enjoying the services of the Sabbath. Men and women mounted on horses or oxen, which were ridden by the women according to the custom of the country in most unlady-like fashion, the men carrying their muskets for defence against wild beasts if necessary, or for aggression should any game appear, might be seen Saturday after Saturday entering the village in quite a picturesque cavalcade; whilst the rear of the novel squadron would generally be brought up by a line of waggons containing the old, young, and feeble, each drawn by a long team of various-coloured oxen. As soon as they had alighted, all tended to the mission house as a centre to announce their arrival and salute the missionary. In this way our Sunday congregations were often large when we had only a few residents. It was a usual thing to see many deeply affected under the Word, though their feelings were generally kept under subjection, so that their tears flowed in silence. Much interest was awakened by a plan of which I gave notice, and which to them was quite new, of devoting a portion of the Sabbath afternoon to the purpose of interrogating them on the sermon delivered in the morning; a plan which I found particularly useful in eliciting whatever information they did possess, and in obliging them to give a closer attention to the sermons they heard, as they often voluntarily confessed. At the same time it operated beneficially upon myself, by showing me the necessity of so preaching as to make every sermon as tangible as possible to their untrained minds. Many signs of good manifested themselves, and under this treatment on the Sabbath, as well as the daily morning exposition of Scripture, their improvement in religious knowledge was very perceptible.

May 24th.—We were suddenly visited by a tremendous storm, without warning from the usual premonitions.

Our congregation was assembled at evening service, when suddenly such a battering on the reed roof of the chapel took place as startled us all. Hailstones as large as a walnut, and some as large as a fowl's egg, falling upon the thatch, beat out such a dust that, despite the candles, I could scarcely see the people in front of me. Hearing, too, being impossible, 'the meeting was broken up. Our river came pouring down, rushing over the rocks, and sounding as if the sea had broken over the land ; whilst none could venture out of the chapel because of the great hail. From the appearance of the country, with white hail everywhere, one might have imagined himself, *pro tem.*, in the polar regions ; but after continuing upwards of an hour, the hail ceased, and was succeeded by deluging rains for nearly the whole night, preventing all from the other side of the river from returning home that night. Roaring winds and a shaking house made us feel that we were in the midst of a tornado.

On June 20th I again visited Blydeverwachting in the waggon, and was accompanied by my wife, this being her first visit. The scenery in the neighbourhood of the village struck her as it had me ; whilst a sight of so many members of the church of the once notorious Afrikaner family was to her one of deep interest and delight. On the Sabbath I preached in the morning and afternoon to attentive congregations of about a hundred and fifty people. In the morning service many literally " lifted up their voice and wept," and I hope their feelings may result in some practical good. Morning and evening a prayer meeting was held by the natives themselves.

On the Monday we went to Jerusalem, the former

residence of this people, at a distance of eight or nine miles, taking with us David Afrikaner; his wife and others following our waggon on oxback. I directed David to draw up our waggon under the tree beneath whose shade the Rev. R. Moffat's mat house formerly stood, which he describes in his *Missionary Labours and Scenes in Southern Africa*, as having been so expeditiously built by the native women; and I felt it an honour to stand and pray with the people gathered around me under the same tree where the noble Moffat had once lived so self-denying a life. It was interesting to gaze on anything that reminded one of former missionary toil, and even on the mass of granite on which Mr. Moffat sometimes reclined to soothe or animate his mind by playing on his violin. Returning to Blydeverwaehting in the evening, I met the members of society in their class meeting, inquiring into the spiritual state of each.

During our stay, which continued nearly a week, a service for the reading and exposition of the Scriptures and prayer was held each morning, and each evening there was either a public meeting or a meeting of church members; and whilst we remained, everything relating to the society and school came under review, and all the members were met and examined as to their religious state. Mrs. R. was also usefully occupied in holding meetings with the women to instruct them in household and relative duties, and also in exhorting them to a more decent manner of clothing themselves—a kind of instruction they much needed, but which could scarcely be given except by the wife of a missionary. It was pleasing to find that these instructions were not in vain, for almost immediately many of the females set to work to prepare more decent dresses than their unseemly karosses. Our departure was much regretted by the people, and it appears that a rather singular expedient had been devised by some of the ladies to keep us a little longer. David's wife, and the wife of one of his brothers, had determined on driving away our oxen to a distance, that by the difficulty of finding them our stay might be protracted. But on consulting the wife of another of David's brothers, who refused to consent, because she thought it wrong, the scheme was revealed and frustrated.

On the 28th of June we safely reached home again, and found all in good order under the excellent care of Mr. Macleod.

Having sent to the Khamies Berg Mission Station, about two hundred miles from the Bath, for a supply of corn for Mr. Haddy in Damaraland, and it having safely arrived thus far, I was glad to obtain some help from the natives in order to send it the remaining distance of five or six hundred miles. It was gratifying to find that several of the people were willing to lend what was necessary in order to its safe transit. A waggon was lent by Jan Ortman. As I could not spare sufficient waggon-gear, the rest was lent by the chief; whilst four oxen of the team were lent by J. Jager, and ten others by Jantje April. As both oxen and waggon were likely to incur much risk and injury by such a journey, it showed a good deal of the spirit of sacrifice on the part of the people; for waggons and waggon-gear are so scarce and expensive in that distant land, that they are reckoned amongst the most precious and costly conveniences they possess; hence in general they are extremely reluctant to lend such articles, except for a valuable consideration. But in this instance, as the object was to forward a necessary supply of food to a missionary, no special pressure was necessary on my part, and nothing was demanded in the way of remuneration.

On the 26th of July I went on another journey to the Afrikaners at Blydeverwachting, and found things in a very satisfactory and prosperous condition; but nothing occurred calling for special remark, except that on this occasion Titus Afrikaner, whom I had not previously seen, on hearing that I was wishful to be introduced to him, came and presented himself. As I gazed upon him I could not help the question arising in my mind: "Art thou the man that made" South Africa "to tremble?" He was now old, nearly blind with age, the mere shadow of his former self, lean and meagre, but still retaining a measure of his former marvellous activity, and very much of the modest and retiring disposition that characterises the family. On the return journey, leaving at half-past two in the afternoon, and intending to travel all night, we offsaddled at midnight; and whilst refreshing our horses with a short graze upon some good herbage, and ourselves with some cold mutton, a troop of zebras, unexpectedly coming upon and catching sight of us, dashed off over some rocky ground with rattling hoofs, and gave us to feel that we were not the only inhabitants of the desert. The occasional "hooting" of an owl by the way, and the yelling of the jackals, were the only other sounds that gave any indications of life amidst the silence and darkness reigning around. Our horses were so full of spirit at the end of that long journey, that they were ready to leap over every bush that stood in their way; and one might have thought they had merely been taken out for an airing, rather than suppose they were finishing a journey of seventy-eight miles. At twenty minutes to four a.m., we safely reached Nisbett Bath.

Our congregations were now greatly improving, and things generally assumed a very encouraging aspect at the Bath. On the following Sunday, our congregation, on being counted by the schoolmaster as they passed out at the door, was found to consist of nearly three hundred persons. This was the largest number we had had since our arrival on the station. For the first two or three months, owing to the want of pasturage in the vicinity of the station, about fifty was the average number, but for some time past there have never been less than two hundred. The reason of the large attendance yesterday was the arrival of three waggons full of people, two of which had come from Riet Fontein, on the south side of the Orange River, and about one hundred- and fifty miles from the station, their object being to remain several weeks that they might hear the Word. An English trader, with his wife and family, had also arrived with five waggons and a number of men, so that our congregation exhibited a few white faces, an appearance quite novel in this country. As I was preaching a course of sermons on the Ten Commandments, I took at the service that which came in regular order, viz., the Fourth Commandment, and it appears to have been very appropriate to some, who, not being quite at ease in their consciences, were led to inquire: "Who has been telling the missionary about me?" Our Sabbath school also was larger than we had ever seen it before, one hundred and ninety being present, among whom were many adults.

Between midnight and two o'clock this morning, a slight shock of an earthquake was felt, accompanied by a hollow rumbling sound similar to the noise of empty waggons travelling over stony ground. The noise, which continued some seconds, awoke many of the natives, and much alarmed them; whilst a swaying motion from east to west was perceived by Mr. Macleod and many of the people. Though I perceived no motion, I was awakened by the noise.

Having announced on the Sabbath that the sacrament of the Lord's Supper would be administered on the next Sunday, during the course of the week many came to the mission house with troubled minds, anxiously desiring to see me. They mostly came in twos or threes, men with men, and women with their own sex, and sometimes several members of the same family. Perhaps a misunderstanding had arisen between them; or they had " fallen out " with each other; or family strifes and alienations prevailed. They came to acknowledge the fact in the presence of each other; and invariably the aggressor would open the case and admit his fault, for they felt that they could not meet at the table of the Lord with enmity towards each other in their hearts, and were anxious for a reconciliation before the Sabbath should dawn. On such occasions, which constantly occurred when the sacrament had to be administered, they would receive suitable counsel, renew their friendship by taking each other's hand, and then go away with light hearts and with a good conscience to " eat of that bread and drink of that cup."

Sunday, 19th August.—The congregation was larger than ever, and almost as many as the chapel could contain. In the morning I baptized a whole family of children, five in number, belonging to some who had recently become members of the church; and then preached on the subject of the Lord's Supper, showing its institution, its design, its obligatory character, and the spirit in which it should be celebrated. This was preparatory to the evening service, at the close of which I administered the Lord's Supper to a solemn and deeply-affected company. Many who were permitted to remain as spectators sat at a distance from the members, and were as deeply affected as the communicants. A rich and hallowing influence of the Spirit pervaded all the services of the day, and seemed a blessed pledge of still richer effusions to be vouchsafed. Only those who live amidst purely missionary scenes, and witness the steady growth in holiness, and in numbers, of a church composed of men and women recently heathen, can form any correct idea of the *peculiar* and hallowed delight that fills the soul of the missionary. He then sees the prophecies in the actual and steady process of accomplishment, and more fully realises himself as an agent in the hands of the Great Head of the Church in advancing their final accomplishment, than seems possible under any other circumstances. None who have laboured with success amongst a heathen race can ever forget the hallowing, heavenly, and peculiar experiences enjoyed whilst with them. He may leave such scenes, and labour amongst civilised races, and have success amongst his own countrymen in the churches of his fatherland; but

THOSE SCENES will stand forth unique amongst them all, and will live portrayed in vivid colours on his mental vision; and the memory of those experiences will be ineffaceably imprinted on the tablet of his heart.

If joy over repenting sinners is a proof of vital piety, then we had many proofs of its vital character amongst our own people, and this was especially the case with our native teachers. As an illustration of this remark, I may state that Job Witbooi, one of them, residing at an outpost about seventy miles distant, visited Nisbett Bath just at this time, and amongst other things he mentioned the case of a young man who had at one time been a member of the society, but had fallen into sin, and been put out of the church. Soon after he became dangerously ill, and during his illness was brought to a sense of his guilt. Alarmed for his spiritual state, he became truly penitent, and resolved, if spared, to dedicate himself afresh to the service of God. God heard his prayers, his health was restored, and he only waited the return of the day on which the class was held to join it again. The native teacher was delighted, and, though a poor man, resolved to mark his return to God and His people in some signal way. And in relating the case he said, " I wish to ask you, Sir, if I have done right." "Well, how did you proceed? " I said. " I had a sheep killed that morning," said he, " and at the appointed time the horn was blown to summon the people together, and when they were assembled beneath the shade of a tree, the young man clothed in new attire stood in our midst. I gave out a hymn, which we all sang. I then knelt down with the people and prayed, and praised God for His mercy in sparing the young man and healing him in body and soul. After this we all sat down and ate together. I had read," he added, " of the prodigal, and of the father's joy on his return, and how it was said, ' Let us eat and be merry ; for this my son was dead, and is alive again ; and was lost, and is found. And they began to be merry.' " Here, I thought, was a simple and beautiful illustration of religious mirth. Here were no noisy outbursts, no boisterous expressions of worldly joy. All was serious, and sanctified by the Word of God, by prayer and praise. They " ate their meat with gladness and singleness of heart."

On September 3rd I sent Mr. Macleod on a visit to the Afrikaners, judging it advisable to remain on the station myself. I was often obliged to employ him in this way, partly as a relief to myself from some of the long and wearisome journeys the working of the mission involved, and sometimes because it was of importance that at that particular time I should remain at the principal station. Sometimes, as in my own case, his journeys were made on horseback ; and sometimes, when his stay at the outposts was continued for several weeks together, in the waggon, in which case Mrs. Macleod would generally accompany him ; and in this evangelising work they were invaluable, Mrs. Macleod having a genuine missionary spirit, and being of great service by her counsels and advices to the native women. During Mr. Macleod's absence the day school was regularly continued by a couple of native young men, under my superintendence.

At this time, having discovered that some of the

members had never been united in marriage except in the native mode, I judged it advisable that since they had become Christians and members of the church, they should be publicly united according to the forms of the Christian religion. The marriage contract is generally so lightly and indifferently entered upon by natives not under the influence of the Gospel, that the obligations of the estate are scarcely recognised, and are too often violated with but little remorse. In order, therefore, to raise the character of the institution in the public mind, and set forth its solemn obligations, I deemed it right to adopt the course mentioned with regard to all the members of the church. The parties were consulted, and all admitted at once the propriety of the course proposed; due notice was given, and at the appointed time eleven couples appeared before God and His people, to ratify their former engagements, and in the fear of God declare their covenant of faithfulness to each other so long as they both should live. By adopting this course the holy estate of matrimony was raised in public estimation, sound views were promulgated, and vice was checked.

Having received a pressing request from the chief of the Velschoen Draagers to visit and preach to him and his people, at the earliest opportunity, I now resolved to take his tribe in connection with a contemplated visit to the north-eastern outposts.

September 6th.—I left home on horseback in company with Dirk Jagers, a young man in my own service, and in the evening reached 'Amas, the residence of our native teacher, Job Witbooi. I remained two days, to preach, inspect the school, meet the members of the society, and inquire into society affairs generally. Then proceeding to Nieuwe Fontein, about forty-five miles further to the north-east, we found our native teacher, Johannes Gagup. He is stationed at this place, and has charge of a portion of the tribe of William Fransman. Here also I remained two days, preaching, inspecting the school, receiving Johannes' report of all matters under his charge, and meeting all the church members in class.

Johannes is remarkable for his activity, zeal, and energy, and for the influence he exercises over the people. He once had a remarkable escape from a lion. He fired, when only a mere lad was with him, and, alas, missed! The lion bounded upon him, and, knowing that any struggling might prove fatal, he endeavoured to lie as quiet as possible. Taking his hand into its mouth, as if playing with it, and placing a paw upon his shoulder, as he lay on his face upon the ground, the lion at length began to crunch the bone of his right arm from the wrist upward. With as much fortitude as he could command, he endured for some time, hoping for some speedy interposition. Meantime, the lad, his companion, had hastened back to the village, where he found all the men away, except one young man. But this brave young man, seizing his gun, hastened to the spot, and, stealthily approaching, knelt down and took aim. He was perceived by Johannes, who saw that if he fired from that position, it would be with great peril to himself. In an undertone, therefore, Johannes ventured to say, "To the other side— to the other side." The lion narrowly observed the movements of the young man, but as he made no fuss, instead of leaving Johannes, it merely lifted its head grandly, and stood watching him. With admirable coolness, he took up a new position, and fired, sending the ball right through the head. The lion just gave a quiver with his lower lip, and fell with his full weight upon Johannes. "Then I thought," said Johannes, "that my life would have been crushed out of me." But the young man was soon at hand, and taking a fore-leg of the lion, and by main strength turning him over, released Johannes from the terrible pressure; and soon obtaining further help, they conveyed him home. The arm was bound in splints, and the bone knit together again; and when Johannes told me of the escape, rolling up his shirt sleeve, he showed me the marks of the monster's teeth, which he will carry with him to his grave.

Thirty-seven miles further to the north-east, lay Stof Kraal, which was so named from the dusty, im-palpable sand, or rather dust, on which the village stands. Here I found a hundred and fifty of our own tribe living. Elias Rolfe, the teacher, holds the school, maintains the services, and regularly meets the members in class. Elias is a most exemplary man, and though not until recently recognised as a native teacher, he has for some time faithfully discharged all the duties of that office; watching over the members with a solicitude and anxiety rarely equalled. To witness so much care and zeal in the work of the Lord, is particularly delightful, especially in a native.

Previous to his conversion he was accustomed to accompany the predatory expeditions which were very common amongst his countrymen a few years ago, when they thought little of shooting down those who opposed them, whilst plundering them of their cattle. The thought of his former mode of life was even now very distressing. Standing one day by my waggon, I perceived that he was in a tremor from head to foot, his lips were quivering and his eyes filled with tears. Thinking that something of a very sorrowful kind must have recently happened, I asked what it was that so deeply affected him, when I found it was the thought of his former mode of life, in contrast with what he now felt it ought to have been. And there was one thought that was to him the most bitter of all, the thought of having, in those reckless days, taken the life of his fellow men. "O, Sir," said he, " I have no doubt that God has forgiven me for the Saviour's sake, and that now I am a child of God; and yet sometimes, when I remember that I have shed the blood of my fellow men, I am ready to wonder how God can, admit me into the heavenly world." Forgiven by God, he felt that he never could forgive himself. In his general character he was modest and retiring, and in religious matters a man of great sensibility and tenderness.

Here at his village I found very interesting occupation. In anticipation of my visit the banns of marriage had been published of fourteen couples, and these were all waiting to be united in holy matrimony in the Christian fashion. This ceremony was performed in the presence of the whole population of the village; after which thirty-seven persons who had satisfactorily passed through their probation were baptized in the name of the Holy Trinity, and admitted into full church-membership. At the close of this interesting and impressive service, during which many tears were shed, four-and-twenty infants were also dedicated to God in holy baptism. There was so much life and animation amongst this people, and they appeared to be in so prosperous and hopeful a state, that I should have rejoiced to spend a longer time with them had it been practicable. I was already a hundréd and fifty-seven miles from Nisbett Bath, and had nearly thirty more to travel over a rugged stony country through which there was only a " baboon's path," as the people call it; so that I could not stay.

Owing to the character of the road we could only travel by day, and as we should be exposed to the sun all the time, we feared a painful journey. At sunrise on Saturday morning, in company with Elias Rolfe and two other members of the society, I left Stof Kraal for Klip Fontein, the present residence of the chief of the Velschoen Draagers. The roads were extremely rugged, the sun intensely hot, and no water to be found. After travelling several hours, unable to endure the sun any longer, we rested for an hour or two in the best shade we could find, which was very poor. About three hours after resuming our journey, whilst passing along the bottom of a narrow, luxuriantly grassy valley, though so strewn all over with loose stones as to make it difficult for our horses to walk, we espied in the distance a few loose ride-oxen approaching, followed by two young natives, carrying their bows and quivers with poisoned arrows. In a minute more the mother of Hendrik Hendriks, the chief of the Velschoen Draagers, made her appearance, walking along the valley in true African style. She was about the ordinary height, very stout, with a remarkably erect bearing, considering her age, which must have been above fifty. She was perfectly destitute of clothing, saving a narrow girdle of skin round the loins, which, being fastened in front, left both ends, cut into narrow strips, suspended as far as the knees. A double necklace of very small blue beads, that reached in a loop down to the waist, a white calico cap, fitting close to the head, and a splendid parasol composed of large black and white ostrich feathers, completed her attire. From head to foot she was so thickly besmeared with grease and red dust as entirely to conceal the real colour of the skin. This unguent was to serve as a protection against the sun. Elias, having several times visited the tribe to which we were going, knew the old lady, and introduced me as the missionary. She had long looked for my visit, and now hailed my arrival with great delight. When the first excitement was past, she sat down to continue the conversation, whilst we still remained in our saddles. But soon the flow of feeling returned, and she rose again to renew her expressions of delight, suiting her action to the animation of her feelings. A young woman accompanied her, but up to this moment she stood a few yards off in silence; now, however, amidst all the tumultuous eloquence of the old lady's rejoicings, the young woman was overheard to say in broken Dutch, and in a movingly pathetic tone, "O, I feel great grief to-day to see a missionary come so far." This, in fact, was the burden of the old lady's exclamations. Wonder, with grief and joy commingled, seemed to fill the minds of both to think that I should have come so far to see and instruct them. After travelling two hours and a half more, we came in sight of the small valley in which the chief and two hundred of his people had pitched their huts ; and as soon as we were seen to descend the hillside sloping down towards the village, all the children, assisted by the young men and women, filled the air with a succession of shouts till we arrived at the place; and these shouts, being accompanied by the barking of dogs, the bleating of sheep and lambs, and the bellowing of cattle just returning home from grazing, produced such a deafening tumult as I had never heard before.

On dismounting near the chief's house, the chief, Hendrik Hendriks, came to offer his salutations, though with a coldness of manner that seemed unaccountable, and that almost made me suspect the genuineness of the wish he had expressed to receive a visit. Perhaps he thought it became the dignity of his position to assume a little distance and hauteur in his manner, lest the missionary should be in danger of thinking himself an equal. The expression of his countenance was by no means prepossessing, and, though firm and manly, it was clouded with a look of sullen sternness. He soon relaxed, however, and became very genial. A chair of native make was brought from his hut and placed by a bush in the open air for my service; some small poles were driven into the ground in a row, and then some native matting, standing on its edges, was made fast to these poles, that I and the men who had accompanied me might be defended against the cool evening wind. As a mark of distinction he ordered a mat to be placed over the part I was to occupy, to serve as a roof, that the dew

might not fall upon me during the night. Whilst these
preparations were being made, seeing that the lower part
of my trowsers was torn into strips from the knees
downwards by the thorn-bushes through which I had
had to ride, to my amusement, I suppose at the insti-
gation of one of my companions, he sent me a needle
and thread that I might repair them, and make a more
seemly appearance at his court! A simple needle and
thread were quite a curiosity in that far distant region,
and must have been conveyed there by a native teacher
in his visits, or by some of our people, as at that early
period no trader had visited his country. As soon as the
cows could be milked, a perfectly new and ingeniously
carved milk vessel was brought full of frothy milk, fresh
from the cow, for my exclusive use. After taking a deep
draught I felt refreshed, and my tongue was loosened;
for till then, in consequence of the rough and stony
nature of the country through which we had passed,
and exposure to the fierce heat of the sun from his
rising to his setting, I was so faint and exhausted as
scarcely to be able to speak. When the evening had
darkened in around us, the whole population assembled
where I and my party were located. A large fire
was made a few yards off, the company surrounded
it, and I preached under the starry canopy on God as
the Creator. During the service all were perfectly
attentive; but long after it was over they continued
together, making their remarks on the missionary, and
laughing with wonder and delight, for I turned out to
be a much more curious object to them than I had
expected. They had heard of a missionary, they said,
but they thought that when he came he would be like

themselves; but I was white. They were also full of
wonder to think I should have come so far; for Elias
Rolfe had told them I had crossed the ocean, and that
my country was at a very great distance. They said
they were troubled that a white man should take so
much pains over them who were black. And when
they looked at my clothes and saw how they were torn
by the angry bushes, they said they were sure I had not
come to take away their cattle, but for their souls'
good. After most of them had retired to their homes,
hearing a loud and angry discussion in the chief's house,
I inquired of Elias Rolfe what was the matter. Smiling,
he said that one man, very anxious to have a full view
of my person during the service, was quarrelling with
another, who, by standing before him, had obstructed
his view; and though the other repeatedly affirmed that
he did not do so intentionally, but merely to gratify
his curiosity, it was with some difficulty that the anger
of the offended man could be appeased.

At sunrise on the Sabbath morning we held a prayer
meeting in the open air. When the time for morning
service drew near, men were stationed at distances of
two or three hundred yards from each other all down
the village, which was situated stragglingly in a long
narrow valley, and the moment I intimated my wish for
the congregation to collect, Elias shouted, " En ka koo "
("Come together "). The next man repeated, " En ka
koo; " the next did the same, and " En ka koo " was
telephoned in native fashion to the extremity of the
village, when simultaneously the whole congregation left
their houses and came to the place appointed; so that in
five minutes we were ready to commence. Only the three

men of my party could sing; but their singing very much struck the congregation, who had never heard such singing before. I preached from Romans v. 8. In the afternoon I again preached from Acts xvii. 30, 31, which was interpreted from the Dutch into Namaqua, as were all the services, by Elias, and with good effect. At night, by star and fire light, I read, explained, and enforced the relative duties as contained in Ephesians v.

During the services I was particularly struck with the devotional appearance of the chief. Whilst we were singing he stood rather behind the rest, having his eyes closed, and seeming by the solemnity of his countenance to be under the influence of deeply serious feelings. Before the evening service I had some serious conversation with him respecting his desire for religious instruction. On asking if he sincerely wished some one to live amongst his people to instruct them, with deep emphasis he said, " O yes, I am exceedingly anxious. I must have a missionary, and," he added, " this is the wish of all my people." " But," I said, " if any one should come to live with you, will more of your people come together ? " " O yes," he replied, " the only reason why they are so scattered is because there is no instruction, and nothing to keep them together. I know where they all are, and I would send for them." I then explained to him the sacrifices a missionary would have to make to come and live in such a land ; the heavy expenses incurred by his coming from so great a distance ; and how all these expenses must be paid by the people of England. He looked very thoughtful, thinking, probably, that if such were the expenses and sacrifices, his was a hopeless case. " Now," I said, " if I could procure a missionary, would you and your people try and do something towards meeting this expense?" He deliberated a moment or two, and then, with a not uncommendable prudence, replied, "I do not exactly understand the matter; but we would do what we could." I then said that I could not promise to obtain a missionary for him, but I would write on the subject. He then said in an impassioned manner, "O, I am in haste, for man is a dying thing, and I and my people may die before we have a missionary." I believe he spoke the deep feelings of his heart; and to me both his serious and earnest manner, and the sentiments he uttered, were inexpressibly affecting; and I thought, If these people are not prepared for the saving Gospel of Christ, where throughout the length and breadth of this world shall we find any that are? Already the incipient workings of the Holy Spirit had been felt in the heart of this chief, and in the hearts of many of his people; a result that, by the Divine blessing, has followed the simple preaching of the Gospel amongst them by our native teacher, Elias Rolfe.

On Monday morning, before day, I was awakened by the voice of prayer, several of the people having left their huts, where they can have no privacy, and gone to the bush to pour out their souls. It was a moving sound, and I hope a proof of the good effect of the services of the Sabbath. At about 7 a.m. we took our farewell of the chief and people, and, after another very tedious and exhausting journey of nine hours, reached Stof Kraal. I was too much fatigued to hold any service that night, and was glad to retire to the nice new mat house which was assigned to me and my guide.

A bowl of milk was brought for my evening meal ; my saddle formed my pillow, some new reed matting spread upon the ground served as a mattress, and, folding my kaross around me, I had no doubt, weary as I was, of a good night's rest. The dogs, however, were an intolerable nuisance, and, as soon as all was quiet, made their way in, searching for food. Several times I started up angrily, and put the prowling beasts to flight. Dash they went out at the doorway, which was merely a reed mat, hanging down in front to the ground. At length, tying the mat firmly to the bamboo framework of the doorway, I once more composed myself to rest, taking the precaution of having my right hand at liberty, and my riding-whip, a strip of solid rhinoceros hide, close by, so that at a moment's notice I could grasp and use it. I was just dozing off when one of these pertinacious marauders was at the door, evidently intent on housebreaking. By-and-by the strings were gnawed through, and the animal had gained an entrance, and was sniffing about for anything eatable. Near me was a chair with my manilla hat lying on it, in which I had put a few pieces of rusk, all my store till I could reach home. Standing on his hind legs, the head of the dog was soon in the hat, crunching the biscuit. In an instant I grasped my whip, and dealt a heavy blow across the loins of the thief, and with a terrific yell he dashed through the matting of the doorway and escaped. I had no more intrusions that night, but slept soundly, and later than usual. Early in the morning, almost before any one else was astir, to his consternation, our native teacher saw my hat lying out on the sand of the village, with sundry strips of paper, on which I had been making notes, scattered about in all directions. His first care was to make for my abode and see if I was all safe ; so stooping down and peeping inside and finding me and my man still asleep, and all right, he carefully kept all till I was up. I had not observed that anything was absent, till, on going out at the door-way for a morning glance, Elias brought them to me. The mystery, so alarming as it was to Elias, was soon explained. The dog, deeply intent on the biscuit at the bottom of my hat, and electrified by the stroke of the whip, dashed off with my hat upon his head, the ribbon which I had kept attached to it, to slip under the chin, evidently answering a similar purpose in keeping it on the head of *canis* till he had burst the bounds of my habitation and got into the open village.

Bidding adieu early the same day to Elias and his people, and on the return journey calling at Nieuwe Fontein and 'Amas, where we rested for a short time, I reached home safely after an absence of fourteen days, thankful for preservation and for all the comfort I had met with in the work of the Lord.

October 10th.—I again left home on horseback for Blydeverwachting, where I preached on the Sabbath morning and afternoon, and at night met all the members of society, about sixty in number. Having noticed that Titus Afrikaner was absent from all the services, on inquiry I found that he was sick. He has suffered from extreme weakness of sight for a long time, and on visiting him, in company with his brother David, I found him unable to open his eyes and also suffering much from toothache. He expressed deep regret at being detained from the house of God, and said " he longed to be able to go there again. His soul was in a comfortable state, and his only trust in Christ." "You are now old, Titus," I said, "and if it should please the Lord to take you away from this world, should you fear?" Roused by the question, he instantly replied, with much emphasis, " O, Sir, I should be exceedingly glad." Several other things he uttered equally delightful—delightful especially from him, who was once the terror of this part of Africa. During Mr. Cook's time he had been truly converted, and so deep were his convictions that for "several weeks he remained under deep distress of mind, and in the night would frequently creep out of his mat hut on his hands and knees, roaring out in the disquietude of his soul, and alarming the whole village in crying for mercy to that God whose laws he had so awfully broken. After his conversion to God, his joy was also so great, that he often left his hut and repaired to the bushes for the purpose of praise, being prevented from sleeping by the ecstatic joy he experienced, as he had been before by the deep sense of his guilt and danger as a sinner." So mightily transforming is the influence of the saving Gospel of Christ!

During this month, Frederick Buys, one of our class leaders, of Dutch and native descent, a very intelligent and pious man, informed me of a party of Bushmen who had located themselves with some of our people at a place called Klip Hoek, forty-three miles to the southeast of the station. He had several times visited them from his own place of abode, and was so much interested in their case, that he came to offer to go with his family and live with them, to establish a school, and endeavour to keep up religious services. I agreed that he should make the attempt, and in a week or two he and his family were on the spot endeavouring to benefit these wild sons of the desert.

In fulfilment of a promise made at the time, I left home on November the 2nd for the purpose of visiting this interesting community. Myself and companion left home on horseback as soon as the sun rose, and had a distressing journey, the sun being insufferably hot, and the atmosphere, loaded with electricity, being extremely oppressive. In vain we looked for the shade of some tree or shrub; for several hours nothing was to be seen in the vast grassy plain that could offer the least protection from the burning rays of the sun, till at last we descried, about a mile to the left, two trees, that, owing to the refracting power of the atmosphere, looked large, and as if they would offer a grateful shade. Reluctant to move a foot out of our path, we were nevertheless compelled by the killing heat, and cantered up to the nearest, which proved much less on our arrival than it had seemed in the distance. Wild animals by multitudes had evidently made it a refuge as we now did, for the sand all round was covered with *zand-luizen*, as the people call them, a species of tick, and other biting insects. There was no remedy, however : so, scraping away the sand and vermin with our feet, we crept under the low branches, for there was no room to sit erect, and lay down with our heads on our saddles. Nearly suffocated with heat, and overrun with vermin, I started up and ran to the tree beyond, when out sprang a poor jackal and fled at my approach. This was no better than the other situation, but we forced ourselves to remain for an hour or two. We anxiously sought for water amongst some rocks near, in the hollows of which we hoped a little might remain from the last rains, but found none. At length we caught and saddled our horses and started, but the fiery air and burning sun absolutely beat us back to our shelter, where for another hour we reclined with bridle in hand, drawing the heads of our poor horses as far into the shade as they could get without trampling upon us. Nature's grand electric batteries, the massive thunder clouds, were piling themselves up higher and higher in huge majesty around the horizon, which accounted for the unbearable oppressiveness of the atmosphere; but again, as with desperation, we went forth to encounter the dreadful heat, fearful lest the night should set in upon us before we found the obscure spot to which we were going, and concerning the position of which we had very vague directions. Just at sunset we reached the place, with bloodshot eyes, blistered lips, fevered frame, and completely exhausted, having had no water, and, with the exception named, no shade during the whole day. Two or three vessels of milk, and also of water, which Frederick brought in a basin, were an unspeakable refreshment, and loosened my parched tongue, which till now appeared to be glued to my jaws; a comfortable bed was made up for me in the body of Frederick's waggon, for the wheels were off and it was under shade, and a profound sleep on a water supper allayed fever, and in a good measure restored me to a feeling of comfort.

I found about eighty people, nearly fifty of whom belonged to the Bushman race, the rest Bondelzwaarts, some of whom frequently resort to this place with their cattle in time of drought, when grass becomes scarce in the vicinity of the station. Several of the Bushmen, I found, had a few sheep, goats, and cows of their own, whilst others were acting as shepherds for our people, from whom they received a few sheep and goats for their services.

The general appearance of the men is far superior to what I had expected. They have in a great measure left off the practice of smearing their bodies with grease and dirt, and, instead of being naked like the generality of Bushmen, some were even decently clothed in trowsers and jackets of prepared sheepskins. The women were far less prepossessing in their appearance, being almost without exception destitute of any other clothing than an open kaross thrown loosely over the shoulders, and hanging as far as the bend of the knee. The holding of Divine service among them by one of our people was at first so great a novelty, and the assembling together of so many persons operated so strongly on their timid minds, that it was with difficulty they could be induced to remain. One man especially was so alarmed that he took to his heels and ran off in terror; and when pursued and overtaken by some of our people, though the kindest language was employed to allay his fears and assure him of their friendship and kind intentions, he could scarcely be induced to credit their assertions, saying " he was sure there would be quarrelling amongst so many people." All this timidity soon passed away; they now sit quietly to hear the wonderful things of God; often feel deeply, and for some time several of them have attended the class with the other members of society, and good hopes are entertained that the civilising and Christianising process thus auspiciously commenced may be carried on to their permanent benefit.

Since Buys has been located amongst them, he has, with the help of the people, erected a small chapel, composed of the stems of young trees interlaced with long grass and bushes, in which he meets his class, holds day and Sabbath schools, conducts prayer meetings, and exhorts ; and as he is a man of unquestionable piety, and more than ordinary intelligence, I doubt not he will be rendered very useful.

With very peculiar feelings and yearning compassion I addressed these wild men and women as they sat in the congregation. Their uninstructed minds had been gradually prepared to understand some of the simple truths of the Gospel ; and whilst I spoke they listened with intense interest ; the bosoms of many heaved, and their eyes filled with tears. The little day school for children was chiefly conducted by the eldest daughter of the native assistant, under the supervision of her father. I left them with an earnest prayer that in the great harvest some of these poor people might be found gathered into the garner of God.

On the 17th November of this year the birth of our firstborn was the occasion of joy and gratitude in the mission family, and throughout the station. Old Sarah, the chieftainess, and the other principal women, manifested quite a maternal sympathy and joy, and offered many thanksgivings to God for the life of the mother and infant. But on the Sabbath following convulsions suddenly seized upon the little infant, and threatened to prove fatal. I dedicated her to Him in holy baptism in the presence of her resigned though weeping mother, soon after which the spirit of the little sufferer was "caught up unto God and to His throne," and heaven became the richer for our loss. In a far distant land the birth of the little one was hailed by the mother with unusual joy, and the stroke of bereavement fell with more than ordinary severity on her newly-awakened maternal feelings. The grace of God was, however, sufficient, and the delicate sympathy of the good women in the place afforded a great mitigation of the sorrow that was inevitable. On one Sabbath our child was born to earth, on the next she was born to heaven.

In this hot country burials follow deaths in quick succession. On the next day at five p.m. the station bell was tolled, and soon the chapel was well filled. The little coffin, covered with white calico, was brought into the chapel and placed upon a table, when a verse or two of a suitable hymn was sung, the usual psalm and lesson read, and prayer offered, during which many wept as though they had lost their own firstborn. When this part of the service was finished, myself and the school-master walked first, four young women followed bearing the little coffin suspended in white linen bands, and the whole congregation of three hundred persons, throwing themselves into order, walked two and two to the grave, nearly a mile distant, the men carrying their hats in their hands as an additional expression of respect. Not a voice was heard, seriousness and silence prevailing throughout that long procession, an example that might well be copied in more civilised lands. Just as the sun was sinking below the horizon we reached the grave, and there, close by the tomb of the Rev. Edward Cook, I committed our dear babe to the house appointed for all living. The people encircled the grave, a short address was given, a funeral hymn sung, the sand was thrown in upon the little coffin, and I left with a full heart. The people followed from the grave in the same order as before, but this time the men with covered heads, till on reaching the gates of the mission house I turned round and bowed my thanks, when every hat was lifted, a serious and polite bow was made in return, and every one retired to his own home. I confess I was much struck by the polite and delicate manner in which all expressed their sympathy and respect. No arrangement had been made previously as to the manner in which the funeral was to be conducted, except with the young women who carried the coffin; so that the orderly marching two and two, the men walking with uncovered heads, the manner of return, and the graceful adieu at the close, were all the spontaneous result of their own instinctive sense of what was right and proper.

The death of an infant makes little impression generally, save in the family where the event has occurred; but, for a long time after the death of our babe, a mollifying influence seemed to rest upon the spirits of our people, and they seemed as ready to receive salutary and saving impressions as the wax under the warming influence of the flame is to receive the impression of the signet. The trial, painful as it was to the parents, was abundantly blessed both to ourselves and our people, whilst the opportunity it gave for the manifestation of their affection endeared them to us greatly.

CHAPTER IV.

DANGERS AND DELIVERANCES.

JANUARY 13TH, 1845.—This morning we made a disagreeable discovery. In a room that had till recently been occupied as a sleeping apartment we found a snake coiled up and concealed under the cradle. The cradle was not occupied, yet the circumstance of finding a serpent in a room so much frequented was peculiarly disagreeable. During the night, unable to sleep in the upper room, in consequence of the excessive heat, I had left our usual sleeping apartment and gone to this lower room, the window of which had been open all the night, and, after pacing about in the dark with bare feet, had thrown myself down on the sofa, if possible to secure a little rest. As the reptile must have been in the room at least that whole night, it was a very merciful thing that I escaped treading upon it and being bitten, which would have been very serious, and probably fatal, for on examination the natives pronounced it to be of a most dangerous kind.

This is usually the hottest month of the year, when a large portion of every night is generally passed, owing to the suffocating temperature, in a sleepless state. It was during such nights, though long before this period, that whilst restlessly pacing my room at two or three in the morning, a sound was heard that somewhat thrilled upon my nerves. At first I could not comprehend it: but, on listening attentively, I felt assured it was a human voice. Soon, other voices broke upon the solemn silence of nature; and at length the fact burst upon me, a delightful, though awe-inspiring fact, that it was the voice of prayer and supplication. The tones were subdued, but full of pathos and earnest entreaty, and proceeded from amidst the rocks and shrubs of the river bed, and soared aloft, "far above these nether skies," whence the silent stars were looking on the dark world below, to the throne of the Almighty God in heaven. For days I felt awed in spirit as often as I thought on the subject; and, on inquiry, I found that it was the custom of many of the pious among our people, when sleepless, to rise and leave their houses, where no privacy was to be obtained, and go to the rocks and shrubs, where, amidst all the solitude and silence, they could pour out their souls before God in prayer; after which they would return home and sleep till morning. I afterwards found how prevalent this habit was amongst the more earnest people, and, when far distant from home, I have been waked many times by the same solemn, subdued, earnest voice of prayer, the very sound of which has often been a means of grace to my soul.

January 24th.—I again mounted my horse and left home on a visit to the Afrikaners, travelling during the whole night with the exception of about two hours, in order to avoid as much of the terrible heat as possible. The sun in this climate, especially at this season of the year, is emphatically " the destruction that wasteth at noonday," and compared to which the " terror by night " is as nothing. Soon after my arrival, David Afrikaner returned from a visit to several small tribes of Korannas living along the northern bank of the Orange River. These tribes belong to one of the leading divisions of the great Hottentot family, speaking the same language, with only a slight difference of dialect, which proves no hindrance in understanding each other, and in general living in the same manner, varying only from the Great Namaquas in a few circumstances, occasioned by the location they have selected along the shores of a great river. They build mat houses of beehive shape nearly close to the water's edge, under the thick foliage of the willows and mimosas, and construct nets out of cord made from the bark of young branches of the mimosa. With these nets fastened at one end on the shore and at the other to the stump of a tree, or pole driven into the bed of the stream, they catch a quantity of fish, some of which are upwards of five feet in length : these are sometimes broiled as soon as taken; sometimes dried, pounded, and put into a goat-skin sack for future use. Occasionally they shoot the enormous hippopotami, the flesh of which, and especially the fat about the ribs, they esteem a most luscious article of food. With these small tribes David spent upwards of three weeks. They received the word with readiness and much interest; and some pressed him to remain amongst them.

This valuable and fine old man was absent nearly five weeks, including his journeyings; and during the whole time he was dependent almost exclusively on wild honey for support, having obtained flesh and pounded fish only seldom, and in small quantities. He seemed mentally and spiritually refreshed by his late mission tour, and to myself the detail of his labours and journeyings was deeply interesting. Klass and Jacobus Afrikaner, David's brothers, had oversight of the work during his absence; and I found the members in a pleasing and prosperous condition; and very much enjoyed the services of the Sabbath, into which David threw unusual animation. Travelling all the night, to escape the heat, I reached our station in twelve hours and a half, the horses showing great cheerfulness on the journey.

In the month of February this year a new and valuable auxiliary to the piety of our people was pretty generally adopted in their own homes. As the result of our singing meetings, the people had acquired many new tunes, which they sang very correctly; and I thought this a good opportunity for inculcating on them the duty of maintaining family worship, as one means of preserving them in spiritual life when scattered by drought to every part of the country where a little water and grass could be found for their cattle, and where they could not enjoy the visits of a missionary or native teacher, except at wide intervals of time. In some families none could be found to read or start tunes; so to meet this case several young men were appointed to certain houses in different parts of the village, to give out the hymn, set the tune, and read a portion of Scripture, when some member present would engage in prayer. The case of every family could not be met, but those who were left without this aid had the opportunity of resorting to the house of a neighbour, and of thus sharing in the service. About eight o'clock at night the signal-bell for prayer was rung; and at eight each morning, in the chapel, the meeting for reading and exposition of Scripture and prayer was, in fact, family prayer for the whole village. On two nights in the week public worship was conducted in the chapel, and on the other evenings the domestic meetings referred to were held, and were much valued by the people. At the evening hour of prayer, I have often left my house and stood beneath the starry heavens to listen to the voice of praise ascending from different parts of the village. "Justification," "Alma," "Helmsley," were some of their new and favourite tunes; and as many families blended their voices, sweetly did they fall upon the ear, wafted by every breeze, inspiring devotion and awakening gratitude at the success which had been graciously accorded to the plan.

For many years past I had been very fond of bathing, and in the summer months I had felt this refreshment as indispensable to my health. But in this country, where, for about nine months out of every year, the temperature was such as to allow of, if not actually invite to, this healthful pleasure, alas! no water of sufficient depth for the purpose was to be found nearer than the Orange River. I had often longed for the exhilarating plunge, and as often had I lingered near the fountain from which the place took its name, and wondered how I could make it available for bathing purposes. At length the idea struck me. At a distance of about twenty feet from the fountain, a bath could be dug thirty feet in length, twelve in breadth, and six in depth; and the water, when let off, could be conveyed to the garden dam, and thus preserved from waste. By a simple contrivance the water from the fountain could be admitted, or shut off from the bath, at pleasure ; and though at the spring it was of the temperature of 105°, by admitting it late at night, it would become sufficiently cool and bracing by the morning. My plans being laid, they were communicated to Jan Rammard, a very useful artisan whom I often employed on the mission premises. Next I called all the young men of the school, among whom were some vigorous half-castes, nearly as white as their Dutch fathers, and all at once entered into the scheme, agreeing to work at the close of the school morning and afternoon. Pickaxes, spades, crowbars, &c., were all in requisition, and some rocks had to be blasted under the superintendence of Jan. They worked with a will, and they worked well. The facing of the bath with stone was done exclusively by Rammard, the materials being brought by the young men. The stone facing being done to the level of the surface, it was further seen that to make all private, so that bathing might not be interfered with at any time, it ought to be surrounded by a wall six and a half feet high ; which Rammard engaged to do for a mere trifle, inserting a door at one end. This bath I found an unspeakable refreshment, and a great contributor to my health and comfort.

February 20th.—This morning I married two of our members, who in company with several of their relatives had travelled a distance of one hundred and fifty miles for this laudable purpose; a pretty strong proof of the importance they attach to the Christian mode of celebrating the union. They and their friends had travelled not exactly in the same manner as Rebekah, who with her damsels " rode upon camels " through the desert, from Mesopotamia, yet in a manner near enough to suggest the resemblance. Our party rode upon oxen, taking their own time, and journeying easily, till they reached the "metropolis." Due notice had been given, the banns published, and the morning had arrived when the ceremony was to be performed. A serious mistake had, however, nearly occurred, owing to the absence of the bride at the critical moment; for, being young, and not fully instructed, the bride had left the bridegroom to go to the ceremony alone, thinking her presence could be dispensed with.

March 19th.—To-day, having committed the station in charge to Mr. Macleod, myself and wife left home with the intention of spending several weeks at the important out-station of Blydeverwachting. The greatest inconvenience on the journey arose from scarcity of water, the only place where it is generally obtained failing to furnish a supply in consequence of the long absence of rain. After digging to a depth of six feet in the bed of the River 'Aams, we succeeded in obtaining just sufficient for ourselves; but the poor oxen were compelled to travel the whole distance of two days and a half in the burning sun without a drop. On the Sabbath morning I preached on Matt. xiii. 47-51, and in the afternoon catechised the people upon the sermon of the morning, which afforded a good opportunity of impressing the subject afresh on their minds. At night I met those members of society who had visited the place to enjoy the services of the day. The impression left on my mind at the close of the meeting was of a sorrowful description, for almost without exception signs of much spiritual languor were perceptible. As I listened to the statements of these few members, so indicative of spiritual faintness, I could not but feel something of the yearning and tender emotion the Saviour Himself experienced when He saw the fainting and shepherdless multitudes. Their frequent absence from the regular means of instruction is one of the greatest hindrances to growth in grace and knowledge and stability of Christian character; yet such is the uncertainty of the rains, such the wandering mode of life occasioned by the search for suitable pasturage, that though the evil may be mitigated by frequent journeyings of the missionary and his native agents, it cannot be remedied.

Often has the writer, whilst stating the peculiar character of the climate and country, been amused with the exclamation, " Why don't they leave the country and seek a better ?" No doubt, if this were practicable, they would do it. It is an idea that has often occurred to themselves; and during my residence there much was said of a land abounding with fountains and good grazing grounds, of which they had heard, and once or twice the chief and all his councillors came together seriously to talk of a removal. But on inquiry this attractive land was found to be already in possession of other and more populous tribes to the north; and though, by dint of powder and lead, the combined tribes of Namaqualand might succeed in driving such tribes further up into the interior and take possession of the country, the act would be a robbery such as no missionary could countenance, whilst the living wave of tumult, once set in motion from the south, would heave and swell in strife, and conflict, and death, from tribe to tribe, till it expired on the lifeless shores of the Great Southern Sahara. I gave them distinctly to understand that I could be no party to so selfish a scheme as the wronging of other tribes, even for the benefitting of themselves; and that desirable as was a better land, could it be honourably found, under existing circumstances I should absolutely refuse to accompany them. This was sufficient, and from those in power I never heard anything more on the subject. Families, and even small parties, of Great Namaquas may improve their lot; but, as a whole people, to move to fairer lands north is out of the question. Barriers lie in that direction that can never be surmounted. To the west lies the Atlantic. East a desert waste. South the British Colony of the Cape of Good Hope. The only way is for the Christian missionary to take the country and people as he finds them, and to deal with them in their present circumstances, conferring all the benefits he can, as God's instrument, and pointing them to that true Canaan which is above, so that they may learn to view it with the " unbeclouded eye " of a living faith, as their own great inheritance through Christ. But it will be evident to all who look at the case, that the missionaries stationed in such a country, and amongst such a people, have special need of faith and patience, for they labour under peculiar disadvantages. It can only be because the God of Ethiopia has not forgotten her that so much success has resulted, and that already so many of her sons and daughters " stretch out their hands unto God."

On Friday evening I met another class of members, from whose experience I derived much greater satisfaction than from those with whom I had spoken on the

Sabbath evening. The reason of the difference is seen in the fact that the former had remained on the place, and had enjoyed regularly the appointed means of grace ; the latter had been necessitated to remove to a distance to procure pasturage ; and, as a natural result, the one was flourishing, whilst the other seemed drooping in the spiritual life.

April 7th.—Yesterday, Sabbath, I baptized eight infants, and preached on 1 Cor. vi. 19, 20, in the former part of the day. Again in the afternoon, from, " If I wash thee not, thou hast no part with Me ;" and at night I closed the labours of the day by administering the Lord's Supper to about eighty members of society. The congregations were large, too large indeed for the chapel to contain them, numbers having arrived on the Saturday evening from adjacent places. This was the third successive Sunday I had spent with them, and each Sabbath had been marked by the descent of gracious influences, but this was pre-eminently the best of all the three.

During my stay here I have held at least one service every day, frequently two. The school has been under daily inspection. I have several times met all the members of society, had a special meeting of the leaders, read and inculcated those portions of the Rules of the Society that can at all apply to a people circumstanced as they are, baptized four adults, eight infants, and administered the Lord's Supper to the members. Mrs. Ridsdale also, twice a week, held meetings for all the women who could attend, for the purpose of conveying such instruction as can be best given to select companies of one sex only. In these meetings opportunities frequently occur of more deeply imprinting on their minds the great truths they have heard preached. Great and visible benefit has already resulted from these select meetings, though there are still many things among the people that need rectifying : and so firmly fixed are their old views and practices, that much patience will be necessary before the efforts for their removal will produce the desired and full effect. Before these, however, and the continued blessing of the Most High, they must finally vanish. Having put several things into a more satisfactory shape, in a final public service I commended them to the blessing of Heaven, and recommenced our journey home.

But there was no possibility of resting long, for another journey to the northern outposts was immediately in prospect. Five days sufficed to look a little into the affairs of the station; one Sabbath's services were held at home, the station was once more committed to the care of our excellent schoolmaster, and before the fourteenth of April closed, our oxen were put to the yoke, and we were once more traversing the wilderness on our great work of evangelising the heathen. On reaching 'Amas, about seventy-five miles from home, messengers were despatched by Job Witbooi, the native assistant, to all surrounding parts, to inform the people of the missionary's arrival. Next day, a large number came, when, as usual, public services were held, and the members met : and during our stay marriages were celebrated, baptisms performed, and everything appertaining to the society matters investigated. One thing struck me very much during this visit. Each morning while it was yet dark, and all the stars were glistening in the vault of heaven, the monotonous sound of the antelope's horn, beginning in a low tone, and gradually waxing louder and louder, roused me from my slumbers, as it did all the sleepers of the village; when, by-and-by, the low and imploring voice of prayer was heard, first from one side and then from another, till it seemed as if all the village was sending up its prayers to God. At the sound of the trumpet, blown by Jantje April, a rich man, upon whom a marvellous spirit of quickening had been shed forth, one and another left his hut and stole away to the rocks or bushes, until the voice of prayer resounded from all sides, and broke the reigning silence long before the first streak of day was seen in the orient. The plan had been proposed some time before by our native teacher; the members on the place had gladly acceded to it, and at the solemn-sounding summons all who had the spirit of prayer rose and cried unto the Lord. The effect of the monotonous summons, the imploring voices striking on the ear in the darkness and silence, was to myself awe-inspiring. It thrilled the soul through and through: it seemed to bring God and man, earth and heaven, intimately near. Indeed, I can never advert to it, even now, without realising something of the peculiar emotion I then felt. What a glorious illustration of David's words! "My voice shalt Thou hear in the morning, O Lord; in the morning will I direct my prayer unto Thee, and will look up." (Psalm v. 3.)

This was my wife's first visit to these parts, and she was as much struck as myself with this deeply interesting circumstance. On a former occasion the people had requested that I would bring her to see them; but such was the state of the roads in the neighbourhood that I told them they were enough to shake her and the waggon to pieces, and until they improved these I should be almost afraid to bring her. A hint was enough: a body of road-makers was soon organised; men, women, and the children of the school, headed by the native assistant and the schoolmaster, went forth to grapple with the difficulty. Fortunately, the stones in general were loose upon the surface, so the men removed the heaviest beyond the line of road, the women what they could manage with facility, and the children soon cleared away the small ones; and on this visit, to my amazement, a very bad and almost impassable road, up a steep ascent, had been so entirely cleared, and rendered so smooth, that my wife could travel over it with comfort.

With many prayers for the blessing of heaven upon the people, we bade them farewell, and proceeded to the next outpost, Nieuwe Fontein, forty miles further to the north-east. Here since my last visit a new and pretty chapel, as it seemed in that country, had been raised under the direction of Johannes Gagup, our native teacher. Until its erection all services had been held beneath the shade of a large spreading camel-thorn tree. Some time before, arrangements had been made with a native builder to erect a stone chapel; but as, in his estimation, the pay was insufficient, nothing came of the agreement. Before long, serious thoughts were agitating the mind of Johannes. "One night," said he, "as I lay sleepless in my house, I began to ask myself, 'What am I doing for the Lord? I say that I love God, and yet I am doing nothing for Him!'" These thoughts so pressed upon his spirit that he called the people together, and told them what his feelings had been, and what he felt it his duty to do: they saw that he was right, and promised to help: waggons for the fetching of wood, and sleighs for the carriage of stone, were promptly put into requisition: whilst the women assisted by bringing a good supply of grey clay for mortar, and the children found genial employment in fetching water in their bambooses and treading the clay. The result was the building we beheld.

After remaining several days at this place, leaving Mrs. Ridsdale and Martha, the servant girl, I took one of my men and proceeded on horseback to the next outpost, Melk-Boom River, a narrow valley with low mountains on each side, the sandy bed of a river running along the base, in which deep holes were dug for a supply of water. The hills were remarkably verdant to the very top, and the euphorbia abounded. This place I had never seen before, though the community were watched over by Elias Rolfe, who on my last visit was at Stof Kraal. Some of our outposts are very shifting things, more especially that with which Elias is connected, he and his people having no fountain around which they can permanently settle. In a country like this, no stationary mode of existence is practicable. A chapel, something like the Jewish booths erected during the Feast of Tabernacles, was set up for their services, and in this primitive place I preached with great comfort and enlargement. During my stay, as usual, a house was allotted to me and my man, which, however, was often frequented by Elias, and occasionally by the people.

After an absence of several days from Nieuwe Fontein, on my return I found the people had been very

busily engaged improving and making some additions to
their recently-erected chapel.   Though the building had
been used by the congregation, the interior required
plastering, and it was deemed that several other things
needed to be done.   So, at the close of the daily morning service, Johannes communicated his intentions to
the people, who at once entered into the scheme, and
men, women, and children were all employed in some
part of the work.   The men brought stones in their
sledges and waggons, the children and youths clay
in dried sheep-skins, and the women water in their
wooden milk vessels : some were soon engaged in plastering the walls, whilst others were building a low wall
to serve as a seat all round the inside of the building.
A pulpit was also built of masonry, for lack of wood;
and a semicircular wall, to serve instead of a commu-
nion rail, was erected, about eighteen inches high.   I
found this very useful in contributing to order whenever
baptismal,   sacramental,   and   marriage   celebrations
occurred.   The masonry and plastering being finished,
all was whitewashed, and exhibited a clean and spotless
hue.   And just when all remaining materials were
cleared away, the shout was raised: " There comes
Mynheer ! " for the horses of myself and man were
seen in the distance cantering towards the village.   On
being led into the chapel, I was astonished at the work
that had been done, the skill and taste displayed, and
the altered and improved state of the chapel.

On Thursday, May 8th, after twenty-four days'
absence, we were glad to reach home.   It was not a
desirable or suitable time of the year for a long journey,
especially a journey to Cape Town; but as our supplies

were nearly exhausted, it would have to be undertaken; and taking the whole case into consideration, the sooner it was completed, and we were again back in the station, the better it would be. Our return had been hailed by our people with so much pleasure that it would have been a delightful thing to ourselves, could we have quietly settled down for some time upon the station after so much of travel and change; but it was imperative that we should start three months sooner than would have been advisable under ordinary circumstances.

On Wednesday, May 14th, all being ready, we bade adieu to our affectionate people, who were assembled around house and waggon, taking with us three men to manage the waggon and oxen (a team of which had to be driven loose, to bring back with us another waggon), and Martha, our native servant. On reaching the Orange River we found its waters low, as they usually are in the winter months, so that our waggons, though with some risk, were driven through at " the Upper Drift." It was an unspeakable comfort to be able to pass with such facility, for we still had a painful remembrance of the difficulties connected with our first passage, and were very thankful that they had not to be encountered again. We met with some loss, however, in crossing. Being so long a journey, it was necessary that a few sheep for slaughter on the road, and a few milch goats, should accompany us, and in passing the river two or three native swimmers living on its banks were employed to get them across. But under the semblance of pushing the animals across as they swam, they managed to keep their noses just below the water, so that, notwithstanding the sharp look out kept upon

the villains, two sheep and a goat when brought to land
were almost dead.   These, to our mortification, we were
obliged to leave in possession of these dishonourable
fellows, who thus got the sheep and goat in addition to
their pay.   Though no members of the Royal Humane
Society, I have no doubt they were quite up to the process of restoring apparently drowned sheep to life, and
that much assiduity would mark their operations in this
way after our departure, when very probably they
would have the happiness of seeing the animals, of which
they had so deceitfully robbed us, nibbling at the grass
and bushes in the enjoyment of perfect health, and
ultimately the still greater one of cutting their throats
and eating them up *seriatim*, just when their wants dictated.   Even in case their efforts to restore animation
should prove unsuccessful, they would lose little, for the
knife is always at hand, and the flesh of all three, cut
up into thin slices and dried in the sun and wind at this
season of the year, would keep ten times longer than
they would be likely to require it.   To us who had to
keep five people exclusively on meat every day in the
wilderness, besides our own smaller supply, the loss was
serious.

We passed the river on Friday, 16th of May, where
our oxen all drank to the full, and where our two water
barrels, for our own use, were replenished.   We were
now in Bushmanland, and at once resumed our journey
through the very heart of the desert.   We had met with
no water at the time of our outspanning on Saturday
night, but we had enough for our own use; and as the
oxen had drunk at the river, and the grass on which
they had grazed was green and full of juice, and the

weather quite cool, we were not anxious, and resolved, according to our constant custom, to rest and "keep holy the Sabbath day" on the spot reached on the Saturday night. We were quite satisfied we should obtain water on Monday. On the Sunday night, however, our oxen showed signs of thirst; they were restless, and could not be kept near, refused to eat, and were bent on wandering, so that the only way of securing them was by having them made fast to the yokes of the waggon as it lay upon the ground. On the Monday we were very anxious, but no water was found; we travelled till it was too dark to travel farther, and then the waggoner said we had better stay, or in the darkness we might pass the place where the water was. We remained, but after the work of the day the poor animals were distressed beyond all endurance. Tuesday morning dawned, the fourth day since they had drunk, and William, on whose knowledge of the region we had altogether relied, started at the first dawn of day and sought, but sought in vain. He thought we must have passed the place, but, as he was evidently uncertain, to retrace a step was out of the question, especially as he knew that by evening we should certainly come to a place where water was always found in the winter months. We therefore yoked in once more, and proceeded with hope and prayer that relief might soon be obtained.

At about ten o'clock that morning we met a Bushman bearing his gun on his shoulder (for whenever this weapon can be obtained, the bow and arrow are laid aside). We stopped the waggon, saluted him, and asked where he was going with his gun. "Op de jagt," was his answer—*i.e.*, on the hunt—and so we supposed. In half an hour we spied some mats set on their edges, and tied to some sticks driven into the ground, as a defence against the wind, evidently a Bushman kraal. This was yet at a considerable distance before us, and to the left of our path. It was a joyful sight, for, " Now we shall have water," we involuntarily exclaimed, and forward we journeyed in good spirits. As we neared the village, eight or nine men came out towards us, as we supposed, to "salute" according to custom, and when within thirty yards of the waggon I ordered it to be stopped. At this moment, just when we were ready to extend the friendly hand and speak words of greeting, the whole party wheeled round and walked away without uttering a syllable. We were all struck with amazement. I felt indignant, and exclaimed, " What do the fellows mean?" for though I had never met with anything like it before, I felt sure that it was intended as an insult. Our men looked suspicious, and knowing the habits of the Bushmen better than myself, they afterwards told us that they were very much alarmed that day. We had our own thoughts, but, whatever others may have felt, I suspected no danger. Two hundred yards further along the path brought the waggon opposite the village—" Span out," I shouted— that is, " unyoke"—and springing from the seat in front, whilst the men were busy loosening the oxen, I ran down the sloping ground to the left, anxious to see and report respecting the water. There was a small hole, not more than eighteen inches in diameter, just at the base of a sudden fall in the plateau, and it gave little promise that our two-and-thirty oxen, ready to " take

in a river," would find a sufficient supply, this being
the morning of the fourth day since they had had water.
As I returned to the waggon, which was nearly two
hundred yards from the water, and on higher ground
than that from which I came, to my surprise there
stood a woman, and a man was in the act of rising
from behind a bush, a little to the left, his gun barrel
peeping out of his kaross. Suspicion of something
wrong instinctively arose, for it was evidently a place
of concealment. "And what's he doing there with his
gun?" was the question that instantly suggested itself.
But immediately it occurred: "Why, it's nothing to
see a man with his gun in this country; every one
carries his gun." Whilst this momentary tumult of
thought and suspicion was going on, as I advanced
towards the waggon, I moved to the man and woman,
by way of recognition, and said, "Good morning."
The woman moved her head in reply, but evidently as
one under restraint. The man looked sullen and angered,
and made no reply. How little did I think that I was
then looking upon my would-be murderer, and upon
the woman who was the means of my preservation!
How little did we imagine that we were encamping in
the midst of enemies!

I mentioned nothing of what I had seen, or of the
momentary suspicion awakened, even to my wife, for,
unaccountably, no remnant of it was left behind, and I
felt as safe and confiding all the rest of the day as I had
ever done whilst living in the midst of the natives. The
oxen being freed from the yoke, the men made loose
the spades, and went to the water to dig the hole larger
and deeper, and make it more accessible to the oxen.

My own post that day was a peculiar one. Standing on the ridge below which the water was situated, and wielding the huge waggon whip, I was obliged, and sometimes with the sharpest strokes my unpractised arms could inflict, to fray away the poor oxen, that, almost maddened by thirst, were ready to rush upon the men who were enlarging the place for them to drink; and even after this was accomplished, though only one ox was allowed to approach at a time, the sand was so often trampled in again, that the men were kept constantly repeating the work the whole day. Several times during the day a Bushman child, generally a girl, was sent to fetch a vessel of water from the place, when I instructed the men to allow her free access and to take as much as she might need. Any petulance or roughness on the part of the men would probably have brought on a crisis, though at the time I suspected nothing, and only acted from a motive of kindness. A garrulous old Bushman came to beg tobacco of our men, but they had none. The eldest son of the Bushman chief was, during part of the morning, standing near observing, and engaged in conversation, though our men had difficulty in understanding his dialect. The skin of an ox, bloody, and evidently just taken from the animal, was spread out to the sun, and pegged down to the earth to dry, which suggested that it would only be prudent to appoint one of our men to guard over the oxen that were grazing at large, whilst the others were waiting their turn to drink, giving strict injunctions to keep them near the waggon and under constant oversight.

Whilst I was down at the water, one or two of the Bushmen had gone and looked into the waggon where my wife was busy sewing, and saw my rifle and fowling-piece slung up, and remarked admiringly on the appearance and contents of the waggon, whilst two or three had sat on the ground watching our servant girl as she cooked our dinner; an old woman also joined them, and through Martha, who was a very good girl, my wife talked with them, and exhorted them to give up their roaming life, and come and settle on the mission station. At noon I was summoned to the waggon to dinner, when for the first time since we had been in the country my wife looked concerned, and said, " I hope these Bushmen will do us no harm." I laughed, and said, " Why, what reason have you to fear? They never have done yet; all I fear is that unless we keep a sharp look-out, they may stealthily get some of our oxen." " I don't like their proceedings," she replied. From the high ground on which the waggon stood she could oversee all, and had marked that at intervals they crept about stealthily from hut to hut, sat as in consultation, and conducted themselves in such a way as to awaken fear in her mind. Our men were amazingly sombre that day, and much less talkative over their meals than usual. Old Kedo especially, a most imperturbable and contented subject in general, was not a little fidgety because two Bushman children had been found by him creeping about almost literally between the feet of the oxen, when he was sent to bring them nearer, and keep watch over them. The little innocents made off on his arrival, but old Kedo was up to Bushman tricks, and he felt that my instructions to him had not proceeded from an *excess* of caution. But his fears, and the fact respecting the children, were both kept to himself till some time after, when a full revelation of our peril came to light.

After dinner the men's task and my own were resumed. The oxen had, during the men's meal time, trampled the pool so full of sand, that not a drop of water could be got by them, so that the opening process had to be recommenced. At half-past four the sun was getting low, and though some of the oxen had obtained no water, we all felt an unaccountable reluctance to sleep at this place amidst Bushmen, who, to say the least, had not acted so as to inspire confidence. No suspicions were expressed to each other, but our men were evidently very anxious to get off: so, as the sun was dropping in the west, at five o'clock we bade adieu to the two or three Bushmen near our waggon, and proceeded on our way. And it was a mercy we did, for, had we known all, we could not have adopted a wiser course.

We travelled seven miles farther and found plenty of water. I ran down a slope to see it, and was delighted to find a pool four to six yards in length and breadth at the base of a rock, and fortunately on my solitary visit found no lions, though a few days afterwards the foot-marks of two were found at that very spot by some people of our own station travelling through the country. Several horses were killed by these same lions, which afterwards crossed the Orange River into Great Namaqualand, when they were hunted and shot. We felt that we were not far enough from the Bushmen to be comfortable, yet we resolved, on account of the water, to remain for the night, and God gave " His angels charge over us to keep us."

When we reached the northern side of the Khamies range of mountains, it being dark, with drenching rain, we came to a halt near the winter residence of a Dutch Boer. What to do with our people that stormy night was a problem we hardly knew how to solve, till, on making application to the Boer, permission was given for them to lodge with his servants. Next morning I went to thank him. He asked if I was a missionary. I told him I was. "Where have you laboured?" "On the other side of the Orange River, amongst the Bondelzwaarts, Afrikaners, &c." At the mention of the latter name he was evidently excited, and exclaimed, "Afrikaner! Afrikaner! he has shed much innocent blood; he was a regular lion!" He wished to know if old Titus was still alive. I said, "Yes, and is converted, by the grace of God, and is now a quiet and peaceable man." "Is that possible? is *he*, then, converted?" I assured him he was. "What, then, is too hard for the grace of God?" After conversing on a variety of topics, I proposed to read a portion of Scripture. He handed me a Dutch Bible, saying he could read, but could not well understand, and was always glad when he could find a missionary to explain it to him. I proposed that several of his people, who were near, might be called into the house; but this was evidently an unwelcome request, though he so far complied as to call them to sit around at the outside of the door. I then read and expounded John iii., and engaged in prayer, all kneeling. Almost before I could rise from my knees, he exclaimed, "But you have not yet sung." "Well," I said, "if you can assist me, I shall be happy to do so;" on which an old Dutch hymn-book was handed to me. I selected a hymn that every Dutchman is likely to know, and to which the notes of Luther's Old Hundredth were printed. So I commenced, and they joined most boldly, without the slightest knowledge of the tune, and such a jargon of roaring and squalling, of harsh unmusical sounds, I never heard. My own puny voice went for nothing in the uproar, whilst my risible faculties were so severely taxed at this outrageous attempt at harmony, that after struggling with extreme difficulty through a couple of verses, I could endure no longer, and was glad to give it up as a bad job! Judging from their agreeable and self-complacent looks, my good friends, however, appeared to derive much satisfaction from the success of the experiment, and no doubt would, in their simplicity, feel all the happier for some time to come.

On wishing him and his family farewell, he accompanied me to the waggon, where, finding the men busy yoking the oxen, he himself took up a couple of yokes and put them on the necks of four oxen, to the great surprise of our people, who said they never saw a Boer do that before. Such was the excess of his good will, though somewhat slow in developing itself.

After about three days of travel through the sublime and rugged scenery of the Khamies range of mountains we reached Lily Fountain Mission Station, and took Mr. Jackson, our missionary there, entirely by surprise, as he had had no notice of our approach. He gave me little comfort. I was altogether too soon for the journey; no rains had fallen; the country was never worse off for grass, and he predicted the loss of all my oxen! I had better hopes, and as circumstances compelled the journey at that early period, after a day or two's rest I resolved to proceed.

On the 20th of June, after a rapid journey of five weeks and one day, " one of the swiftest on record," I should think, in missionary annals, we reached Cape Town *without the loss of an ox*, and in the enjoyment of a measure of vigour much greater than when we left our station.

Our object in visiting Cape Town was twofold : the first and most important was to obtain supplies for another two years' residence in the interior; and the second, to procure a boat to facilitate the passage across the Orange River. In order to obtain the latter, the liberality of the members and friends of our society in Cape Town had to be appealed to. A public meeting was held in the chapel, at which the writer gave an account of the mission, and especially a detail of the difficulties and dangers attendant on passing a deep river with rapid current, and five hundred yards in breadth, by the native rafts. A collection was made at the close, when a Sergeant Churchill, from the barracks, came up and presented, in addition to the collection, a donation of £5. The amount requisite was soon raised, the boat procured, and after spending three weeks in Cape Town, during which plenty of work both in the Dutch and English departments was found for me, we commenced our return journey for the interior with a new waggon in which to travel, whilst the other served the purpose of a pack-waggon, bearing the novel article of a boat, inverted above the general load, and covered by the waggon tent.

On July 11th ourselves and our people all felt it to be a positive relief to escape from the narrow limits of a town and launch out again into the open space and breathe the free air of the wilderness. Sundry snappings of our tackle told of the weight we had stowed away in our pack-waggon, and at the same time put us to no small inconvenience. On the day after starting, whilst the men were greasing the fore axle of the pack-waggon, they managed to slip off the wheel, when down came the point of the axle upon the ground, the waggon being much strained by the weight of its load. Unable to raise it, we were detained there all the Sabbath, a dreary day, rain falling from beginning to end; but on Monday all was made right, our spirits rose, and we once more resumed the journey. As we passed along, occasionally near the houses of the Dutch Boers, the sight of the boat awakened their curiosity, and elicited many questions. After travelling for about a fortnight in the ordinary monotonous way, we met with a Dutchman who was very friendly and chatty. He was quite up with the times, and, amongst other matters, had the most recent information from Bushmanland. He told me of the depredations of the Bushmen, and of their having killed a Dutchman. " Well," I said, " if people will go out to shoot Bushmen, you can't wonder if the Bushman shoots in return." He wanted to know where I was going, and, on being informed, told me that I must not think of venturing through Bushmanland, as no one could travel there in safety. I bade him farewell, assuring him that I must go nevertheless.

We had thought nothing more of the Bushmen, since we were at their village, and had mentioned the circumstance to no one, simply because it left no abiding impression on our minds. And all that the Boers now told us, passed away as an idle tale.   A week after, at ten o'clock one night, whilst our waggon-wheels were monotonously grinding their way through heavy sand, a man appeared in the darkness, close by, and hailed in Dutch: " Is that Mynheer Ridsdale's waggon?" Recognising his voice as that of my old servant, Dirk, " What," I said, " is that you?"   He had lived with me for eighteen months, at Nisbett Bath, and was now on a journey to Clanwilliam in company with another man.   He and his companion had lain down to sleep for the night, but hearing the waggons, and suspecting them to be mine, he had come to see.   At his request the waggon was stopped: he had something important to communicate.   He stated that we had been in great danger on our way to Cape Town: that the Bushman chief 'Nosop had intended to murder us; that his wife had remonstrated; that, vexed at allowing us to escape, he had flogged her severely with a sambok, and vowed that on our return with loaded waggon he would murder us, and have a prize; that he was then with his party on the look-out for our return, and that we must not think of proceeding beyond the Khamies Berg Mission Station.   Still, as it now seems to me, unaccountably slow of heart to believe, I did not hesitate to express my conviction that there was no truth in the matter; when poor Dirk, finding his word questioned, felt as if he had received an insult, and wound up by saying: " Well, you'll hear all about it from Mr. Jackson."   That last reference produced its full effect, and opened my eyes to the reality of the case; and I became anxious to meet Mr. Jackson, and understand the matter fully.

During the journey, in consequence of the copious dews of the night, a keen south wind, and a hot sun, we found the weather exceedingly trying; especially after the climate of Namaqualand. In the sun we were too hot, in the shade too cold; shivering, sickness, and headache followed, and soon I was very seriously attacked with fever. This continued for ten days, during which the sail of our new waggon was our only defence against rain, of which we had an abundance, and it found its way through in half a dozen places, falling in all directions upon the bed, which was a sore affliction to my poor wife, who had the care of her sick husband. When nearing Mr. Van Zyl's, of the Uitkomst, though necessitated by our circumstances, we felt exceedingly reluctant to call at the house, because of their children; but on finding that I had been ill, they insisted on our going into the house. A large room was given up for our use, the kindest attention shown, and there we remained till my strength was so far recovered as to be able with safety to resume our journey.

After having been exactly a month on the road, at midnight on the 11th of August we once more reached Lily Fountain Station, and were glad to leave the waggon, and shelter ourselves beneath the roof of the mission house. The family had been at rest for an hour or two, but rose to welcome us with all the enthusiasm of missionary affection; a sentiment that can only be fully appreciated by those who have lived and laboured in foreign lands.

Mr. Jackson soon confirmed all I had heard respecting the Bushmen, and said it would be impossible to

proceed to my station in safety, except under the escort
of a large body of armed men.   The murder of William
Threlfall was not yet forgotten, and that alone was
sufficient to operate as a salutary check to the adoption
of any presumptuous course of action.   'Nosop, we
understood, to insure his prize, had placed scouts on
a mountain just at the point where the main path
branched out into two, so that whether we had taken
the road leading to the upper, or that leading to the
lower drift or *ford* of the river, in either case we should
have been full in view of the scouts.   These were
reasons why we should take due precaution : but our
stay for a season at this station was rendered all the
more necessary by Mrs. R.'s circumstances, which made
it impracticable to travel over the rocky and precipitous
roads of this lofty mountain-range without great inconvenience and danger.   The weather, too, was very severe,
and of itself was sufficient to put a veto on all waggon
travelling.   Snow covered the ground, and in these
grand highlands an innocent game of snowballing was
carried on by the children of the mission family, in
which the fingers of the writer so itched to take part,
that he found it impossible to refrain ; and so in honour
of Old England, and in remembrance of her brave white
winters, he threw himself with enthusiasm into the fun,
till his cheeks, pallid with the everlasting sweats of Great
Namaqualand, glowed with the crimson flush of a frozen
clime.   Icicles hung down from the roof of the mission
dwelling, all round, from twelve to eighteen inches
in length ; a scene so new again, and a contrast so
entire to anything I had seen since leaving England,
that I could scarce believe I was in Africa.   The great

drawback at such a season is the scarcity of fuel. For
coal one might search for ever in this granitic region,
and to collect a load of good hard wood a waggon must
travel many miles over tremendous passes. Of late,
however, a winter's residence has been erected in the
Onder Veld, a portion of the country two or three
thousand feet lower down, where the cold is much less
severe, and where perhaps more fuel is to be found.

After we had been about a fortnight on the station,
the dubious intelligence was brought: "Old Abraham
has made 'Nosop still." Mr. Jackson first heard the
rumour, and asked what I thought it meant. "I
suppose," I said, "that old Abraham and he have come
to terms, and that 'Nosop has promised to keep the
peace." "I don't think so," said Mr. Jackson, "I
believe Abraham has killed him." But this was an idea
that I was very slow to entertain, as I had not heard
so much of the ravages of the Bushmen as Mr. Jackson.
I now learned that soon after we had passed through
them, they commenced depredations on the flocks and
herds of a trader in the vicinity, and he applying for
assistance to the nearest "veld kornet," an armed
party was sent against them, headed by Pieter
Engelbrecht, a principal man in the community at
Kok Fontein. The Bushmen took refuge in a low
mountain, and, ensconced behind the shrubs and rocks,
fired on their assailants. Engelbrecht at the head of
his party advanced recklessly, and was shot down, on
which his companions with dastardly cowardice fled,
leaving their wounded leader in the hands of his
enemies. The Bushmen, seeing their enemies flee, left
their concealment, and whilst their victim was still

quivering with life, they cut away the flesh about the wound to search for the ball, that they might reserve it for future use.   Soon fresh depredations were committed on the flocks and herds of another farmer, and while out in search for them, suspecting that they had merely wandered, he was fired at by the concealed Bushmen, and the ball, striking his thumb, tore it from the hand.   At the same moment he was wounded by a poisoned arrow in the thigh ; but being on horseback he escaped, and afterwards recovered.   They sent threatening and alarming messages to Boers in the neighbourhood, and also to the people of Lily Fountain Mission Station, saying they would save them the trouble of reaping their harvest, for they would come and do it for them : and though this was puerile boasting, as their numbers were too few to accomplish anything against a community, yet the alarm spread amongst many of the people : whilst to those Boers who were living on solitary farms, with very few servants to aid in defending them in case of an attack, their threats were full of terror.   They had passed over the Orange River into the territories of our chief, and had robbed and plundered, and scattered the few people living near the river.   This seems to have aroused the ire of our chief, and with a body of men he went against them, the first announcement of which proceeding was the dubious one already mentioned. Soon other rumours of a horrifying nature were brought, to the effect that all the men had been killed, and that wanton barbarities had been perpetrated on their bodies after they were slain.   But no reliable information could be obtained for some time.   Eventually, the intelligence was brought on good authority, that all the men had been shot by our chief's party, and the women and children spared.

It was these women from whom the particulars were afterwards learned with respect to myself. On the day when we first met with them, they saw our waggon approaching long before we saw them: the old chief 'Nosop took up his position behind the bush, where I saw him, as the waggon drew near, levelled his gun, and only waited till we should pass, when his intention was to send the bullet through myself and the driver, who were both seated on the fore-chest, side by side, and very favourably for his purpose. The woman remonstrated, and said, " That's a man of peace, and a missionary; if you shoot him, not one of your children will be spared to you." But he was sullenly fixed in his purpose. Providentially the waggon was ordered to stop before coming opposite the bush, and at a distance of fifty yards on the other side. The women testified that the intention was by one shot to dispose of myself and driver, when it would be easy to dispose of the other members of the party, to take possession of the oxen and all our articles, and then to take the waggon to a " kloof," or ravine in a mountain, and burn it, that no trace of us might remain, and no one ever know what had become of us.

On September 5th, Mr. Jackson left the Khamies Berg Station, having received an appointment to Wynberg, near Cape Town, so that I was left alone till the arrival of his successor.

Early in November, I received a letter from the Civil Commissioner of Clanwilliam, enclosing an account of the attack on the Bushmen by our chief Abraham.   It was written by a trader, in the chief's name, and forwarded to the Secretary of Government immediately after the transaction, and gave me the first account of the affair that was at all to be relied on.   His Excellency the Governor having directed the Civil Commissioner at Clanwilliam " to make inquiry, with a view of ascertaining the accuracy of the statements, and to report the result," he wrote to me, requesting that I would make inquiry, send him what information I could, and accompany it with my opinion as to whether the chief acted properly throughout; " as," it was added, " his Excellency will be happy to reward him for his conduct."   In reply, I stated that I was then at the Khamies Berg Mission Station, but that as soon as I reached Nisbett Bath, I would endeavour to ascertain the facts, and immediately communicate all the information I could gather.

During my stay at Khamies Berg, I found a good measure of employment.   I had all the services on the station to conduct, besides occasionally visiting those living in the Onder Veld.   Amongst other matters that engaged my attention was my boat, which had been brought in safety thus far, and which was now carefully deposited under cover.   By exposure to the sun on the road, the wood had shrunk very much, so that many of the seams between the planking were half an inch wide. I tried my hand at caulking and painting the little craft, a novel occupation for me, devoting three hours a day for several days, till the work was done to my satisfaction.   At the end of November several of our people arrived from Nisbett Bath to assist us over the remaining part of the journey; our waggons were repacked, and everything in readiness.

On Wednesday, December 3rd, we took our leave of Mr. Bailey, the new missionary, and the people, and after an unavoidable detention of more than sixteen weeks, we descended from this elevated region to travel once more through the burning plains of Bushmanland. Some of the heights from which the waggons had to descend were frightful, and though thongs were attached behind the waggons to prevent too rapid a descent, and at the sides, to prevent their canting over where the roads were very much lower on one side than on the other, I had many fears lest the pack-waggon should go over, and my boat be smashed among the rocks. By the good providence of God, the lower country was reached in safety, and our Sabbath was spent at the house of a Boer at Riet Fontein, by whom we were most kindly received, and in whose house I preached twice to all his household, increased by our own party; and, as a number of his friends were visiting him, I had a congregation of forty persons. The heat was suffocating, and probably we felt it more owing to the sudden change in our position. On the last Sunday, being on the mountain height, the thermometer stood at 57° in the shade: to-day it was 100° in the shade, with not a breath of wind stirring. As we travelled through Bushmanland, we could not help thinking of our providential escape a few months before, though at the time no fear of danger was permitted to agitate our minds. He who had before saved us from the danger itself, imminent as it was, now saved us from all fear. The heat was dreadful, midsummer being near at hand, and water extremely scarce, so that we all suffered from both these causes, the poor oxen the most, as is always the case, it being impossible to carry water for them, though we may often manage to do so for ourselves. On reaching Quick Fontein, rather more than sixty miles on the south side of the Orange River, I despatched a man on horseback to our station to request that, by a date mentioned, Mr. Macleod would meet me at the river, to assist me in rowing the boat.

On Friday evening, the 12th, we reached the Orange River, and were much better prepared to cross it than we were two years previously, when we had to rely on native swimmers. This time they came to offer their services, but to their amazement they were not required. The first thing was to launch the boat, when, to my delight, I found that my first experiment at caulking had been very effective ; for after exposure to the heat of the sun for nine days, and a tremendous jolting over the Khamies Mountains, she only took a gallon or two of water on first putting into the river, and, after lying to soak a little and swell, was nearly water tight. Our Sabbath we spent on the hot and dusty banks of the river in our usual way, in public worship and quiet reading. On Monday, being impatient at Mr. Macleod's non-arrival, and being unable to obtain any aid from the natives, who had never seen a boat before, I ventured across the river with a light load, and a man to help to deposit the cargo on the northern shore. How to get back was the difficulty. In crossing, the current had borne the boat far down the stream, so that the cargo was landed more than a quarter of a mile below

the point from which I had started. The only way
was to keep nearer the northern shore and row dead up
against the current a sufficient distance without attempting to cross ; a very exhausting labour, and one
which was only accomplished inch by inch. Having
succeeded in getting up sufficiently far, literally flooded
with perspiration, panting for breath, and prostrate
with exhaustion, I leaped ashore to rest awhile before
attempting the passage over. This I found very easy,
as I crossed at a slant, and was aided by the current.
Twice I crossed with loads, and returned, by myself. I
had just reached the northern bank with the third load,
and was so weakened from the heat and exhaustion
that I scarcely knew how I could row myself and man
up stream again, when to my joy Mr. Macleod and a
native came up on horseback just in time to take an
oar and share my labour. Two pairs of hands were a
vast relief, and we soon found ourselves in high spirits
on the other side among our friends.

The heat was really dreadful, and what to do with
our new-born babe, five weeks old, we could scarcely
tell. Mrs. R. and the servant ran with him from
bush to bush and tree to tree for the best shelter ; but
in the best place the shade was only partial and the heat
insufferable. At last, as the best protection we could
devise, we placed him on a camp stool, and put that
under a small camp table, both standing beneath the
imperfect shadow of a large tree on the river's bank,
and only a few yards from the water's edge. Having
just come, weary and exhausted, from rowing the boat,
I sat on the ground resting my elbow on the camp
stool and my head on my hand. Just then a long thin

snake, coming from the brushwood behind, glided along the sand, with head erect, close by the side of my leg, and when just past my naked foot (for, being constantly in and out of the water, I had taken my shoes and stockings off) the alarm was given; it turned and fled, springing into the low branch of a fallen tree, where it was soon killed by some of our people. Had I started on seeing it, no doubt I should have received a bite, but being perfectly still I escaped unscathed.

Whilst remaining at Khamies Berg, I had procured a small mast and bowsprit for my boat, and had got a native woman to make me some rope out of several old rice bags, and to hem a sail I had shaped out of an old tilt sail of a waggon. On Monday afternoon a violent wind blew from the west, which was just favourable for my experiment. My mast and little bowsprit were soon fixed, my foresail hoisted, and with that sail alone the breeze took Mr. Macleod and myself up the stream against the powerful current at a great rate, when, having gone as far as we felt disposed, sail was struck, and we came back at our ease with the stream. That was the first white sail ever spread, I believe, on the waters of the Orange River. The natives were amazed, and, as *per saltum*, I rose to the highest point in their admiration. " Before you came," said they, " we were everybody; " meaning they were indispensable; " but now you have made us to be nobody!" Subsequently, the boat was rigged with foresail, mainsail, and gaff-topsail, like a cutter, though the latter had to be used judiciously, and only in gentle winds; but I found it very useful sometimes to boom out the foresail on one side and to lay the mainsail back

on the other, when the strong winds of the afternoon
would carry the boat up river against the powerful
current at great speed, to the astonishment of our men.
With all the aid and comfort of our boat we were
detained four days at the river, as our waggons had to
be reduced to small portions, wherever this was possible,
the boat being only twelve feet by four. The body
and tent of the waggon, being inseparable, could not be
taken over in safety by the boat, and had to be conveyed by swimmers on a raft. At length the waggons
were repacked, and, going on before them on horseback, I reached my station on the night of the 17th
of December; the waggons with Mrs. R. and party
reaching home before breakfast on the morning of the
18th in peace and safety, after an unexpectedly long
absence of nearly seven months. The chief and people
gave us a hearty welcome, and we once more felt as if
we were at rest. Our hearts were filled with gratitude
to God, for the truth of His promises had been most
signally displayed in our preservation, so much so, that
the ninety-first Psalm seemed an exact description of
the various interpositions we had experienced; and as a
suitable expression of our gratitude, we devoted the
second Sunday after our arrival to the Lord, as a day
of special thanksgiving for mercies received.

CHAPTER V.

1846.—At the earliest opportunity I undertook the delicate task of inquiring into the truth of the statements made by our chief respecting the destruction of the Bushmen in his letter to the Government. On stating my object, and requesting the chief and several of the leading men who had accompanied him on the commando to meet in my house, he came, evidently under great excitement, shaking either with fear or wrath. I stated that the governor was wishful merely to know the facts of the case, and that if the chief had " made no unnecessary use of fire-arms, he would be happy to reward him." I then took down their statements, read them *seriatim* before them, and they were confirmed as true by all present. Next morning, however, two of the principal men came to the mission house, wishing to see me. They commenced by saying : " We are ashamed to tell you, but we cannot rest without doing it. We told you falsehoods yesterday." I had spent two or three hours with them in getting their several testimonies, and weaving a connected account, which on hearing they all agreed was correct. Now it appeared all my trouble went for nothing ; but, being resolved to send off no false statement, I ran the risk of exciting the anger of the chief by summoning him and the same men once more, and then called on the confessors to point out what part of the statement made on the preceding day was false.

They had made it appear, as the chief did in the account he sent to the governor, that the Bushmen *fell in fight*; whereas the real facts were that when Abraham ordered 'Nosop to surrender, he replied, something like another Leonidas: " If you are a great chief, come and fetch us." On this the chief ordered the bushes on the small island, on which the Bushmen had taken refuge, to be fired, in order to compel a surrender; but they were too green to burn. The women, however, on hearing the order, became alarmed, and, with the children, waded through the water and came to the chief's party, having received the promise of protection. Almost immediately, all the Bushmen, except three, followed the example of the women, coming unarmed, having left their guns behind. The women were then sent to fetch the guns, which they brought, with the exception of one retained by Klass, 'Nosop's son, and which he refused to yield. Then, finding that there was no escape, a party of armed men being on each side of the river, the remaining three waded through the water, as the others had done, Klass bearing his gun in his hand, and cursing savagely as he came. The chief, standing near the water's edge, upbraided Klass with the murder of Pieter Engelbrecht, which only increased his rage, and as he held his gun in a threatening position, the chief retired and ordered his men, as soon as he reached the shore, to disarm him. All the Bushmen who had previously come to the chief were seated on the ground, near his own men. But instantly on Klass's gun being taken from him the word was given by Abraham, " Fire." Five of the Bushmen fell at once. Klass was attempting to run into the water, but was shot and fell at its edge; whilst two others, who had fled into the water, were shot and fell there. This order was quite unexpected by the chief's own people, one of whom had seated himself in the midst of the Bushmen, and was asking one who sat next him how he came by his gun, when the order to fire was given, and, starting to his feet, and raising his hands in the air, he cried out: " Don't shoot me." The chief said, unhesitatingly, that when he left the station he went resolved to shoot them: they had already committed murder; had threatened to murder others; no one could travel through the country with safety; and therefore the only way to remove the danger was to remove them out of the way.

Such was the account I finally received. All admitted, when read sentence by sentence, that it was now perfectly right, and ever after they affirmed this to be the only true version.

Thus it appears that the Bushmen, instead of falling in fight, were shot after they were disarmed and had surrendered; a fact that makes a mighty difference, and one that the chief had studiously concealed in the account he had forwarded to the governor.

Under these circumstances, an account of which I forwarded to the civil commissioner, and through him to the governor, it is scarcely necessary to say that it never pleased his excellency the governor to reward the chief for his conduct. No reply was ever returned, from which Abraham rightly concluded that his conduct was not approved.

It is remarkable that these poor creatures were shot on the 22nd of August, about the very time we should in all probability have become their victims, had we merely called at the Khamies Berg Station on our way, as we originally intended, instead of meeting with the providential detention of several months. Whilst we were kept there, they were taken out of the way.

Again I was called to thankfulness for a merciful interposition of God's providence. One day wishing to obtain some corn for family use, which was kept in a loft above Mr. Macleod's kitchen, a ladder was brought and so placed as to enable me to ascend and unlock the door of the loft. After obtaining the corn, the door was locked, and the ladder removed. But by some means a stone in the building had become loosened, where the framework of the loft door was inserted in the wall. Of this none of us were aware; but soon afterwards, when ascending the steps to enter the kitchen, I was stunned by a terrible shock, which for the moment made me leap upwards and instantly fall backwards to the ground. There I lay helpless till assistance was rendered. The stone from the building had fallen just at the instant that I was ascending the steps, and struck with terrible concussion the right leg just above the cap of the knee. The marvel was that it did not break the bone, and the greater mercy, perhaps, that it did not strike the skull, which must have happened if the head had been inclined forward. It had fallen from a height of about twenty feet, and was nearly fourteen pounds in weight. I was so maimed as to be kept a close prisoner for some days.

On the 13th of January, anxious, after my long

absence, to visit the Afrikaners, I set out on horseback for Blydeverwachting. On my arrival I found David Afrikaner absent, having gone on a visit to Jonker Afrikaner, the chief, in Damaraland. Jonker had now abandoned his evil practices, and received a Wesleyan missionary, and had sent urgent and repeated messages to David and his people to come and settle with him. Until now they had disregarded these messages, being so attached to David that they were extremely unwilling to leave him and the quiet they had long enjoyed. This had been the state of things for years. But it was one that placed David in an unenviable position, as Jonker was chafed by disappointment and jealousy. David, at length, anxious to remove wrong impressions from the mind of his chief, to whom he was uncle, resolved to visit him, though at a distance of six hundred miles, taking with him all who had any inclination to remove. And as he had left home in June and intended to return by the end of the year, it was feared by his brother Nicholas that he was being detained by Jonker against his will. In consequence of David's long absence, I expected to find things in some degree of disorder. My pleasure and satisfaction, therefore, were great on finding that though their head was absent, such excellent arrangements had been made, and so faithfully carried out, that nothing of consequence had been neglected. The services had been held by Nicholas, the school daily maintained by Jacobus, and the classes regularly met by the leaders, and on meeting the members, sixty in number, I was thankful to find that they had advanced rather than retrograded in their Christian experience and character. One old woman, referring to our escape from the Bushmen, said her heart was full of joy to see her missionary again; and when she thought of the goodness of God in so preserving me, it was " too great " for her. She had thought what great love the Lord has for His people. He always knew where they were. On that long journey He knew where Mynheer was every day, and He preserved him every day, just as a man knows where any precious thing is that he has put into a sack, so that he always knows it is safe, and always knows where he can find it. (A " sack " is their only safe.) I returned home on the 21st.

The missionary meeting this year, though held seemingly at an unpropitious time, proved a success. Our congregation did not number more than seventy, yet much interest and feeling were awakened, whilst I was recounting the chief spiritual and temporal blessings they had received, since the Gospel was first preached among them. Instead of being involved in perpetual war with the Afrikaners, tranquillity reigned, and as the result the population was increased, the men and women in general lived to a good old age; their young men were spared instead of being destroyed by the ravages of war; their flocks and herds, instead of being scattered or carried off by marauding bands, had multiplied. They were now clothed in decent English clothing, and appeared more like a civilised people than they had ever done before, &c. Several other speeches followed from Mr. Macleod, John Ortman, the principal councillor, and from old Hendrik, a tall fine old man. The stately form, and hoary head, and genial countenance of old Hendrik made him quite a patriarch amongst the Great Namaquas. The younger people

all spoke of and treated him with great respect. He
said:

"It is all true, all true; it is the very ground of the
truth that Mynheer has spoken. Mynheer has not
said too much: he has spoken less than the truth. I
have not only heard it from others; I have seen it
myself. I was in the middle of it, and so were others
now present. *Now*, when we are on a journey, we can
unyoke our oxen, or offsaddle, whenever we will, and
can lie down and sleep on the plain wherever we are,
without fear of an enemy. But before the Gospel
came, we were afraid to offsaddle or to sleep on the
plain: we must then seek the mountains and go and
hide ourselves and sleep there. If we were thirsty, we
dare not go to the fountain in the day, but must suffer
thirst, and then, when night came on, we must creep
one by one to the water, and lie on our faces and
drink. Or if we saw the *spoor* of men, we were so
afraid that we were almost ready to suffer thirst and
die, rather than go and run the risk of being shot.
Then we dare not send our sheep and cows out of our
sight to graze, lest they should be stolen; but now we
can send them wherever we like: every place is a place
for them now; and we, too, can go and stay wherever
we will. And every place where we live to-day, and
have our doings, is a place from which we had fled in
former times. But now we live in peace; and all
this is through the Gospel. Now we have horses and
waggons, and our oxen and sheep are increased; and
this is all, all through the missionary and the Gospel.
Now the missionary is our Father. Who else is our
Father? What other Father do you wish to have?

We also had fathers. I had a father. I was a grown up young man; and my father taught me: ' If any one fights you, fight him again; if any one does you wrong, do wrong to him again; what anybody does to you, do the same to him again.' That was our fathers' teaching; that was the instruction they gave to us. But now, the missionary is our father; and he teaches us to-day what is good, and what is evil, and all that he teaches us is to keep us from evil. Some there are who say they don't know whether it is good to have a missionary meeting, and whether it is right to give their things: they don't know whether this has been so of old. But these people are foolish. I have seen many missionaries, and they have all said the same thing. And old Albrecht, the first missionary I ·saw, said: ' Come, let us hold a missionary meeting, and give of our things, that they may go to the Cape, and be sold, and by that money we shall help to send other missionaries to the heathen.' So that it is an old thing, and good and right, to give of our goods to help to send the Gospel to others."

On the previous evening, he said, with reference to the same period: " Then we dare not take off our clothes at night when we slept, lest we should be suddenly surprised in the night by the enemy. Then, if we heard a dog bark in the night, we said: ' It is war!' and we instantly made ready to flee. But now we can sleep in peace, and never think of war. Now, if we hear the dogs bark in the night, it creates no alarm; for we think it is only a jackal, or a wolf, or may be it is only the missionary with his man and horses returning from one of his distant visits to the people. And I believe that many of us would have died from hunger if the Gospel had not come and restored peace, since which our flocks and herds have multiplied."

February 19th.—This morning, whilst standing in the waggon-house making an engagement with a native builder, a snake that had concealed itself in the crevices of the stone wall, protruded its head several inches, and, shortly afterwards came completely out; but on perceiving me slightly move, it fled to another hole in the wall, where it remained several minutes without making its appearance again. There being no possibility of destroying the reptile in any other way, I went for my fowling-piece and charged it with small shot. Soon after my return, on perceiving its head projected about two inches from the wall, I fired and wounded it in the neck, when it sprang out of the hole to the ground, where, though wounded, its activity was great, and we had some difficulty in despatching it.

March 2nd.—This evening the announcement that an Englishman was at the door, and wished to see me, produced quite an excitement, being a most extraordinary occurrence in this land. He was sitting on his ox, with a brace of pistols in his belt, and his gun on his shoulder. It was Mr. A. Searle, of Cape Town. About five months since he had left Cape Town with two waggons, intending to visit the mouth of the Orange River; but, having changed his purpose, he crossed it at some distance from its mouth, and, travelling northward, passed the Nisbett Bath Station considerably to the westward.

Mr. Searle stayed with us for the night, and about half-past six a.m. we left home for a bath. I had plunged in and swum several times round, and whilst we were dressing on the narrow path running between the surrounding wall and the bath, we heard a sound, which we thought was occasioned by a stone thrown over the wall and striking against the opposite side. A minute or two afterwards we left. We had not, however, gone more than fifty yards, when we were startled by a loud rumbling noise, and, on turning to look, we saw the whole of the bath enveloped in a cloud of dust. On returning to examine it, we saw that the heaviest portion of the wall, composed of large and massive stones, had fallen just at the spot where I had stood to dress, so that had it occurred two or three minutes sooner, I must inevitably have been forced into the water by the weight of the wall, and drowned, being kept under by the weight, and so bruised as to be quite unable to make an effort. The outer wall had been built too near the water, and this gradually sapping the foundation led to the collapse. God in His mercy watched over us, and gratefully we exclaim: " Thanks be unto God, Who delivered us from so great a death." Soon after breakfast Mr. Searle left on oxback, equipped in true African style, with a cutlass at his side, a rifle slung at his back, a brace of pistols in his holsters, and a white ostrich feather in his hat. In this manner he travelled to the Bath, having sold one of his waggons, and sent on the other by a different route to that taken by himself; and in this manner he left us for the south.

On March 5th, I felt it necessary to leave home on a visit to our two north-eastern stations of 'Amas and Nieuwe Fontein, and on the afternoon of the third day reached Wortel. Here I met with the chief Fransman, and a number of his people, on a journey to my station.

His intention was to complain, as he said, before Abraham, the chief, and myself, of one of our native assistants, Johannes Gagup, who is stationed, with a portion of his people, at Nieuwe Fontein, at some distance from the residence of their chief. He accused him of several things, the most serious of which was that Johannes had appointed another chief in his place, saying that Fransman was no longer chief of the 'Karakikooika! As I was on the way to Johannes' place, I endeavoured to persuade Fransman to accompany me, when I promised to investigate the matter. This he was unwilling to do, and seemed bent on visiting the Bath Station, and conferring with Abraham, our chief, to whom he had sent notice of his approach. Why an independent chief should wish to have such a cause adjudged by the chief of another tribe, I cannot conceive.

March 8th, Sunday.—Still at Wortel. This morning I preached to a good number from the parable of the Ten Virgins. Late in the afternoon, to avoid the great heat, I met about twenty members and had a close conversation as to their spiritual state, and was pleased to find that the service in the morning had induced some to search their hearts, " examining themselves whether they were in the faith." At about eight o'clock, by moonlight, I again preached on the General Resurrection, from John v. 28, 29, when the people listened with deep solemnity.

This morning, the 10th, we reached 'Amas, an outpost that is regularly visited; but as I intend remaining here a day or two on the return journey, we only rested two or three hours to refresh ourselves and our oxen. Soon after we reached the place, Job Witbooi, our native teacher, arrived from a village to which he had gone to hold services with a number of Fransman's people, who are located temporarily at about fifteen miles' distance. In this way our native teachers may be said to go "everywhere preaching the Word," sowing the seed of the kingdom, and exercising by their simple ministrations, and by the piety of their example, a powerful and very salutary influence upon the people, and that far beyond the range of the outposts which form their special charge. Before leaving this place, myself and Mrs. Ridsdale entered the chapel, where we found about eighty scholars (for the chapel serves as a schoolroom too); and instantly on our appearance all order was at an end, all, from the least unto the greatest, crowding towards us to give us their salutation. In order to despatch the business, we were obliged to grasp two or three extended hands at a time, and that with our left as well as with our right hands.

11th.—Whilst the day was yet dark, we commenced travelling, and at about two o'clock this morning the oxen, being frightened by some wolves or jackals, concealed amongst bushes, turned abruptly out of the path, and ran the waggon under a mimosa tree, the low branches of which tore and much injured the front of the waggon-sail. We were thankful that the waggon was not overturned, and a greater injury sustained. At sunrise we reached a place called Zwaartwater, where we found about one hundred Bondelzwaarts, amongst whom regular religious services were kept up and school held by Abraham Witbooi. At considerable labour, they have constructed a very tolerable chapel, and, considering that it is intended necessarily as a temporary place of worship, it is especially laudable in them. Abraham was absent on my arrival, having gone some distance to hold services on the banks of the Ky 'Kaap. Before sunset he arrived on oxback, accompanied by several others; and in the evening, by the serene light of the full moon, I held a missionary meeting.

Nieuwe Fontein, Friday, March 13th.—Last evening I reached this place about sunset, and the distance from Zwaartwater being only short, several of those people followed us on foot. The people of this place belong to Frausman's tribe, named the 'Karakikooika. Before sleeping, I held service with them. This morning, after all had assembled in the chapel, at the sound of a koodoo's horn, and I had read and explained a portion of Scripture, I met twenty-seven of the members, leaving seventeen women to be met in the afternoon by Mrs. Ridsdale. During the day a number of people have arrived from various surrounding parts, having heard that I was here. Some have come in waggons, and many more in true native style on oxback, the women sitting astride their steeds in the same manner as the men, the use of the side saddle being entirely unknown amongst the people generally. I believe the first side saddle was taken to the country by myself; and whenever used by Mrs. Ridsdale, both she and it were objects of immense curiosity. In the evening I again preached to a congregation of more than two hundred persons.

14th.—This morning, after the usual service, during which I baptized eight children, I called together Johannes Gagup, the native assistant, Jan Koper, the alleged new chief, and fifteen others, who, as stated by

Fransman, were all implicated in the same crime, for the purpose of making known to them the charges brought against Johannes. Not one of the whole company knew anything of the "abominable things" alleged by Fransman to be said and done on the place; of the election of a new chief, &c. Indeed, the whole of the charges were astounding to them, as they neither knew nor had heard of any of them, till they heard them from my mouth. And I can easily conceive that the origin of all Fransman's suspicions is his jealousy at the flourishing state of the society here, by which a number of his people are induced to attend the services held by Johannes, and to settle on this place, instead of living nearer the chief.

Some time since Fransman came to my station to ask permission, as he put it, to remove to a considerable distance north of his present place of residence, and to take with him Johannes and all the members of society who formed his special charge. With regard to his own removal and that of his people who were not members, I said I had nothing to do, he might act as he pleased. But with reference to Johannes and all the members, I said I must decidedly object, especially as they were reluctant to leave. If he 'removed them, which of course he had the power to do, I said it must be in opposition to my wish; and were he thus causelessly to break up a portion of the Church of Christ after so much labour and expense had been incurred, he would certainly bring upon himself the Divine displeasure. He admitted the truth of all I said, but was still bent on his favourite scheme of removal, which I believe implied nothing less than the plunder of the lands and cattle of the tribes of Damaraland.　On that occasion he remained for three days at the Bath, visiting me each day in order to obtain my consent.　But as he was unable to extort a compliance with his wishes, he has become irritated against Johannes and the members at Nieuwe Fontein, and ready to receive any idle tale that may be repeated to their disadvantage.　I have no reason to believe that Fransman is opposed to missionary operations in themselves; he is very anxious to have a missionary of his own, but he is jealous that so many of his people should prefer living at such a distance from himself in order that they may become members of Christ's Church, and enjoy all its privileges.　I was, therefore, especially thankful that none of the charges he has brought against this portion of his people have the appearance of truth. The formal charge has yet to be preferred.

Sunday, 15th.—Every day since my arrival in this place numbers have come from various surrounding parts, some from a great distance; and this morning at about seven o'clock Elias Rolfe, our native teacher at Bak River, came with about twenty others, men and women, all riding on oxback.　They had left their homes on Saturday at sunrise, but the distance to this place being upwards of fifty miles, they were not able to reach us before this morning, though they had travelled nearly all the night through.　In consequence of the arrival of so many persons we have had nearly four hundred people on the place, and the chapel being much too small for the congregation, we were obliged to erect a shade along one side of it to screen some of those who were unable to gain access to the interior.　It being too hot for service in the afternoon, I held none, but had the horn blown for the Sunday school; and whilst this was being held, I had a conversation with three of our native teachers, who had met me on this place, examining them as to their knowledge of the principal doctrines of Christianity, and giving them some instruction on the subject of preaching.

Monday, 16th.—After the usual short service this morning at eight o'clock, at which I baptized seven children and married eight couples, I met forty-three people in class, which, with the other services, occupied nearly the whole morning. After a short interval of rest I met seventeen adult candidates for baptism. This being concluded, Mrs. R. held a meeting of all the females on the place, and at an evening service I publicly baptized the candidates with whom I had conversed during the afternoon. This day, like every other since I came, has been one of incessant occupation, and of much bodily fatigue and exhaustion. Every day has been so completely filled up from morning to night, that anything like study, or even reading, has been out of the question, and literally, on some days, we have scarcely had time even to eat. The languor and exhaustion induced by such incessant speaking have often been distressing; but still in the pleasure and satisfaction I have generally enjoyed, I have had sufficient recompense for all my toil.

Tuesday, March 17th.—This morning when we were just ready to take our leave, a man arrived saying that the two chiefs, Abraham and Fransman, were approaching; that their coming was "met scherpte," with severity, Abraham having ordered one of his great men to be flogged at one of the places through which he had passed. Not being assured of the truth of the report, I despatched a man on horseback to 'Amas, a distance of more than forty miles, to ascertain its correctness, resolved, if it were true, to stay till their arrival, that I might endeavour to temper the anger of the chieftains, and defend our native assistant from their wrath in case the accusations preferred against him should prove false. At about eleven o'clock at night the messenger returned, having met with the chiefs at the above-named place. He states them to be now on their way, accompanied by a body of men on oxback, armed with guns, so that we expect their arrival on the morrow.

Wednesday, 18th.—At four o'clock this afternoon the chiefs arrived, preceded by about sixty men on oxback armed with guns. On the two waggons in which the chiefs travelled being drawn up at the entrance of the village, at a distance of six or seven hundred yards from my own, the oxmen wheeled round in quite a fine manœuvre to the rear of the waggons and dismounted. Soon-after, the chiefs left them, and walked at the head of their men towards mine, when, descending from it, I went out and met them half way, saluting each chief, by shaking hands, as usual; and this cere- mony being completed, they sat round the front of the waggon, the chiefs on chairs, and most of the others on the ground. Just at this moment, a smart clap of thunder burst over our heads, and a few drops of rain fell, but subsided as unexpectedly as they came. For some time all sat in silence, when by degrees they glided into a familiar conversation, grouping together into small parties; but nothing was said on the subject of their visit till I myself alluded to it. This was just

as the chiefs were about to return to their waggons for
the night, when I intimated a wish that the accusations
laid against Johannes might be gone into early on the
following morning, as I designed leaving in the afternoon, my stay having been already protracted two days
beyond what I had intended, solely in consequence of
the reported approach of the chiefs. This being
assented to, they all returned to their encampment at
the entrance of the village.

Thursday, 19th.—This morning, just after sunrise,
Abraham sent to inquire whether I intended holding
the usual morning service before the charges were investigated, to which I replied in the affirmative, and
immediately ordered the horn to be blown. The chapel
was well filled, and both the chiefs attended. On leaving
the chapel and inquiring if they were ready, they said
they were; but as they wished to have a little private
conversation with me, before entering on the general
business, I accompanied them to a wide-spread camel-
thorn tree, a short distance from the chapel, beneath
the shade of which we seated ourselves : but after some
minutes had passed in silence, and they seemed scarcely
to know how to commence the solicited conversation, I
opened it myself by referring to the serious charges
Fransman had made against the native teacher here, and
the great surprise and grief I had felt on hearing them.
Each of those charges, I said, I wished to be thoroughly
searched into, in order that the innocence or guilt of
Johannes might be clearly established. At this point
Fransman said he wished to see Johannes alone, "that
he might understand the man himself:" and both
chiefs desired that whilst they should converse with him,

I would withdraw, adding that if it were found necessary for me to be present, I should be called. As I had reason to suspect that there was some sinister design in the request, I resolved not to comply, and instantly said that as Fransman had brought to me accusations against Johannes, and as Johannes was appointed to his special office by the missionary, I must be present at his examination.

Whilst Johannes himself steadily denied any knowledge of the things laid to his charge, Fransman addressed him at some length and in great anger. But all present could see there was no real cause for the exhibition of such a temper; and Abraham, perceiving its unreasonableness, stepped in as moderator, saying to his brother chieftain, " Speak softly; speak according to justice," when Fransman desisted. After a little conversation amongst themselves, the two chiefs said they " found nothing " in Johannes: they acknowledged that he was " guiltless," and added, " He is now free; we have done with him." I therefore arose and said, as they had discovered no guilt in Johannes, and had pronounced him free, that was all I wished to know. I had no desire to be present during their examination into other matters, and I would therefore leave the council, which I then did.

At three several times the chiefs wished me to leave; but this I steadily refused to do whilst the case of Johannes was pending, and I am now particularly thankful that I resolved on remaining till that was settled.

'Amas.—Late last night, 20th, we reached this place, where our native teacher, Job Witbooi, is stationed.

The whole of this morning and afternoon I was engaged meeting the members and candidates, sixty-three in number, and after the incessant labour I had at Nieuwe Fontein, and the excitement and anxiety connected with the visit of the chiefs, I felt much exhausted. The people here are in a distressing state of want, in consequence of the long-continued drought, and I think I never saw our native teacher so emaciated. The Lord has visited the people literally with " cleanness of teeth," and our native teacher himself stated that, for a considerable time, he had tasted absolutely nothing in the shape of food. The only thing by which he had kept soul and body together for several months was by eating the gum of the mimosa. " But," as he emphatically added, " that is not living, Sir !" Yet, in these days of famine, he has omitted none of the usual services, though I cannot imagine how he has had the strength to continue them. Nearly all the other people of the place have long fared no better than himself; and the only mitigation of their sufferings is an occasional recourse to the pipe, which is literally the shin-bone of a sheep, into which a few leaves of the tobacco-plant are thrust, by inhaling the fumes of which, the keenness of hunger's edge is blunted, and rendered in some degree tolerable.

Wednesday, 25th.—This evening we reached 'Harrees, but were grieved to find only a few houses, instead of the large number we had expected. We were consoled, however, by witnessing an answer to our prayers in one respect. The sky was covered with dark and massive clouds, a delightful prospect in this dry and burning land : the red lightnings darted and glared incessantly from every quarter of the darkened heavens; whilst the thunder burst in rapid and terrific peals over our heads, so that our waggon and the very earth quailed under its reverberations. Our only habitation was our waggon: yet we felt no alarm, knowing the Lord of the tempest to be our defence. At length the thick clouds were rent asunder, and the danger from the electric fluid diminished by the descent of floods of rain upon the scorched and thirsty earth. Our hearts beat high with gratitude and delight, and we were lulled into a sweet slumber by the music of its descent upon the tilt-sail of our waggon during the whole night. This morning I called together the few persons on the place, and held a short service with them. Here I found Hans Jager, one of the chief's Raadsmen, who, being somewhat turbulent, had made himself offensive to the chief, who had ordered him to be held down by four men and flogged. I found him scarcely able to move yet, from the severity of the strokes he had received; expressed my sorrow at his sufferings, and gave him some friendly counsel as to the future. He seemed pleased at the call, and appeared to receive my counsel in a right spirit.

Friday, 27th.—Reached home at noon to-day after an absence of rather more than three weeks, and was exceedingly thankful to find that abundant rains have fallen all around the neighbourhood of the station. There are very few families remaining, most having left with their sheep and cattle, in order to prevent the new grass being consumed as soon as it appears. For the same reason the chief has removed to a distance of about twenty miles from the station: but in six or eight weeks he will return, and numbers of people from all sides will flock to the place.

After remaining some days at home, the fewness of the people affording a good opportunity, I again left on a visit to Blydeverwachting.

After remaining nine days, I again left and reached home on the 14th instant. Since the late rains, our journeys have been enlivened by vast numbers of springboks, gemsboks, zebras, quaggas, and ostriches, which all in turn inspect and then take fright at our waggon, as it travels slowly over the grassy plains. In addition to the jackals, wolves, and tigers that are already numerous, wild dogs and lions will before long follow in the rear, all " seeking their meat " from the beautiful and harmless animals of the plains. About six months since, springboks being abundant, two large male lions appeared, and were shot, not far from the station, one of the skins of which was brought to me as a present.

On Tuesday, April 28th, I left home on horseback about an hour and a half before sunset, travelled about fifteen miles, and slept outside a village where some of our people were " lying," with the intention of being some distance on the way when we should resume our journey in the morning. At sunrise I arose and, after a drink of milk, left. It proved to be a very hot close day, thunder filling the air, and our poor horses being covered with sweat, as if lathered all over with soapsuds, the hot steam from their bodies made it almost unbearable to the riders. At noon we offsaddled at a large shallow " vlei," or rain pool. Here I ate about an ounce of cold mutton, and drank all the water in my bottle. We derived a little shelter from a low bush, beneath which we rested, and where I scribbled a few pencil notes of my journey. After a long rest, owing to the oppressiveness of the weather, we left at half-past three, expecting to reach 'Amas at a little after sunset. We travelled on till dark, when, finding from the position of the moon that we were going altogether in a wrong direction, we resolved to remain where we were till the light of the next day should enable us to judge more accurately of our position. My lips were parched with thirst, my head felt twice its usual weight; we had no water for tea, for, being certain of reaching 'Amas by about dark, we had omitted to replenish our water bottle at the " vlei." I had no inclination to eat, and was so wearied out that I was unable to do anything but lie down just as I was, on the bare ground, without making loose my kaross. After a time, finding the ground rather cold with the dew that had fallen, I aroused myself and attempted to loosen my kaross, but in the act of stooping I was seized with a fit of vomiting, after which I obtained some relief. On spreading my kaross and preparing for the night, another fit of vomiting seized me, when exhausted I lay, and wrapped myself in my kaross, and soon fell into a dreamy slumber, my mouth dry and hot, and my whole body burning with fever.

During my slumber I imagined some one bringing me a vessel of frothy milk just drawn from the cow; but before I could partake of the 'delicious draught, a slight shivering coldness, accompanied by a fit of retching, aroused me from my slumbers. Several times during the night I was awoke by the same cause, and sometimes the retching was very distressing. And it was specially disagreeable to be obliged to sleep again without a drop of water to quench the burning thirst. At daybreak I arose, when we were both confirmed in our belief that we were in the wrong path, and travelling on the road leading from 'Amas to Blydeverwachting. Just as the sun appeared above the horizon we mounted our horses to retrace our steps. My head was light and dizzy, for I had eaten only an ounce of food since the noon of the previous day, and that had all been ejected; and as my somewhat wild horse bore me along, I was so weak as to be scarcely able to sit him. For safety's sake I directed my man to travel in front, my horse being exceedingly apt to shy, and I felt that, should he do so at such a time, I should certainly be thrown.

For two hours we travelled hard over a good road, and were then just as much at a loss to know the exact position of 'Amas as at starting. We had just resolved on going about an hour's ride further to a village, the dust of which we had seen to our left on the previous afternoon, when my man, who had eyes like a telescope, discovered some oxen. Before I could make out the oxen, he had made a more important discovery, and exclaimed, "I see a man!" At once we rode to him, and to our astonishment and joy we found it to be one of our Nisbett Bath people, who, with his family and a few others, had come to this neighbourhood for the sake of grass and water for their flocks and herds. He directed us to his father's place, which we found, after about a ten minutes' ride, along the sandy bed of a small periodical river. Here our first call was for water, not having tasted a drop since the previous midday; and whilst we yet sat in our saddles, a bamboos full was brought; but

the glands of my throat were so swollen with feverish-
ness and long-continued thirst, that I was not able to
swallow a drop. So I ordered my little copper travelling .
kettle to be filled and put on the fire, in which, as soon
as it boiled, I made some weak tea, with copious draughts
of which myself and my companion were soon refreshed.
As soon as that repast was finished, I stretched myself
on my kaross on a clean mat laid by my friends under
a shady shrub, and slept soundly for more than an hour;
then, calling for water, shaved and washed under the
privacy afforded by some bushes, and felt unspeakably
restored and refreshed.

Friday.—Having slept out for the third night in succession, I was roused by the galloping of my horses,
which Adam was bringing to me in all haste, and was
greeted with the howling of some wild beast; and on
asking Adam what it was, he answered, looking very
serious, "That's a tiger, Sir." From the sound of his
voice the animal was certainly not more than three
hundred yards distant; so I said, "Then the sooner
we're off the better." My horse was soon saddled and
bridled, but as Adam had not only his own horse to
saddle and bridle, but the pack-horse to make ready, he
was longer, and meantime I kept a look-out. However,
the beast never left cover so as to show himself, though
he kept up a continuous howl; and when we wished him
good morning and rode away, he still kept up his
" morning carol," though he neither alarmed nor gratified us by a sight of his person. At about eight we
arrived at the Ky 'Kaap River, took our simple but
refreshing breakfast, left at nine, and reached Nieuwe
Fontein at ten o'clock.

May 2nd.—At half-past two p.m. yesterday we left for Stof Kraal, Elias's place, and came by the new path he has made. At about five we offsaddled for a short time, and then resumed, riding on and on till we were stiff' and out of patience, wondering when we should recognise any part of the country I had previously seen in travelling to this place. Nothing appearing, we travelled on till about ten o'clock, when we came in sight of a hill, beneath the shoulder of which I believed Stof Kraal to lie. Yet we saw and heard nothing that could lead us to suppose that any one was living there. " Here," I said, " we will offsaddle for the night; " and just when our karosses were spread, and we were ready to sleep, we heard a cow lowing in the distance, from which we concluded the village to be a little further forward. Worn out with fatigue, we soon fell asleep; but whilst it was yet very early in the morning, and dark, the voice of prayer was heard amongst the grass and low bushes, the first real indication we had of the vicinity of human beings; and in such a place it sounded peculiarly grateful, when neither missionary nor native assistant was in their midst; for by hearing it under such circumstances I was persuaded that prayer was engaged in for the love of it, and not made to attract the attention of the missionary, whom they supposed to be at his station a hundred and fifty miles away, but to gain the ear of God. At sunrise all the bustle of a native village was heard—the lowing of calves and cows, the bleating of flocks, the barking of dogs, and the shouting of men—a perfect contrast to the stillness of the night. Our horses were soon saddled, when, riding up to one or two men we saw near the village, we found it was not the residence of Elias, but only a cattle post belonging to him and his people, he and they having come nearer than Stof Kraal, and being now at Melkboom River. So after a good draught of milk, which we took as we sat on our horses, and saluting all 'the people at hand without telling them that we had encamped outside their village, we rode forward, and in an hour and a half reached the place—a nest of green grass, and green bushes in abundance, encircled with high and noble mountains, whose sides and tops are clothed with verdure, the river running along the base of the mountains. Late last night, as we travelled, a zebra from a high krantz, hearing the clatter of our horses' hoofs amongst the stones, saluted his supposed mates with a shrill short whistle, which I should not have recognised as the neighing of a zebra but for my man. At Elias's a new house was awaiting my arrival, clean, comfortable, and orderly, qualities that were always highly acceptable to me, never more so than when among the natives.

Sunday, May 3rd.—A day that the Lord has made. This is true in the general sense, but also in its special signification ; for, being without a chapel, in consequence of this not being a fixed out-station, and also, and chiefly, because of the recent coming of the people, we should have felt it very severe to assemble to worship under the beams of a burning, cloudless sun. But God mercifully " covered the heavens with clouds," so that we were enabled to worship in comfort, screened by the cooling canopy. My subjects for the day were " the Ten Talents " and " the General Resurrection." At night we assembled by firelight in our circular but roofless chapel, and had some conversation with twenty-eight persons who had long been candidates for baptism and membership. Having been under the instruction of Elias already, this was immediately preparatory to the administration of the rite.

Monday, 4th.—This morning, at the close of the service, I baptized twenty-eight adults and thirteen children, and married four couples. Afterwards I met thirty-one members in class, which kept me closely engaged till half-past eleven. After a short rest, and taking some refreshment, the day being cool, clouded, and slightly rainy, we saddled up, and at half-past twelve left, and, the horses travelling briskly, we reached Nieuwe Fontein at nine o'clock p.m. Many had retired for the night, but hearing of our arrival they aroused themselves, and by half-past ten our new house was constructed, and by eleven we lay down to rest.

Anxious to reach home, after holding a morning service at this place, and attending to sundry Society matters, we again left for 'Amas, Johannes accompanying us on the new road he had made for the first two hours, when, having come through the " poort," or opening between the shoulders of a hill, we reached the great waggon path. This road is much shorter than the old path, as we reached 'Amas in five hours, though for the first two hours we only travelled at good walking pace, to adapt ourselves to the rate of our companion, who rode on oxback. Reached Job's place at seven, and as we were unexpectedly soon, the house was not made. But by the diligence of several native women, one was very soon extemporised over one of the hardest and best floors I have seen, and before long the village was all silent and wrapped in slumber.

Thursday, 7th.—I was much pleased by observing the great improvement in the singing. Held a service in the morning, met the members, and had a conversation with Job respecting several Society matters, and examined the school.

Friday, 8th.—After holding the morning service, and meeting the remaining members, we started for home at half-past nine. The sun was not hot, mid-winter approaching, a fresh and rather cold wind was blowing from the south, and our horses, full of mettle, were ready to scour over the plain at good speed; so we gave them the rein, and after travelling at a rattling pace for some time, rejoicing in their might, we reined in a little and took it more gently, when all at once my man exclaimed: " Sir, I see a waggon !" Having on many occasions before had proof of his superior vision, I could not disbelieve ; but after deliberately gazing in tho direction to which he pointed, all I could do was to confess that I did not see it. Once more our horses resumed a rapid pace, shortly after which the man exclaimed : " It looks just like master's new waggon." This I thought out of the question; besides, it seemed impossible to discriminate with so much nicety what I was as yet unable to detect at all. As we drew nearer, he insisted that it must be my new waggon ; but I felt sure that no native would venture to ask for its use ; or, if he should do so, that Mrs. Ridsdale would never comply with such a request. Still, our horses advancing at a smart canter, once more he said : " I see a man :" and soon after, " I see a maid with a child in her arms." I could now unmistakably see the waggon ; but all the rest I had to take on trust. Meantime I was extremely puzzled and perplexed. Again he cried, " I see Martha," our servant, " and master's child." Every moment brought us nearer, and the event proved the truth of Adam's statement, and the astonishing accuracy of his vision, even at a distance at which my own was perfectly useless. As we neared the spot I saw all as he had done long before, and at length my wife was seen to descend from the waggon, that she might welcome her husband in the heart of the desert. Whilst yet the mystery was unsolved as to what had brought her to such a spot, I ordered the man to take off saddles, and bridles, and pack from the horses, and liberate them at once, when at their own leisure they grazed by the way, making towards the fountain on the station, yet many miles distant, and we heard and saw nothing more of them till they were required for another journey.

Meantime, my first anxiety was to know what had induced my wife to venture on so novel an expedition. That was soon learnt. The losing of our path, and the severe attack of sickness that had followed the exposure to the terrible heat to which we had been subjected, which we had fondly imagined would never be known till our return, had come to the knowledge of my wife several days before. Next morning she despatched a man to the plains to seek the oxen, and whilst waiting for their coming, a selection of medicines was made from the medicine chest, and, all being ready, she started in the direction by which she expected her husband to return, ready to minister to his needs should she succeed in finding him. For two nights she tra-velled over the plains, a sharp look-out being kept by

the men for our return.   On the third morning, fearing
that we might have travelled by another course homeward, she commenced the return ; and in the early
afternoon of that day, having outspanned on a gradual
ascent of the road, all eyes were directed to the quarter
from which they hoped we might possibly come; and
Jan Rammard, the waggon-driver, scrutinising with
eagle eye every object in the distance, at length cried :
" I think I see a dust, mistress ; " a few minutes enabled him to speak with certainty.   Awhile he kept
silent, and then once more he exclaimed : " I see three
horses ; it must be master."   We in time came near
enough for all to see for themselves, and soon we were
in the midst of them ; the kettle was boiling on the fire,
tea was awaiting us in the midst of the wilderness, and
so unexpected a pleasure was greatly enjoyed.   The
medicines might have been " cast to the dogs ; " and
finding us well and in excellent spirits, all the solicitudes
of my brave wife were dismissed and her heart was
at rest.

On July 28th Mr. Macleod, whom I had found invaluable as a schoolmaster, and as one I could always
leave with confidence in charge of the station, when
obliged to be absent, left for Cape Town, chiefly to
obtain supplies for himself ; but I availed myself of this
opportunity of sending off the missionary subscriptions
of the Great Namaquas of my circuit for the two past
years 1845 and 1846.   They consisted of thirty-two
oxen, two cows, two calves, four hundred and ninety-
eight sheep and goats, besides ostrich feathers, antelope
skins, ox hides, samboks, bambooses, &c., which would
all have to be disposed of to the Dutch farmers along

the road, or in the market at Cape Town; contributions which I think highly creditable to our people.

August 4th.—Mr. Haddy, his wife and son, reached our station from Damaraland, having left his mission with Jonker Afrikaner two months ago. Notwithstanding the length and tedium of the journey, they are all in the enjoyment of good health, and anticipate resuming their work as soon as they can return to the station. But the length of the journey involves a terrible expenditure of precious time. After a rest of only one week, they bade us adieu amidst our good wishes and prayers, and proceeded to Cape Town.

About this time Frederiek Buys visited the station with his wife and family, and their provisions failing on the road, he felt that his only resource was an earnest prayer to Almighty God that He would send some wild animal within the range of his gun. For some time he and his family were in great distress for want of food; but waiting confidently for the answer to his prayer, and scrutinising every object on the plains with his keen vision, he at length detected in the distance a zebra. Approaching, by creeping on his hands and knees, and availing himself of the shelter of any bush that might occur between himself and the animal, he at length came within what he considered safe shooting distance; when, touching the trigger, the game was struck and fell, and at once his heart bounded with joy because relief had come to his family, a relief which was manifestly an answer to prayer. It was a young animal, in good condition, and unusually delicious. He arrived at the station during my own dinner time, bringing, as a *souvenir*, a small portion of zebra flesh; so, setting aside the mutton off which I was dining, and which was an everlasting dish, I partook of the zebra flesh instead, partly as a rarity, but also because of its own juicy and excellent nature.

To-day, September 25th, I had some conversation with Frederick Buys, whom I appointed nearly two years since to hold services amongst a number of Bushmen. After some encouraging signs of the blessing of the Lord on his efforts, and many discouraging circumstances, those hapless Bushmen threw off all restraint, resumed their former habits, and are now scattered in all directions. During his residence amongst them one died, who, previously to his last sickness, had become enlightened in some measure, and manifested earnest desires for salvation. After much and patient instruction, Frederick thought there was hope in his death; and this was a source of much consolation to him, for it proved to him that though, owing to their extreme ignorance and to the wildness of their habits, they are difficult to reclaim, even Bushmen are included amongst " the redeemed of the Lord." Our conversation to-day related chiefly to his being stationed amongst the Velschoen Draagers. They have been regularly visited by Elias Rolfe, from his outpost, and it is not long since I baptized twelve persons who had been candidates for many months; but occasional visits, and such services as they have had, have only awakened desires for constant instruction, and fresh requests have recently reached me from the chief. Frederick Buys, being no longer required by the Bushmen, is now at my disposal; and, as he is perfectly willing, I have resolved to send him. His wife is like-minded, and desirous to be engaged in the work of the Lord. I have engaged to meet him ten days hence at our most distant outpost, that together we may see the chief of the Velschoen Draagers, preparatory to his appointment to reside with him and his people.

Sunday, 27th.—In the afternoon I held a love-feast, when some very satisfactory and interesting statements were made. Amongst those who spoke was Frederick Buys, who said, in anticipation of his being appointed to labour amongst the Velschoen Draagers, that he was willing to go wherever the Lord should direct; and that if he were certain that he should meet with death itself in the execution of his Christian duty, he should not for a moment hesitate: his purpose was fixed. This was not the effervescence of youthful zeal, but the matured and calm determination of a man of forty, who has a wife and many children. I was rejoiced to hear so many testify of the grace of God, some of whom are the seals of the late Rev. E. Cook's ministry.

Monday, October 5th.—At Nieuwe Fontein, nearly the whole day was employed in meeting the members. I had a sorrowful task to perform in the expulsion of fourteen members who had disgraced their character and religion by dancing according to their former custom. So severe a stroke I never before found it necessary to inflict since I came to Africa; but as I have lately heard of many dances amongst the unconverted natives, I was resolved, if possible, to make a salutary impression on the minds of all by cutting off from the church those members who had become the first aggressors. May God give them repentance. At night conducted public worship, and was much moved at the distress manifested by many of the people at the act of discipline just exercised. I have no doubt the effect will be very wholesome.

Tuesday, 6th.—Early this morning we proceeded to Kroon Krantz, where Elias Rolfe, our native assistant, is living. · After passing through some most ruggedly romantic scenery, we reached it soon after dark, though too late for any public service. This was the place at which I had appointed to meet Frederick Buys; and, faithful to his engagement, he had arrived, and came with Elias to meet us on our approach.

7th.—This morning I despatched a messenger to Hendrik Hendriks, the chief of the Velschoen Draagers, to announce our arrival at this place, and to request him to visit us, that I might converse with him on the subject of having a native teacher appointed to labour amongst his people. Held a short service at about eight o'clock, and then met the members; after which I met, in order to converse specially with, the native assistant and class leaders. At night I preached on the humiliation and exaltation of the Redeemer.

8th.—As soon as I arose this morning, which was with the sun, I heard that the chief of the Velschoen Draagers had arrived. At eight o'clock I commenced our missionary meeting, at which, besides myself, Elias Rolfe and Frederick Buys spoke; and at the close twenty sheep and goats were promised, besides four young oxen and a few antelope skins. In the afternoon Mrs. R. met all the females on the place to impart such instruction on their duties in general as they need. At the same time I had a special conversation with the

chief of the Velschoen Draagers, stating that in case of
a teacher being appointed to live with him it would be
necessary to choose such a place of residence as will
afford sufficient grass and water for the sheep and cattle
of a large number of his people, so as to receive constant instruction; that the native teacher must have
unrestrained liberty to visit any portion of his people,
at any time, in order to hold religious services; and
that the chief must not imagine he was conferring any
favour by allowing the Gospel to be admitted amongst
his people, but rather should esteem it a high honour
and unspeakable privilege to have it offered for his own
and his people's acceptance. After he had distinctly
assented to each of these propositions, I stated that it
was determined that Frederick Buys should return
home and make preparations for his new sphere, and in
about a month remove his wife and family, his habitation and goods, to the village of the chief; when, in
order to facilitate his movements, the chief promised to
assist him with a waggon, in addition to his own. In
the evening I held service as usual.

9th.—At about seven o'clock this morning we took
our leave, and proceeded on our journey to Nieuwe
Fontein. Whilst travelling through a wild and rocky
ravine, we came upon a small village, consisting chiefly
of members under the care of Johannes, by whom we
were informed that on the same day that we passed on
our way to Kroon Krantz, a lion was seen on the side
of one of the adjoining mountains, following zebras,
and was supposed still to be in the neighbourhood.
We expected to see his majesty before completing our
journey, but were not permitted to enjoy the privilege.

This is the ninth lion of which we have heard within the last four weeks, an unusual number for this part of the country, where powder and lead are so abundant. Two were shot by the chief's sons about three weeks since. We arrived at Nieuwe Fontein late at night.

10th.—During the short service this morning a most gracious influence descended, and a spirit of mourning seemed to be imparted to all. One man remained after the congregation was dismissed, overwhelmed with grief on account of those who had fallen and been cut off from membership with the church. He could only sob and weep; utterance was completely taken away by the depth of his emotion. About an hour after I went out to take a solitary walk along the side of the rocky mountain that towers above the village, when I heard indistinctly a subdued voice of mourning and supplication. At first I could not discover any one, but at length saw amidst the loose rocks an individual prostrate on his hands and knees, with his head bowed to the very dust, pouring out his soul in prayer. His hat was placed on a large stone by his side, a little circumstance, but still one that pleasingly indicated the reverence of his spirit. As I passed softly on through the sand, lest I should disturb him in his devotions, I was not perceived, but my heart was filled with thankfulness to see that God's Spirit was producing the right effect on the minds of those who still retained their place as members of the church. This humiliation amongst the people I regarded as a sign of the speedy restoration and exaltation of those who have fallen, and I rejoiced to think of the words of Eliphaz: " He woundeth, and His hands make whole." In about half an hour I passed again by the same route, on my return to the village, and, to my surprise, I found the man in precisely the same position, but praying still more earnestly, and in tones so imploring and pathetic as quite affected me. It was then only that I discovered him to be the same person that was so overcome with sorrow in the chapel at the morning service. I expounded a portion of Scripture again at night.

Sunday, 11th.—The early prayer meeting was held as usual at sunrise. At about 9 a.m. I preached on Psalm li. 14, with special reference to those on whom it had been necessary to exercise discipline, and during the service a solemn and fixed attention was manifested. In the afternoon I spoke on the influences of the Holy Spirit. The services of the day were closed by a prayer meeting at night.

12th.—Having published during the previous week that I should hold the missionary meeting on this day, I held it accordingly. It proved the most productive of any missionary meeting I had held on this place; for, out of a congregation of about eighty people, we had promised six young oxen, four cows, five calves, thirty young goats, five sheep, besides a few ostrich feathers, antelope skins, shoe soles and samboks. Such a degree of liberality I had never witnessed in so small a congregation. In the afternoon we left, and travelled homeward by a new path which the people were still busily engaged in making, in order to shorten, as much as possible, the long journeys we must take before we can reach them.

15th.—This morning we reached Nisbett Bath, having travelled hard since Monday. In the afternoon I had an opportunity of conversing with our chief, when I

s

spoke to him faithfully of his rejection of the Gospel, and of the pain it gave me to see him unaffected, while so many of his own, and of surrounding tribes, had received it to their salvation. I afterwards learnt that several of the members had been expostulating with him on the same subject. One old man, Old Hendrik, said : " It was you who first requested to have the Gospel, but now that it is come you receive it not. Many are nourished by it, but you are hungered. It is just as if you had slaughtered an ox, and distributed it amongst us until it was all given away, and you yourself had nothing to eat."

26th.—This morning, at nine o'clock, our missionary meeting commenced, and though I feared the contributions would be small, my fears were not realised. The contributions are, in fact, larger than I have ever received at any meeting held on the station since my arrival; a success which is perhaps chiefly attributable to the spirited, earnest, and convincing speeches delivered by three of our aged and leading members. On this occasion were promised eight young oxen, two cows, seven calves, seventy-five sheep and goats, five bambooses, besides samboks and skins of wild animals. Three or four years ago it was no great sacrifice for these people to give an ox or sheep occasionally, when no other demands were made on their possessions; but now that so much traffic is carried on in the land by traders, and wants are felt that were never before experienced, and which have to be supplied by exchanging their sheep and cattle for goods of European manufacture, one sheep or ox is worth as much as eight or ten were a few years ago.

November 5th.—At four p.m. I mounted my horse, and, accompanied by my man, commenced my journey to Blydeverwachting. With the exception of a short interval of rest, during which we turned our horses to graze, we travelled till half-past ten, intending when we left home to travel all the night, as we had heard of lions being in the vast plain across which we had to travel, and we deemed it better to keep in motion. The weather, however, was so extremely oppressive, that we seemed unable to travel farther, and I felt that, lions or no lions, I must sleep. So, hoping that if they were anywhere in the plains, they might be a long distance from us, we offsaddled, boiled our kettle, drank some tea, and, committing ourselves to the care of Him Who " neither slumbers nor sleeps," spread our karosses upon the sand, and lay down for the night. For some hours I slept soundly, when I was awaked by the howl of some wild beast. Not knowing what it was, I called to Adam, who was half a dozen yards off. I had to call several times before he was aroused, when, suddenly starting up on all fours, his kaross hanging down to the ground on all sides, " Yes, Sir," said he, in rather an alarmed way, and looking very much like a wild beast himself. " What is that sound ? " I said. After listening a moment or two, again it was heard. " That's a wolf, Sir." " O, then, lie down and go to sleep," I said, which he did very quickly; after which we had no further disturbance. At about four o'clock the day broke, and we resumed our journey till about seven o'clock, when, the sun being very hot, we dismounted at the 'Amse River, where we obtained an abundant supply of delicious water, on digging about a foot deep in the loose sand of the bed of the river, boiled our kettle, and refreshed ourselves with breakfast. As it was insufferably hot, we were compelled to pass the remainder of the day under the shade of the aged mimosas that line the banks of the river. However, being anxious to proceed, at four p.m. we remounted our steeds, though the earth was still glowing with intense heat, and, after travelling three hours more, reached the Afrikaners about an hour after sunset.

7th.—Held a short service this morning at eight, and then met all the members on the place. In the evening I held another short service. During the day five waggons, filled with people from the surrounding parts, arrived in the village, together with a number of others, mounted and on foot, messengers having been despatched to announce that the missionary had come.

Monday, 9th.—Yesterday being the Sabbath, I baptized eight infants, and preached morning and evening. After the latter service I met about thirty members, when I was completely exhausted with the heat and labour.

This morning, at about seven, the horn was blown as a summons for the people to the missionary meeting. Three of our principal men addressed the congregation besides myself, and the results were very encouraging, surpassing those of the preceding years. On this occasion were contributed two oxen, one cow, two calves, forty-nine sheep and goats, one hundred and eleven ostrich feathers, and nine shillings in money, which the owner presented " *if it was of any use,*" for it was of no use to him in a country where no coin was current. At the close of this meeting I publicly united ten couples in Christian marriage. They were all elderly people who have long lived together as husbands and wives, but, being now admitted into the Church of Christ, they renewed and confirmed their previous engagement on Christian principles.

10th.—Yesterday at four p.m. I took my farewell of the people at Blydeverwachting; but we soon had cause to regret having left so soon, as the burning sun glaring full upon our faces from the west, and the hot winds issuing from the same quarter and blowing upon us as from a furnace, produced violent headache, and such a feeling of suffocation as was scarcely to be endured. On resting and drinking copious draughts of weak tea we felt refreshed; and in order to escape the sun's intense heat the next day, we travelled hard almost the whole night, and at a quarter to nine this morning we reached home, having been much longer on the journey than we were in general, owing to the close and suffocating state of the weather. How strange it seems! but in this climate, especially after a night of travel, we fear the approach of the sun to the horizon, more than we should fear the approach of a demon, so deadly is the exhaustion it produces.

In the last month of this year I wrote to the missionary secretaries, and as the letter presents a general view of the mission, a few extracts from it may suitably close the year 1846.

" For the last several months we have had at least five hundred persons resident on the station, and on this, as on every former occasion, when there has been sufficient rain and pasturage to allow of their collecting in any considerable numbers, we have been delighted at the evident *influence the Word* has produced on their minds. The most interested and earnest attention is depicted on every countenance, whilst frequently their dark eyes glisten with delight, or express the serious concern and solemnity of their feelings, as the various truths of the Gospel are unfolded to their view and applied to their consciences. And when the services of the sanctuary are closed, they may frequently be seen sitting in groups near the chapel, conversing together on such parts of the sermon as have most particularly arrested their attention. It is very refreshing to myself and Mrs. Ridsdale *to meet our classes*, as then we see most decidedly their improvement in grace and knowledge. The references there made to the instruction that has been administered either in sermons, or in the regular morning exposition of Scripture, are often very intelligent, and sometimes remarkably striking : so that though we often go to those means with a feeling of languor and exhaustion, we often return refreshed and quickened in spirit. Never did we experience more pure spiritual enjoyment, even in our delightful class meetings in England, than we do whilst listening to the simple and artless, but sincere and intelligent, Christian experience of many of our Namaqua members. We feel that they are ' fellow heirs, and of the same body, and partakers of His promise in Christ by the Gospel.'

" Our *Sabbath worship* begins at early dawn, for at sunrise the natives hold a prayer meeting conducted by one of themselves. In the morning and evening I preach, beginning early in the former case, and late in the latter, to avoid as much as possible the great heat of the day; and in the afternoon the Sunday school is held, which is attended by old and young, and by the members generally, both male and female. All the drudgery of learning to read is omitted on that day, and is reserved for the week days. Those who belong to the Bible class read the chapter from which the morning text is taken, and are then examined on the sermon ; whilst those who are not far advanced sit in small circles, with a teacher appointed to each, who endeavours to impress on their minds those parts of the sermon he can best remember or best converse on ; and at the close of this part of the school duties, a short account of the lives and deaths of pious children is read. In this way the *Memoir of Christopher Dove* has been read, and various selections from the *Child's Magazine*, &c., &c. By this course of instruction the Sabbath school is rendered as profitable to the children as the other services are to the adult hearers, and it is equally appreciated by young and old.

" In taking a view of the circuit generally I am much pleased and encouraged at the advancement that has been made, not only by the Gospel, but *by civilisation*, its natural accompaniment and result. In various parts of the circuit we see ' temples of His grace ' standing that have been raised by men who build nothing for themselves, who are content to dwell in houses made of light reed matting, and who are naturally averse to everything laborious. Yet their chapels have cost them much labour and expense too, and have been erected without any assistance from the society, or even from the missionary, save that which arises from his encouragement and approbation. True, they are not buildings to be scrutinised by the eye of the architect, but they are, nevertheless, decent and seemly, and are alike honourable to the judgment and ability of those who have engaged in their erection. In several parts of the circuit, at the expense of great labour, new roads have been made, and old ones shortened and improved. We have read to them the language of the prophet: ' Prepare ye the way of the Lord, make straight in the desert a highway for our God ; ' and in a very literal sense they have done so. By these improvements the circuit is considerably diminished in its extent, and we are enabled to reach our most distant outposts with much more comfort than formerly, and with a considerable saving of time. The *dress also* and general habits of the people have become greatly altered for the better. The native costume is entirely laid aside on the principal station, and by the majority at the outposts. The change is, in many instances, the result of Christian principle, for we have laboured to make them perceive and feel the connection between a demoralised appearance and immoral conduct. Many have, therefore, acted in this matter from a conviction of its propriety, and of the incongruity with their Christian character of their former indecent and filthy habits."

CHAPTER VI.

JANUARY, 1847.—Early in this month Mr. Macleod returned in safety from his long journey to the Cape, having left at the end of July, and being obliged to travel slowly, in consequence of having the missionary subscriptions with him for 1844 and 1845. The amount obtained for the Society was as follows : For oxen, £55 4s. ; sheep and goats, £110 18s. ; skins, £7 16s. 6d. ; ostrich feathers, &c., £19 1s. 9d. : making a total of £193 0s. 3d. The expenses amounted only to £2 8s. 6d., leaving as clear contributions the sum of £190 11s. 9d. for the two years. This is a truly noble amount, considering all the circumstances of the case.

Since the sale of the above subscriptions, the meetings for 1846 have also been completed, and have proved even more productive than either of the former years. The total amount of things promised is : 232 sheep and goats, twenty-two oxen, seven cows, two heifers, twenty calves, six bambooses, twenty-two pairs of shoe soles, six skins, and 138 ostrich feathers ; which, at a moderate calculation, I estimate will bring in £140 or £150 for the one year. These very liberal contributions proceed not from a people who are living in abundance, but from those who, during a great part of the year, are in extreme need, and who often lead what appears to us, who have no such powers of endurance, a life of extreme want and hunger. And, moreover, they are all contributions voluntarily offered, no pressure of any kind being employed, save that of the facts and arguments adduced in their missionary meetings; and that, chiefly by leading men of their own tribe, who speak from experience, and who can appeal to the people themselves as witnesses to the truth of what they say.

When I consider the success of the Gospel amongst this people, the character of the work, and the many decided and practical proofs that are furnished of its genuineness, and yet the feebleness and comparative inefficiency of the agents by whose instrumentality so large a portion of it is accomplished, I am constrained to say, with the late Rev. Edward Cook, and as the only adequate explanation: "This is a people eminently prepared of the Lord."

February.—I recently received a copy of the new Stations of ministers, as settled by the late Conference, from which I find that I am appointed to Wynberg, a very salubrious suburb of Cape Town. This appointment was a complete surprise to myself, as I was not aware of any probability of a change; and yet I could not but regard it as providential, and hail it with thankfulness; for, owing to the deadly languor and exhaustion I suffer for about nine months of the year, arising from the intense heat of the climate, and also from the immense amount of labour that must necessarily fall on a missionary, where only one is appointed to a circuit of such vast extent, I have long felt that a change of station was absolutely necessary.

Long before the copy of the Stations arrived, Mrs. R. and myself had said between ourselves that we should be compelled to request a change of station on that account alone.

We were now in the heat of the summer, and six months would yet have to elapse before we could travel to the Cape; and I found, as the summer heats continued to try me, that the change was not a moment too soon, and that God's good providence had arranged for timely relief before the entire failure of health should disqualify me for further service. For a long time to come we deemed it advisable to give our people no information as to our removal from the station, as it might have an unsettling and injurious effect.

March.—We have now a larger number of people on the station than we have ever had before,—at the lowest calculation seven hundred; consequently, we have some difficulty in finding accommodation for our overflowing congregations, especially on the Sabbath. Our chapel, which will hold only about three hundred and seventy people, is far too small, and for several weeks past it has been necessary to have the waggons drawn out, and the waggon-house cleared every week for the convenience of a separate Sabbath congregation; so that whilst I am conducting service in the chapel, Mr. Macleod occupies the waggon-house for the same purpose. Both, however, are insufficient, and many who cannot find admittance to either, unable to endure the heat of the sun, are compelled to return to their homes.

March 10th.—For the last three weeks some of our native teachers have been on a visit to the station, for the purpose of receiving some special instruction.

About two hours every morning I devoted to their improvement in reading and writing, as they are far from
being either skilful readers or penmen; and I have
generally spent two hours every afternoon in giving
them instruction in the principal doctrines of revelation.
The period of their stay was far too limited, as they
themselves felt, but it was as much as could be secured at
once; and although it was so short, I am confident they
returned to their out stations with clearer views, with
quickened and improved intellect, and I trust with
improved piety. One good effect of their visit has been
to give them a more humbling view of their own weakness and inability than they had before; for now, without exception, they confess that "they are not worthy
to speak to their fellow-men in the name of the Lord."
They are not, however, unduly discouraged by this new
sense of their insufficiency for the work they have to
engage in; but seem resolved to use such power as they
possess for the glory of their Lord. Though their
knowledge is necessarily exceedingly limited, yet they
are destitute of neither gifts nor graces, for to some
extent the Spirit of Christ has enriched them with both.
They have all a sound experience, and a ready utterance:
some of them are very striking orators, and a powerful
unction often attends their exhortations; whilst under
the moving, melting, pathetic prayers of David Afrikaner, I have sometimes witnessed such effects produced, as I have never seen under the prayers of any
other person. They are humble-minded and sincerely
pious men, and I can say of them in general, with a
most comforting assurance: "I have confidence in you
in all things."

For some time past the number of people on the place has been steadily increasing; and this morning I went round the village, and estimate that, at this time, there must be nearly nine hundred people; a very large number for any one place, especially when their subsistence is derived almost entirely from the milk and flesh of their flocks and herds. We have now, at the lowest calculation, ten or eleven thousand sheep and goats, and upwards of a thousand head of cattle, including milch cows and draught and slaughter oxen, belonging to the people, and all dependent on one fountain, and on the pasturage surrounding the station.

March 15.—About this time I was called up very early one morning by a member of William Bukas's family to go and if possible relieve him, for he was very ill, and suffering from great pain. For some years past our house had been the constant resort of the people in their ailments, and might be regarded as the dispensary of the village. Not only was "advice given gratis," but medicine also, so that we were pretty extensively patronised. Dr. Graham's *Family Medicine* was our constant reference; the ailments treated usually yielded to simple means, and the people had great confidence in medicines that almost infallibly cured. From the information now given concerning William, I felt sure that internal inflammation was going on, and I promptly concluded that the bleeding of the patient was necessary. But such an operation I had never performed; however, dismissing the messenger with the promise of a speedy visit, I looked into my " directions for bleeding," and at once prepared my bandages and pledget, and, taking my lancet, I proceeded in confidence to the house.   There I found the sufferer sitting on the ground, grasping a couple of thongs made fast to the bamboo frame-work of the house, and writhing with agony, the members of the family standing concernedly around.   I rolled up the shirt sleeve of the sufferer, tied the bandage around his arm, and soon succeeded in getting a very excellent vein for the instrument.   I introduced the lancet, and immediately a fine jet of blood sprang forth, and having taken a small basin, half full, I applied the pledget, and bound up his arm, with the direction to carry it in a sling for a couple of days, and all would be well.   The bleeding operated like a charm; and to the amazement of the man and his household, the pain immediately ceased, and I heard no more of its return.   My wife sent a few little niceties suitable for an invalid; and to my great delight gradually and slowly my patient gathered strength, and ultimately he was enabled to engage in his usual occupations.   A great sensation was produced amongst the natives, which soon spread far and wide.   On the day following, a young woman appeared, complaining that she felt very poorly, and expressing a strong desire to be bled.   I told her that we never bled any one for trifling ailments, but only in cases of great emergency : she might need a little medicine; and I gave her some to carry away with her : but as to bleeding, I absolutely refused, to her great disappointment!   A week after this a strong young man, about thirty years of age, came to me complaining that he felt very heavy and continually drowsy, and said that he would feel very much obliged to me if I would please to bleed him!   I again expostulated; but in vain.   Still his cry was to be bled.   So I looked at him: I thought, "Well, you are a strong young man, full of blood; to take a little will do you no harm." So I prepared him for the operation, and took a small quantity of blood from him: at which he went home highly delighted, and perhaps feeling less "heavy and drowsy" for the loss.

On the 24th of March, our waggon being prepared, the oxen inspanned, and the people standing around, I embraced the opportunity of reminding them of what I had some time before told them, that an eclipse of the moon would take place on the night of the 31st, explaining, as I had done before, what occasioned it. I also stated that at the commencement of the eclipse Mr. Macleod would ring the station bell, so that they might come out of their houses and watch its progress; and that since they had first been told of this several weeks before its occurrence, that would show them the superiority of knowledge to witchcraft, or any such rubbish. Wishing them farewell, I left for the north-east, and arrived at

Nieuwe Fontein on Saturday evening. Since reaching this place, I have heard of the death of a young man who was on trial for membership. He was killed during a late thunderstorm by a stroke from the electric fluid, which broke his neck, and laid the flesh open to the bone between his shoulders. On the previous day, which was the Sabbath, he had spoken much with his parents and other friends on spiritual things, and on the uncertainty of life; and looking at the setting sun he said: "I do not know whether I shall live to see that sun go down to-morrow." It is very remarkable that on the following afternoon, before sunset, a storm suddenly broke over the place, and whilst he was passing from one house to another, the lightning struck him, and in an instant he was removed from time into eternity.

Tuesday, 30th.—Yesterday, at eight o'clock a.m., I conducted a short public service, and was afterwards engaged for three hours in meeting the male members, so that it was noon before I could obtain any cessation from my labour. This following the services of the Sabbath makes the toil very severe in this debilitating climate. In the afternoon Mrs. Ridsdale assisted me by meeting the females.

On the night of March 31st we had a fine view of the eclipse of the moon, to which I had previously called the attention of our people on the station, and to which I had, since commencing the journey, more especially referred our people who were travelling with us; particularly Old Tonnis, our waggon-driver, who had been a *toovenaar* or wizard. I took some pains to explain how it was occasioned; for I was very anxious to uproot all his superstitions with regard to witchcraft, and to make him feel the superiority of real wisdom and knowledge to superstition and mere trickery. So when the moon arose that night, round and large, I called his attention to it: "Tonnis, it does not look as if the moon would be eclipsed to-night, does it?" "No, Sir," he said, "it won't be eclipsed;" almost laughing in his incredulousness at the idea. "Ah, but it will," I said, "only it's too soon yet." Soon we outspanned, a fire was made, and the kettle set on for tea. Meantime I told Tonnis to slaughter a sheep, "and when you have finished that and hung it up for the flesh to set, you may look at the moon." He was soon busy about this necessary work, and every now and then cast a glance upwards towards the moon, showing that some commotion was going on within, and that he still thought there was some possibility of my words proving true. At length all being finished, and the eclipse having visibly commenced, I said, " Now, Tonnis, look." He seemed still in doubt, as it was not very visible. " Well," I said, " wait a short time." At about half-past nine he looked again, and said, " It seems as if one side of the moon was cut off!" " Was it like that when the moon rose?" " No, Sir, it was altogether round and full." His interest was now fairly enlisted, and as the eclipse advanced, for some time I sat up with him, watching the phenomenon ; at length, weary with long travelling, I retired to rest. Tonnis, however, was wide awake, and sat up till the close, and first thing in the morning, on leaving the waggon, he exclaimed frankly, and in high excitement, " Ah, Sir, I sat up till the eclipse was all over, and the moon became round and full again as when it rose ; and everything came to pass *exactly* as you had said." " Well," I said, " I told you of this some time before it took place, and the time when it would begin and end. There was no trickery there; you know I could not get up there and draw a veil over the face of the moon." " No, Sir," he at once replied. " Well, you see how much better knowledge is than sorcery ! Clever men calculate everything concerning eclipses to the minute, days, months, and years beforehand, and publish it to the world, so that men may have the opportunity of testing the truth of what they say." He seemed much impressed, and I doubt not he then learnt lessons which he would tell to others, and carry with him to the end of his days.

Saturday, April 3rd.—This morning we arrived at Schans Vlakte, a village of the Velschoen Draagers, and at present the residence of the chief and his principal men, and of Frederick Buys, our native assistant. For a considerable distance before reaching the village our attention was arrested by the amount of labour the people had bestowed in road-making. On former occasions I had visited this tribe on horseback; but as they had for some time past expected that I should visit them with the waggon, bringing my wife with me, which they felt to be an honour, they had with great labour, and no implements more powerful than their hands, torn up enormous stones and made a clear open road for a waggon, of many miles in length. From the wild and rugged nature of this part, there can never be what an Englishman would call a good road : still, this is one that can be travelled without danger, and it reflects great credit on its inexperienced makers. It is the commencement of a civilising process that has followed the introduction of the Gospel.

On entering the village the laborious work of shaking the hand of every man, woman, and child, on the place, all marching up in regimental order for the purpose, was commenced ; and as several hundred were presented in succession, we were glad when the tedious ceremony approached its termination.

During the course of the day the chief sent his slate for my inspection. It contained the whole alphabet in capitals and small letters, and was very tolerably written, considering that it was almost his first attempt. It had probably been reserved for my inspection for some days. In front of the village is a low mountain, which is surrounded at the top by a wall, the entire length of which must be eight or ten hundred yards, low in places difficult of access, and five or six feet high in those parts that are most easily available. This wall, which consists of a double row of loose flat stones piled one above another, was thrown round the mountain by the Afrikaners at the beginning of the century. After shooting the Dutch Boer, Pinaar, to whom Old Afrikaner and his clan were at that time subject, and by whom they were oppressed beyond all endurance, Afrikaner and his people fled to this place. Here they resolved upon making a stand against the commandoes sent in pursuit of them by the Colonial Government. Within this entrenchment, at the top of the mountain, they built their houses, had kraals for their calves, and in fact everything necessary to a Namaqua village, and considered themselves able to defy all their enemies. They seemed scarcely able to conceive of a valour that would proceed in the face of their bullets, scale their fort, bound over its walls, drive them over the fearful precipice on the opposite side, and plunge them into the abyss of black waters beneath. The opportunity of defending themselves in their impregnable fortification, however, never occurred, as the commandoes of Boers from the Colony pursued them no farther than Nisbett Bath. This entrenchment remains unimpaired to this day, and is at least a proof that the Afrikaners possessed an energy of character much greater than that possessed by the Namaqua tribes generally. I felt much interest in viewing this relic, calling up so vividly as it does the scenes of war and bloodshed, of rapine and murder, in which the Afrikaners were formerly engaged, as all contrasts so strongly now with the changed conduct of that part of the tribe which forms a portion of my charge. I next inspected the new stone chapel in course of erection. The walls, in nearly their entire length, are raised to the height of six feet, and are two feet thick, and when the building is completed, it will hold about three hundred hearers. In the evening I conducted public service, the present chapel being well filled.

Monday, 5th.—Yesterday being the Sabbath, an early prayer meeting was held, and, about 9 a.m., I preached from Gen. i. 27. In the afternoon I examined ten adult candidates for baptism, explaining to them the nature of that sacrament, and the obligations they were about to take upon themselves in the reception of it. At night my theme was, the " Saviour, Jesus " (Acts xiii. 23). I felt unutterable delight in speaking concerning Him, and the attention of the people was powerfully arrested by the glorious subject, throughout the entire service. When the Saviour Jesus was exhibited to this yet half heathen people as their only Hope, and as the only Restorer of the lost moral image of God, the whole congregation was moved with emotion. O, it is in these lands, where we see man in his lowest state of sin and wretchedness, yet sighing for deliverance, that the very name of Jesus is as music, thrilling music, in our ears. I rejoice in the assurance that a mighty hand has been already laid on the kingdom of Satan, in this region: he may struggle to maintain it, but it shall finally fall, and great shall be the fall thereof.

This morning I again held service, and at the close publicly baptized the candidates I examined yesterday. This is always felt to be a very impressive service. After this I united eight couples in the bonds " of holy matrimony." This service being finished, I was occupied for three hours in meeting the members and candidates for membership. We have now amongst this people twenty-four members, most of them the early fruits of Elias Rolfe's visits, and thirty-four on trial, the result chiefly of Frederick Buys's recently commenced labours—the commencement, I trust, of a large church to be gathered out of this tribe.

This afternoon we took our leave, amidst abundance of shaking of hands, but were accompanied a considerable distance by many of the people, before they seemed willing to part; and we could not but lament that the great distance of this outpost from the station prevented the possibility of its being visited with the frequency it deserves.

This visit has given me great and unmingled satisfaction, and I could not help contrasting the present state of the Velschoen Draagers with that in which I found them in 1844. Then there were neither candidates nor members; now we have fifty-eight regularly meeting in class. Then they had no place of public worship, and no schools; now they have a large stone chapel in course of erection, and a hundred and fifty children in the Sunday and week-day schools. We have also twelve Sunday-school teachers selected from amongst themselves. Then they were only occasionally visited by one of the nearest native teachers, though residing at a considerable distance, who at such times held service in the open air; now they have a native assistant living in their midst, and enjoy stated instruction. They were at that time almost all destitute of any decent clothing, the mother of the chief herself being perfectly naked, with the exception of a small strip of skin round the loins; but since my first visit traders have found their way thither, and now a large number are clothed in articles of English manufacture, and the Sunday congregations nearly equal in respectability of appearance the congregations on the principal station. Then they had neither waggon-roads nor waggons, but now, considering the character of the country, they have made a tolerable road, and are in possession of eight waggons. So that a few leading steps in civilisation have followed in almost immediate connection with the introduction of the Gospel. Whatever may be the opinion of others, missionaries in such lands are in no doubt as to what is the great civiliser of the nations.

For forty or fifty miles before reaching Schans Vlakte the character of the scenery is totally different from any other in the circuit, or indeed from any other I have seen in South Africa. It is as wild and gloomy as the imagination can conceive. Rugged and barren ravines, skirted with a succession of terrible and abrupt precipices, here and there rent by gloomy fissures, fill the mind of the solitary traveller with an irrepressible feeling of awe. The towering height of these lofty precipices makes the passer-by most impressively to feel his own nothingness in contrast with their mighty magnitude, whilst their grey and age-worn appearance is in perfect keeping with the brown and faded aspect of the trees and shrubs around. Along these ravines an

African river invariably courses its way in time of storm, though generally leaving nothing for the eye to gaze upon but its bed of dry and burning sands, with here and there a stagnant pool of black or green water, of unknown depth, deposited at the base of a high and massive precipice.

The age-worn precipices, and the pools of dark water at their base, the withered aspect of the vegetation around, and the black prostrate arms and trunks of trees lying in the most fantastic and serpentine forms, the holes in the face of the rocks suggestive of tigers' dens, and the deathlike stillness only broken by the shrill screams of the wild geese disturbed in their pools, or by the gruff salutation of the baboon as he spies the puny traveller from the top of his rocky heights, invest the entire scene with an air of almost depressing melancholy. One feels as if he were treading regions that had never been trodden by the foot of man before, and can easily imagine them to be the abode of every doleful creature. And if it be his first visit to these dreary scenes, without the rattle of a waggon's wheels or the smack of the driver's huge whip to cheer his spirits and drive away the awful solemnity of the reign of silence, the traveller is almost ready to imagine that at every step he takes some direful monster from the rocks, or holes, or mountains, will stand before his view.

We have heard fearful accounts from the natives of enormous serpents that infest the rocks and mountains, which, they say, are too terrible to look upon, and of which they are infinitely more afraid than of lions and tigers. On first hearing their descriptions, I was much inclined to treat all as fiction, or gross exaggeration, as

I had not previously heard of the existence of the boa constrictor in these parts, with which alone their descriptions agree. After more minute inquiry, I am compelled to believe in the existence of some kind of large rock serpent, as the accounts of the natives so nearly accord with the descriptions that have been furnished by naturalists. From the information the natives give, they must be thirty or forty feet in length. They have "beards and eyebrows," they say; "they sometimes make a blowing noise, like the noise of a smith's bellows, and sometimes like a small whirlwind passing through the rocks;" they have a horrible fœtor, which none of all the snakes or serpents I have seen and *handled* possess, and they glitter in the sun like burnished metal. In all these particulars they so nearly agree with the accounts naturalists have published, that I can doubt no longer, especially as the natives have never seen or heard of the descriptions we have been accustomed to read from childhood.

The people told of a woman who came unexpectedly upon one of these monsters among the rocks, when it immediately reared to a frightful height. The woman fled, but soon fell with fear, and arose and fled, and fell again, till at length she escaped.

Hearing that some of these monsters might possibly be seen up in the entrenchment at the top of the hill, and being very incredulous, I took my rifle, and, accompanied by Elias Rolfe, who was also armed, we ascended the hill, and went on a tour of inspection. Fortunately, if there were any, they were too sleepy or too lazy to show themselves.

After leaving the Velschoen Draagers, we called at Cook's *Boom,* or " Tree," which was the farthest spot to which the Rev. E. Cook extended his journeys in this direction. Here Elias Rolfe is at present residing with his people. During a brief visit I met all the members, baptized two adults and six children, and married two couples. After leaving this place we were amused, during an outspanning, with watching some baboons on a high krantz, who, doubtless, were similarly amused with watching us from their lofty elevation. One of them, who appeared to us to be upon the very edge of a precipice, with his legs hanging over the front, just leaned on his right arm, gave a twist to his body, and leaped down in most human style to a lower ledge, which we could not see from our low position, appearing to be as much at home on those precipitous heights as we were upon the plain below. I happened to be looking at him through my glass at the moment, and was much amused at his unconcerned appearance, and at the adroitness he manifested. One might infer that these gentlemen are not much troubled with giddiness in the head, however great the elevation.

Whilst in this rocky and precipitous region, I obtained a couple of rock rabbits, which we had for dinner. I shot them at a height of about thirty feet up the face of one of the precipices, and laying my gun down at the bottom, I ascended with ease, and secured my game; but how to descend the perpendicular face of the rock again was the difficulty; and as the waggon and men had passed on a considerable distance, I felt some concern, as it was evident I should have to drop from some height upon the loose stones below : and in case of a sprained or dislocated ankle, I did not see how I could make them acquainted with my position. Mercifully I escaped without injury.

On another occasion the alarm was to my party, not to myself. I thought they had seen me walking in advance of the waggon through a defile with rocks on either hand. My intention was to look for a stray antelope or other game, which would be sure to take fright at the sound of a waggon travelling over a rocky road. Intent upon my purpose, I had walked on a considerable distance in advance, as the waggon could only travel slowly over such roads. Suddenly, the inquiry arose: "Where is master?" No one had seen him for a long time. In a panic, whilst one man was left in charge of the waggon, the other two were despatched in search of me, but all in vain: meantime I was marvelling at the long delay of the waggon. The sun was setting and casting long shadows, and very soon the darkness of night would cover all nature. I stood, knowing that the waggon must travel that road. I shouted, and waited, and fired my gun, and grew impatient at the long delay. At length, proceeding towards the direction from which the waggon ought to come, I caught a distant sound of its rumble over the rocks, and in due time we met, to the great relief of all.

On the station I found all in very good order; and the services having been regularly conducted by Mr. Macleod, things generally were in a state of prosperity.

On the 5th of May, after a residence on the station of nearly three weeks, I again proceeded to visit the Afrikaners, when as usual I met the members, examined the school, and inquired into affairs generally. In some respects they were not in so satisfactory a state as I had generally found them, and I felt it necessary to rectify some irregularities, and to reprove some of the leading men for negligence, which I had very seldom found it needful to do at this place. As I did this with a reluctance which they could not fail to perceive, I hope the effect will be salutary.

On the 14th I returned, intending to travel through and reach home that night; but owing to the carelessness of Links, my attendant, this was frustrated. We had travelled to within five-and-twenty miles of home, when I resolved to offsaddle and benefit ourselves and our horses by rest and a little refreshment, before commencing the final stage. But as it was already dark, I gave special directions to my man to be sure to "span" the horses, and not merely to knee-halter them as we do in the daylight. When we were ready to resume the journey, I directed him to fetch them, anticipating no delay. He was a long time absent, and at length he returned, saying he could not find them. In all my journeyings such a thing had never happened before; and on inquiry I found he had not spanned the horses, which would have kept them grazing near to us, but had merely knee-haltered them. Immediately I ordered him after them, as they could travel at a good speed with merely the knee haltered, and they would be sure to make for the nearest water, many miles away. In that case we should lose them for the night, and for hours on the following day. He seemed very reluctant, but as the case was urgent, he obeyed. After sitting on the grass by a small fire, till I was tired of that position, I made loose my kaross and spread it upon the ground, and arranging my saddle for a pillow, I lay impatiently waiting for Links and the horses. Suddenly a dash, as of hundreds of animals, startled me; and away they went over the plain. Immediately I sat up, peering into the darkness over the embers of my little fire, but of course I could see nothing.

It seemed to me like the rush of a herd of antelopes that had suddenly taken fright at something—a wolf, a tiger, or a pack of wild dogs perhaps, neither of which it was pleasant to think of being near. This was about the only time, in all my journeyings on horseback, when I happened to carry a brace of pistols at my saddle-bow. At once I made them loose, examined the nipples and caps, and saw that they were all right. As they were very small, only pocket-pistols, and could not be depended on for straightness of aim, I determined that if necessary to use them, I would not fire at a distance, but wait, till an attack was actually made, and then fire at close quarters, into whatever wild beast might pounce upon me. Lifting up my heart to God for calmness, and nerve, and protection, I waited, expecting to see the glaring eyeballs of some fierce animal confronting me; but, after a while, none appearing, I ceased to expect it. Soon, however, I heard something in the distance, and it appeared to be approaching, for in those silent plains sound travels a long way; so, standing up, I shouted, " Is that you, Links ?" " Yes, Sir," was the instant reply, and at once I was greatly relieved. It was near midnight, and he had returned without the horses; but though very much disappointed at his not having them, I could say nothing more to him in the way of reproof. " I stooped down," said he, viz., that he might see any object projected above the horizon, against the sky; "and sometimes I thought I saw them: but when I ran up, I found they were only bushes. This I did many times, but still I found only bushes: at length I felt very much terrified." How he found his way back to me I cannot tell, as for some time past my fire had been reduced to embers. And although in his state of trepidation I did not venture to accuse him of not having gone after the horses, I have often thought since, that he must have remained within sight of my fire. After all, it was the best plan he could have adopted; for as the horses had evidently gone to the water, and it was impossible to see their footmarks, the only wise plan was to return before he became lost himself. It was a bad job; but all we could now do was to make the best of it. Before I awoke in the morning, the poor fellow was off, and I was again alone, in all probability, for some hours.

The sun soon mounted the horizon, and at once began to pour forth its wonted heat, which even at this hour of the day I always felt to produce a feeling of much faintness. It appeared to be hotter than usual, and I had no means of counteracting the feeling by taking an early breakfast, for all our refreshments had been consumed the previous night. At length, as the warmth increased, in self-defence, I lay down again upon my spread mantle, put my head upon my saddle, and drew the mantle over my face. For some time I dozed off in a state of happy forgetfulness; but, on awaking again to consciousness, I threw down the kaross from off my face, to the disappointment of several crows which were hovering about, a few yards above my head, evidently puzzled with that strange something on the ground, which for some time had been as still as death, but which now showed unmistakable indications of life.   Higher in the heavens, wheeling in large circles, was a vulture; so that in case of death by hunger, thirst, or violence, there were pretty plain indications that clean bones would soon be all that was left of me.   After the revelation of *life* these rapacious birds had witnessed, it is astonishing how quickly they disappeared. Evidently there was nothing for them there !

Waiting thus in the plains hour after hour with nothing to do but wait, was inexpressibly tedious. At last, looking towards the south-west, I thought I saw a dust : five minutes later it was certain, and something visible was moving. At length *two* men on horseback were seen, which was discouraging, as I supposed them travellers by the path across the plain who would never see me, but pass on unconscious of my presence. Still they drew nearer, and other horses were with them.   Hence I could not think them mine, for here were two men and four horses ! Still they bent their course towards me, and as they drew nearer and nearer, at length I saw my man on one of my horses and leading another, and Andries Abraham, one of our own people, riding another horse, and leading that we used as a pack-horse. All was soon explained. The poor horses had made for an outlying place, where a few of our people had gone for the benefit of the water and grazing for their flocks, and evidently the horses were acquainted with the spot, and had reached it early. Having slaked their thirst, they contented themselves with grazing in the immediate neighbourhood of the water. Andries was the first up in the village, and at once saw the horses. Finding them to be knee-haltered, and recognising them as mine, he at once opined the facts of the case, and immediately prepared his own horse, which fortunately was at hand, with the intention of bringing them to us, who he concluded were far away on the plain. His first duty was to find the *spoor*, and thus ascertain the direction from which they had come; and having soon succeeded in finding this, he was galloping upon it as his guide, bringing on my three horses at a smart rate, when he met my man. It was now about ten a.m., and hungry and faint, with the prospect of a journey of twenty-five miles before we could breakfast, we soon equipped and mounted our horses, and in due season reached home, very thankful to God, Whose good angels had " encamped round about us, and delivered us."

As soon as I return from my circuit journeys to the principal station, I have always been accustomed to resume my daily morning expositions, taking up the place at which I left off; and as soon as resumed, the old interest shown by the people returns. Indeed the continuous narratives of some of the historical books have seemed completely to fascinate the people, and at the same time to be a means of supplying them with many valuable and instructive lessons. I am now reading the First Book of Samuel, and am anxious to complete it before these meetings for exposition are brought to a close by my leaving the country. In a few days I shall have to read about the combat between David and Goliath, and intend to show them a sling, and its use, that I may be able to give them some idea of its terrible power in the hands of a skilful slinger.

About the *end of June* I once more had to pay the monthly visit to the Afrikaners, which would probably be the last time I should be able to go before leaving the circuit. As usual, the society, the school, and all the affairs belonging to the society were carefully inquired into, and they were found as satisfactory almost as could be wished. Though my impression was that I should not have the opportunity of visiting them again, I could not muster the courage to tell them so, especially as possibly another opportunity might present itself. I therefore said nothing on the subject, though in bidding them farewell I felt the wrench as terribly as though it were the last. Had the people known my thoughts and feelings, I fear their laments would have been so distressing as completely to unman me.

On returning to the station I resumed my morning exposition, and the combat of David and Goliath having been read as part of the service, great interest was shown by the people ; and after the service a crowd of men being gathered together outside the chapel to talk on the subject, I showed them a sling, made probably of the same materials as the sling of David, viz., of prepared sheep or goat skin. I told them of the skill of the Benjamites, who could sling stones " to a hair's breadth, and not miss ; " of the force with which stones could be hurled by those who were practised, as they had just heard in the case of David, who hurled a stone that pierced the forehead of the giant, and brought him to the ground. Putting a smooth stone into the sling, I said I was altogether unpractised, but I would try and show them how it was used; when, requesting them to stand back that I might have room to swing my arm, I sent the stone into the air with a loud, continuous whiz, which excited their astonishment; but from which they could infer, that, since an unpractised slinger could throw with such force, David, who was accustomed probably to sling from his boyhood, might easily hurl a stone with force sufficient to break into the skull of Goliath. In this way, when it could be done, I had pleasure in illustrating outside the sanctuary anything they might have heard within, and rendering it more vivid to their perception.

July 21st.—I met my class this morning, and could not help realising in a very vivid manner that the time of my departure from the people and station is very near at hand. The allusions made to it by the members were very touching, and it excited sorrowful emotions to think my ministrations in this part are so nearly over, perhaps for ever. We have had abounding joy and consolation in our labours here, and nothing less than the absolute necessity of a change to a less trying climate could reconcile us to the idea of leaving. But to remain would almost inevitably destroy my health permanently; for the heats of Great Namaqualand are truly dreadful, especially after the constitution has once begun to feel their debilitating influence; whereas a timely removal to a cooler temperature will, I doubt not, restore lost energy, and prepare me for future years of labour, if necessary, in the interior again.

August 1st.——This has been a solemn Sabbath, probably the last I shall ever spend in this part of Great

Namaqualand. I strove to realise the idea, and gazed with peculiar feelings on the various objects in the station and surrounding it, as far as to the verge of the widespread horizon itself, together with the hills and long, low range of mountains which break it to the south and south-west, never expecting to see them again enlightened by the beams of a Sabbath sun. A multitude of varying and commingled thoughts and emotions were excited, but amidst them all thankfulness for ever having been sent to this part of the mission field, and for the manifold .blessings I have enjoyed during my residence here, prevailed. God has caused us to " sing of mercy," almost entirely unmingled with "judgment," and He has made His " pleasure to prosper in our hands."

In the morning I preached on Acts xx. 32 : " And now, brethren, I commend you to God, and to the word of His grace," &c. And I felt a hallowed delight and satisfaction in the thought that I was delivering up my charge into the hands of that same Great Shepherd of the sheep, who had for a season placed them under my pastoral care. And if in any measure I had fed this part of His flock according to His will, I felt that that was a full and abundant recompense for all the labours and watchings my charge had imposed. The people felt deeply, and were nearly overwhelmed with emotion. In the afternoon, instead of the Sabbath school being held as usual, I repeated all the leading points of history in the Old Testament, from Genesis to the end of the First Book of Samuel, in order the more deeply to impress on their minds the facts they had heard read and remarked upon for a considerable time past in the regular daily morning service, as well as to give them a general and connected view of the whole.

Tuesday, August 3rd.—This morning, at about eleven o'clock, our waggons being packed, and our oxen caught and inspanned, I had the station bell rung, when the people who had been standing about all the morning accompanied us into the chapel.

I gave out a hymn and began to sing with a good courage, but was suddenly compelled to stop by irrepressible emotion. Out of the chapel full of people there were only two or three voices that were able falteringly to proceed, so that after singing two verses I proposed prayer. But the sobs of the whole congregation were so overwhelming, together with the deep emotion of my own mind, that for a considerable time I could not proceed. At length, however, I mastered my feelings and was able to continue with tolerable calmness. On leaving the chapel and taking the hand of first one and then another, the scene was renewed as painfully as before, and to very many I could not utter even a word of salutation. Our people were even more powerfully affected, and so distressing was the parting that I was thankful when it was finished.

August 8th, Orange River.—Having got our waggons and everything we had in charge through the river on the previous day, we were able peacefully to enjoy the Sabbath. A number of our people had accompanied us in their own waggons and on foot from the station as far as the river, and many others had arrived on the previous evening at our encampment, having come from various places along the river on horseback, on oxback, and on foot, so that our congregation amounted to nearly one hundred persons.   In the morning, assembled under the trees by the river side, I preached to them from : " Dearly beloved, I beseech you as strangers and pilgrims, abstain from fleshly lusts, which war against the soul " (1 Peter ii. 11).   And in the afternoon from : " There remaineth therefore a rest to the people of God " (Hebrews iv. 9).

Monday, August 9th.—This morning I held a service with the people before finally parting; and at the close I married the youngest son of the chief.   In the afternoon, being almost ready to leave the river, I rowed Sara, the chief's wife, and Marie, the wife of Jan Ortman, the chief's principal councillor, to the north side of the river; and as they were much distressed, I spoke cheeringly to them by the way.   On handing them out of the boat to the river bank, they sat down upon the bank in silent, but inconsolable grief, their heads bowed, and covered up with their shawls. Taking their hands, I said in a tone of forced cheerfulness, " Good-bye, Sara; good-bye, Marie ; " got into the boat, and rowed back.   Most of the remaining people would easily wade through at the ford, as the river happened to be low; and as delay would only increase the difficulty of parting, we gave the signal to move on; " Trek, loop," cried the waggon-driver, and away we went, never to return.   But standing on the waggon forechest, and looking from the high bank over the tree tops to the other side of the river, I beheld those poor, disconsolate women, still sitting on the same spot, their heads covered and bowed in sorrow, as when I left them.   That scene has remained indelibly engraven on my mind ever since.   It so overpowered me at the time, that, ashamed to be seen so affected by the waggon-people, I descended, and walked on in advance of the waggon for three hours, during which my sorrow was repressed and renewed again many times over. This sorrow of parting from the first scene and people of my mission was one of the greatest sorrows of my life.

Printed by Beveridge and Miller, Fullwood's Rents, High Holborn.

My Black Sheep. By EVELYN EVERETT-GREEN. Crown 8vo. Three Full-page Illustrations. 2s.

Miss Meyrick's Niece. By EVELYN EVERETT-GREEN. Crown 8vo. Illustrated. 2s.

Mad Margrete and Little Gunnvald. A Norwegian Story. By NELLIE CORNWALL, Author of 'Granny Tresawna's Story.' Crown 8vo. Three Whole-page Illustrations. 2s. 6d.

Raymond Theed, a Story of Five Years. By ELSIE KENDALL, Author of 'Friends and Neighbours.' Crown 8vo. Frontispiece. 2s.

For the King and the Cross. By JESSIE ARMSTRONG. Crown 8vo. Frontispiece. 2s. 6d.

The Two Harvests. By ANNIE RYLANDS. Crown 8vo. Frontispiece. 1s. 6d.

Among the Pimento Groves. A Story of Negro Life in Jamaica. By Rev. HENRY BUNTING. Crown 8vo. Six page Illustrations. 2s.

The Happy Valley: Our New 'Mission Garden' in Uva, Ceylon. By Rev. S. LANGDON. Crown 8vo. With Map, Portrait of Mrs. Wiseman, and numerous other Illustrations. 2s.

Brookside School, and other Stories. By MARGARET HAY-CRAFT. Small Crown 8vo. Frontispiece. 1s.

The Spring-Tide Reciter. A Book for Band of Hope Meetings. By MARGARET HAYCRAFT. Small Crown 8vo. 1s

Severn to Tyne: the Story of Six English Rivers. By E. M. EDWARDS. Crown 8vo. Fifty-two Illustrations. 2s. 6d.

Grand Gilmore. By REESE ROCKWELL. Crown 8vo. Six page Illustrations. 2s.

Psalms and Canticles.

(*Pointed for Chanting.*)

Words Only, Limp cloth, 4d. ; Stiff cloth, red edges, 6d. ; Paste Grain roan, gilt edges, 2s.

With Chants (343), Staff Notation, Limp cloth, 1s. ; Cloth boards, 1s. 6d.

With Chants, Tonic Sol-Fa, Limp cloth, 1s. ; Cloth boards, 1s. 6d.

With Chants, Organ Edition, 4to, Cloth, red edges, 3s.

'The book supplies a great want in a way that should make it popular in our congregations.'—*London Quarterly Review.*

Psalms and Canticles (Words Only), WITH SACRAMENTAL, BAPTISMAL, AND COVENANT SERVICES. Limp cloth, 8d.; Stiff cloth, red edges, 10d. ; Cloth boards, 1s.

London: C. H. KELLY, 2, Castle Street, City Road, E.C. ;
AND 66, PATERNOSTER ROW, E.C.

Wesley's Hymns with Tunes & Psalms

and CANTICLES with 343 CHANTS, in One Volume. *Staff Notation.*

Crown 8vo. (8 x 6 in., 1¼ in. thick.)			Crown 4to. (9 x 8¼ in., 1¼ in. thick.)		
For Choirs.	*s.*	*d.*	*For Organ and Pianoforte.*	*s.*	*d.*
Cloth	4	0	Cloth, red edges . . .	10	6
Linen Cloth, red edges . .	5	0	Linen Cloth, red edges . .	11	6
Limp Roan, gilt edges . .	6	0	Half Persian Calf, marbled		
Half Persian Calf, marbled			edges	13	6
edges	6	6	Half Morocco, gilt edges .	17	0
Persian Calf, grained, gilt edges	9	0	Persian Calf, grained, gilt edges	17	6
Morocco, gilt edges . .	14	0	Morocco, gilt edges . . .	24	0
Morocco Antique, red under			Morocco Antique, red under		
gilt edges	17	6	gilt edges	30	0

The General Hymnary.

Containing 500 Hymns and Eight Canticles, for Mission and Special Services.

SMALL TYPE.			LARGE TYPE.		
Paper Covers		2d.	Limp Cloth		6d.
Limp Cloth		3d.	Cloth Boards		9d.
Cloth Boards, red edges . .		6d.	Linen Cloth, red edges . .		1s.

THE HYMNARY (LARGE TYPE) is also kept in Superior Bindings :—

	s.	*d.*		*s.*	*d.*
Limp Roan, gilt edges . .	1	9	Persian, padded sides, round		
Roan, stiff boards, gilt edges .	2	6	corners, red under gilt edges .	4	0
Paste Grain Roan, red under			Morocco, stiff boards, red under		
gilt edges	2	6	gilt edges	5	0
Paste Grain Roan, red under			Morocco, padded sides, silk		
gilt, round corners, gilt side .	3	6	lined	9	0
Persian Grained, gilt edges .	3	0	Morocco Yapp, red under gilt		
Persian, gilt side, grained, gilt			edges, round corners . .	9	0
edges	3	6			

This Hymn-Book is intended for Mission-Halls, and especially for Mission-Centres, in which the Evangelistic Services are surrounded by a system of Social and Philanthropic Agencies; but it is not designed to supersede the *Hymns and Songs for Mission-Services and Conventions.*

The General Hymnary Tune-Book.

Containing 406 Tunes, 34 Single Chants, and 42 Double Chants.

	s. d.
Paper Covers	1s. 6d.
Cloth Boards, plain edges, blind lettered .	2s. 0d.
Cloth, bevelled boards, red edges, gilt lettered	2s. 6d.
Persian Morocco, limp, red under gilt edges .	6s. 0d.

This Book has been prepared by a Sub-committee, the convener of which was the Rev. Dr. Stephenson. The Musical Editorship has been entrusted to Mr. Alfred Rhodes, A.R.A.M., to whose skill and interest the Committee are much indebted. It is right to say, however, that Mr. Rhodes is not responsible for the selection of the tunes.

It is obvious that in a book intended for use in great popular gatherings, many compositions must be included which do not meet the demands of severe musical taste. Their utility for the purposes contemplated in the publication is the justification of their presence.

The unusual metrical form of very many of the hymns has called for many new tunes. In supplying them the Committee are happy to have been able to secure the assistance of several able composers.

Cheap Editions of Popular Religious Books.

By the Rev. W. L. Watkinson.

Lessons of Prosperity; and other Addresses Delivered at Noon-Day in the Philosophical Hall, Leeds. Crown 8vo. Paper covers, *1s.*; cloth, *1s. 6d.*

Noon-Day Addresses delivered in the Central Hall, Manchester. Crn. 8vo. Paper covers, *1s.*; cloth, *1s. 6d.*

The Influence of Scepticism on Character. The Fernley Lecture of 1886. Demy 8vo. Paper covers, *1s. 6d.*; cloth, *2s. 6d.*

John Wicklif. With Portrait and Eleven other Illustrations. Crown 8vo. *2s. 6d.*

Mistaken Signs ; and other Papers on Christian Life and Experience. *Fifth Thousand.* Crn. 8vo. Paper covers, *1s.*; cloth, *1s. 6d.*

The Beginning of the Christian Life. *Sixth Thousand.* 16mo. *1s.*

The Programme of Life. *Fifth Thousand.* Demy 16mo. *1s.*

By the Rev. John Bamford.

My Cross and Thine. Large Crown 8vo. Red lines round pages. Ten full page Illustrations. Cloth, red edges. *3s. 6d.*

Hugh Axe, of Hephzibah. Crown 8vo. Six Page Illustrations, *1s. 6d.*, gilt edges, *2s.*

Father, Fervent. *Sixth Thousand.* Crown 8vo. Eighteen Illustrations, *1s. 6d.*; gilt edges, *2s. 6d.*

A Week of Life. Small Crn. 8vo. With Frontispiece, cloth, *6d.*

Elias Power, of Ease in Zion. *Eighteenth Thousand.* Crn. 8vo. Seventeen Illustrations, *1s. 6d.*; gilt edges, *2s. 6d.*

John Conscience, of Kingseal. *Ninth Thousand.* Crn. 8vo. Eighteen Illustrations, *1s. 6d.*; gilt edges, *2s. 6d.*

By Charles R. Parsons.

The Vicar of Berrybridge. Crn. 8vo. Thirty-seven Illustrations, *1s. 6d.*; gilt edges, *2s. 6d.*

The Man with the White Hat; or, The Story of an Unknown Mission. 21 Illustrations. *Seventeenth Thousand.* Crn. 8vo. Paper covers, *1s.*; cloth, *1s. 6d.*; gilt edges, *2s. 6d.*

Roger Wentwood's Bible. Crown 8vo. Numerous Illustrations. Gilt edges. *2s. 6d.*

Purity and Power. Crown 8vo. Cloth, red edges, *2s. 6d.*

Farmer Read's Kingdom ; the Story of One Poplar Farm. Eighteen Illustrations. Crown 8vo. *1s. 6d.*

The Little Woman in Grey ; Scenes and Incidents in Home Mission Work. Twenty-two Illustrations. Crown 8vo. *2s. 6d.*

By Mrs. Robert A. Watson.

Poet-Toilers in Many Fields. Biographical Sketches of Lucy Larcom, Daniel Macmillan, Henri Perreyve, Mary Carpenter, James Clerk Maxwell, Toru Dutt, John Duncan, Wives and Mothers in the Age of Homespun, Oberlin, Edward Denison, Annie Keary, Alfred Saker. Crown 8vo. Portraits and Illustrations. *2s.*

Building her House. Small Crn. 8vo. Five Illustrations. *1s. 6d.*

Roger Haigh, Chartermaster. Crn. 8vo. Six Page Illus. *2s. 6d.*

Crabtree Fold : A Tale of the Lancashire Moors. Small Crown 8vo. Five Illustrations. *1s. 6d.*

The Good Luck of the Maitlands. Crown 8vo. Five Page Illus. *2s.*

Elias Power, of "Ease-in-Zion." By Rev. JOHN M. BAMFORD. *Eighteenth Thousand.* Crown 8vo. Fifteen Illustrations. Gilt edges.

John Conscience, of Kingseal. By Rev. JOHN M. BAMFORD. Crown 8vo. Eighteen Illustrations. Gilt edges. *Ninth Thousand.*

The Hallam Succession. A Story of Methodist Life in Two Countries. By AMELIA E. BARR. Crown 8vo. Frontispiece.

Fought and Won. By RUTH ELLIOTT. Crn. 8vo. Frontispiece.

Undeceived : Roman or Anglican ? A Story of English Ritualism. By RUTH ELLIOTT. Crown 8vo. *Eighth Thousand.*

"Than Many Sparrows." By A. E. COURTENAY. Crown 8vo. With Frontispiece.

Orphans of the Forest; or, His Little Jonathan. By ANNIE E. COURTENAY. Foolscap 8vo. 300 pp. Four Illustrations.

The Opposite House, and Other Stories for Cottage Homes. By A. F. PERRAM. Crn. 8vo. Frontispiece.

The Shadow of Nobility. By EMMA E. HORNIBROOK. Crown 8vo. Frontispiece.

For the King and the Cross. By JESSIE ARMSTRONG. Crown 8vo. Frontispiece.

Mad Margrete and Little Gunnvald. A Norwegian Story. By NELLIE CORNWALL. Crown 8vo. Three Page Illustrations.

Miss Kennedy and Her Brother. By FRIBA. Frontispiece. Crn. 8vo.

The Little Woman in Grey. Scenes and Incidents in Home Mission Work. By CHARLES R. PARSONS. Crown 8vo. Numerous Illustrations.

The Vicar of Berrybridge. By CHARLES R. PARSONS. Crown 8vo. 37 Illustrations. Gilt edges.

The Man with the White Hat; or, The Story of an Unknown Mission. By C. R. PARSONS. *Seventeenth Thousand.* Crown 8vo. Twenty-one Illustrations. Gilt edges.

General Gordon : Hero and Saint. By A. E. KEELING. Crown 8vo. Portrait and Eight Illustrations.

Sunny Fountains and Golden Sand. Pictures of Missionary Life in the South of the Dark Continent. By ARTHUR BRIGG. Crown 8vo. Nine Page Illustrations.

The Nine Famous Crusades of the Middle Ages. By ANNIE E. KEELING. Crown 8vo. Illustrated.

Severn to Tyne : The Story of Six English Rivers. By EDITH M. EDWARDS. Crown 8vo. 53 Illus.

History of the English Bible. By Dr. MOULTON. New and Revised Edition. Crown 8vo.

Nature Musings on Holy-days and Holidays. By the Rev. NEHEMIAH CURNOCK. Crn. 8vo. 41 Illus.

Rambles and Reveries of a Naturalist. By. Rev. W. SPIERS, M.A. Crown 8vo. With above 60 Illustrations.

The Sabbath for Man : an Enquiry into the Origin and History of the Sabbath Institution. By Rev. W. SPIERS, M.A. Crown 8vo.

Price Two Shillings.

Nathanael Noble's Homely Talks for Years and Youth. By Rev. H. SMITH. Crn. 8vo. Numerous Illus.

Parson Hardwork's Nut, and How He Cracked It. By Rev. W. W. HAUGHTON. Illustrations. Crn. 8vo.

Sprattie and the Dwarf ; or. The Shining Stairway. A Story of East London. By NELLIE CORNWALL. Crown 8vo. Illustrated.

Dickon o' Greenwood ; or. How the Light came to Lady Clare. A Village Picture in Martyr Days. By KATE T. SIZER. Crown 8vo. Illus.

Eighty-seven : A Chautauqua Story. By 'PANSY.' Crown 8vo. Illus.

Avice Tennant's Pilgrimage ; a Tale of Bunyan's Days. By KATE T. SIZER. Crown 8vo. Six full-page Illustrations.

London: C. H. KELLY, 2, Castle Street, City Road, E.C.; AND 66, PATERNOSTER ROW, E.C.